WHEN BONDING FAILS

Volume 151, Sage Library of Social Research

RECENT VOLUMES IN
SAGE LIBRARY OF SOCIAL RESEARCH

WHEN BONDING FAILS

Clinical Assessment of High-Risk Families

FRANK G. BOLTON, Jr.

Foreword by George D. Comerci

Volume 151
SAGE LIBRARY OF
SOCIAL RESEARCH

 SAGE PUBLICATIONS
Beverly Hills / London / New Delhi

For information address:

SAGE Publications, Inc.
275 South Beverly Drive
Beverly Hills, California 90212

SAGE Publications India Pvt. Ltd.
C-236 Defence Colony
New Delhi 110 024, India

SAGE Publications Ltd
28 Banner Street
London EC1Y 8QE, England

Printed in the United States of America

Library of Congress Cataloging in Publication Data

Bolton, Frank G.
    When bonding fails.

    (Sage library of social research; v. 151)
    1. Family violence. 2. Parent and child. 3. Family violence—Forecasting.
I. Title.   II. Series
HQ809.B64   1983   306.8'74   83-4425
ISBN 0-8039-2079-2
ISBN 0-8039-2080-6 (pbk.)

FIRST PRINTING

CONTENTS

This work is dedicated to

W. Boyd Dover and Bill Jamieson, Jr.,

for encouraging the acquisition of the knowledge within it,

J. Kipp Charlton, M.D., Dorothy Smith Gai, and Sandra Palmer Kane

for demonstrating how the knowledge can be applied, and

the memory of Larry Rork, M.D.,

who dedicated his career to the parents and children described by this work.

FOREWORD

My earliest experience with family violence was in Philadelphia when, as a young physician, I was confronted with a comatose young girl whose frightened mother was unwilling to explain the child's multiple facial bruises and the indisputable evidence of intercranial hemorrhage found later at autopsy. At the child's funeral, the mother, out of concern for herself and the safety of her other children, disclosed that the injury was inflicted by her teenage son. The year was 1960, a time when Henry Kempe was preparing to publish his first article on "the battered child syndrome." The turbulent 1960s followed and the time was right for a theory of child abuse that emphasized the role of an impoverished environment and its contribution to the individual's potential for abuse. Crisis, isolation, and limited family resources were emphasized as major factors leading to maltreatment in infants and children. Influenced by the times and the then current research in child maltreatment, I was eager to view the problem as one of "nurture" rather than "nature." I saw the perpetrator as a victim of circumstances and someone that could be helped if only the right kind and amount of resources were made available.

As I increasingly was confronted with seriously dysfunctional and chaotic families, I studied the background of parents who had abused children and was impressed by the degree of impairment of early bonding and attachment between parent and infant that could be historically documented. In an attempt further to explain this phenomenon to medical students and residents, I began to use references in my teaching to Harlow's early studies with rhesus female monkeys, which, having been "reared" by wire-mesh surrogate mothers, were unable to have normal sexual relations. After conception by artificial insemination, they bore physically normal offspring, only later to reject them completely.

During the 1970s, as I began to observe failures in certain families, regardless of investment of time, energy, and community resources, I came to realize there were certain perpetrators that, given a certain set of circumstances, exercised what seemed to be an "evolutionary" mechanism to ensure their own survival and to cope with limited physical and emotional resources. I began to stress that humans are not alone in this slaughter, and not only did it occur in other species but it seemed almost systematic. I pointed out that investigators during the late 1960s were beginning to identify and report dozens of species that killed their own. This was contrary to the writing of Konrad Lorenz, who argued that man was the only species that regularly killed its own kind; lions, hippos, bears, wolves, hyenas, and at least fifteen types of primates other than man did so as well.

Other examples of situations in which resources have become severely limited are striking in their relationship to child abuse as observed with young parents, those with multiple pregnancies in quick succession, and the effect on survival behavior in the parents. Infanticide has been used by many societies as a method of population control during times of economic stress, and cannibalism of infants and young children is known to have occurred under conditions of extreme famine. Colen Turnbull describes so well in his book, the *Mountain People,* the deterioration of a culture when deprived of its basic beliefs, rituals, and tradition.

In *When Bonding Fails,* Bud Bolton beautifully weaves into a synthesis sociobiology, attachment (mother-infant bonding) theory, and existing child maltreatment knowledge. The result is a single clinical/academic approach to the problem of violent families. The last twenty years of research and theory development have suffered from a lack of applied development and a narrowness that prohibited other areas of theory from expanding its horizons. With the publication of this volume, this is no longer true. Each theoretical approach, until now, seemed to lack an important element—that having to do with the mechanisms which drive humans and their offspring toward survival. *When Bonding Fails* addresses the mystery of why some families engage in violence when confronted with certain stresses and others do not.

This book is a first. The theoretical approaches it takes are controversial enough to excite the academic never confronted by an abused child. The hard applied suggestions are adequate to serve the clinician as a manual for dealing with child maltreatment cases and violent families in general. Finally, the massive literature reviews in each topical area are attractive to the professor of medicine, psychology, nursing, sociology, and social work, as well as any form of social and medical science who finds the study of the family to be at its heart.

There are no true competitors for this work. The early child maltreatment literature growing out of the work of Henry Kempe and co-workers at the University of Colorado Medical Center is medically focused and beginning to age in the face of new findings. The mother-infant bonding work of Klaus and Kennell in the late 1960s has not been well replicated and now finds itself in some doubt. The attachment theory work of John Bowlby in England remains the classic work in the field but is inaccessible to all but the most committed reader due to its length. Finally, the new works on sociobiology by Wilson and Barash ignore the natural aspects of child maltreatment other than as it applies to incest. The only work remotely approaching this manuscript is a Grune and Stratton work (1980) by Paul M. Taylor entitled *Parent-Infant Relationships,* which takes an academic medical approach to recent biological research. It does not approach the child maltreatment issues.

I am fascinated and intrigued by Dr. Bolton's yeoman accomplishment in providing the theoretical and research foundations for what I have struggled with over the last two decades. For me the book has served to organize my thoughts and has provided information needed for more effective teaching. As a guide for practitioners it offers an approach to conduct by (a) providing methods for easy identification of the high-risk family, (b) suggesting ways of screening out families not likely to benefit from known interventions, and (c) giving a theoretical explanation for the etiology of this difficult family and social problem.

When Bonding Fails is a landmark work for the practitioner, teacher, and researcher. It will provoke controversy and learning, argument and discussion, thought and direct help in the area of violent families. *When Bonding Fails* is gratifying to me in that it encompasses my own maturation as a student, practitioner, and teacher in the conceptualization of family violence.

—*George D. Comerci, M.D.*

PREFACE

Benjamin Franklin has been given credit for uttering the advice to "either write things worth reading or do things worth the writing." Trying to fit into either of these categories is the constant struggle of the clinician who also attempts to record his or her clinical experiences through the development of theory. It is impossible to know, without unrestrained examination by colleagues, just when you have done something worth writing about. It is equally impossible to know when your own writing about it is worth someone else's reading it. As such, books like this one are rarely developed solely by the author. This book is no exception to this general rule.

Three persons have played a privotal role in the development of this book. The first is Dr. John Scanzoni of the University of North Carolina. Dr. Scanzoni's critical reviews of the various drafts of this work forced its continual refinement. The second is Dr. Richard Gelles of the University of Rhode Island. Dr. Gelles's clear and honest examinations of this work not only directed me toward a better product, but also educated me in those aspects of theory building more familiar to the sociologist than to the psychologist. His urging gave me the initial courage to believe that there was a theory to be developed from this information. Finally, Dr. John Johnson of the Arizona State University has provided continual support throughout the long periods of tedious examination and reexamination of the information used to develop Family Resource Theory. Without the counsel of any of these social scientists, this book would be destined to rest in that vast storehouse of projects I wish I had accomplished.

The information and theory presented in this book are a product of watching violent families from a research and clinical perspective for nearly ten years. This work is also built on watching clinicians who have elected to deal with these families and the price they pay for their professional choice. The information in this book is intended to help those who are victimized by family violence as well as those who are victimized by their choice of focusing on violent families in their clinical work.

The utility of the work is that it provides organization to the morass of data that batter the clinician when first examining the violent and potentially violent family. It provides a means to set priorities, throw out extraneous detail, and begin more solid prediction. Most important, it does something that is almost never done for the behavioral clinician: It gives some idea of when to consider surrender. It is the constant battling with the "almost well" violent family that takes its toll upon the clinician in this area. Knowing when to back away from a given family and focus on a more productive therapeutic relationship elsewhere may be the only survival mechanism available to the clinician in the family violence area.

Developing this knowledge for all clinicians is impossible. Providing guidelines from which they can make their own determination is not. This book provides those guidelines.

Violence is certainly not a unitary phenomenon, and the application of theory to the examination of the violent family reflects the multidisciplinary knowledge demanded. Part I provides the clinician with the basic theoretical background from which to begin an examination of the violent family in general and the parent-child relationship in particular. Research from the past twenty years of child maltreatment research is examined. The unlikely admixture of physical and social sciences that generated the study of sociobiology is reviewed. Finally, the core of this theory, attachment and bonding, is reviewed from the psychiatric, psychological, and medical foundations from which it has grown. Taken as a unit, these three theoretical formulations comprise the heart of the assessment scheme presented in this work.

Part II examines the special relationship between parent and child. The roles played by the parent are reviewed as they affect the child. The impact of the child on the parent is noted. An interactionist approach to the relationship is established to allow the clinician to reaffirm the regularized observation that each member of the family must play a specific role if the family is to develop successfully.

Also within Part II are detailed examinations of the special times of parent-child relating. The demands of pregnancy, labor, delivery, and the early neonatal period are viewed in detail. This detailed review opens points of assessment and critical incident examination that have been left to chance in the clinical setting for too long. The section ends with a view of the relationship between parent and child that should provide a foundation for continued growth and development—and suggests why it sometimes does not fulfill its promise.

Part III brings the view of the family down to that family with a special need. Thorough examinations of the premature child, the premature (adolescent) parent, and the low-birth-weight or failure-to-thrive child are presented to alert the clinician to unusual problem predictors. These family issues are known to cause stress, and the whys and hows of these stressful family events are reviewed.

In the fourth and final section, the "how-to" elements of Family Resource Theory and the Graduated Resource Assessment scheme are presented. For the clinician, this section will be the "meat" of the work, although without a good understanding of the material in the sections that precede it, its application will suffer.

This work does not promise final answers to the problems facing clinicians and researchers in the family violence area. It does promise some guidelines for assessment, a manner of arranging the approach to the family, and some warning signals that a family may be drifting along a precarious path. For the student, clinician, and researcher alike, this work provides a solid review of what we know of these families and their origins. If, from these origins, the clinician and the researcher can begin to predict outcomes, then this work and the clinical examinations that have led to its being written will have met Franklin's criteria.

PART I

INTRODUCTION

Chapter 1

FAMILY RESOURCE THEORY

Range, Purpose, and
Limitations of This Work

There is no greater contradiction than that between the perception of the family as a warm, safe, and happy place and the record of known family violence. Family advocates suggest that it is inconceivable for parents to respond to their child as though it were merely an "inanimate thing" (Newson, 1977: 50), but they do. A complete failure to respond to the child's needs is unthinkable, yet it occurs regularly. Violence is a part of some families—a part that may never change.

The purpose of this work is to develop and offer a theoretical perspective on violence between parents and children. This is a perspective to be used most frequently by the clinician, not the researcher. Because this theory provides the clinician with a tool to assess the emotional, environmental, and educational resources in the family, it is termed *Family Resource Theory*. This theoretical model has two major purposes: (1) It will allow the clinician to "screen" parent-child relationships prior to the onset of a maltreatment event, to allow for prediction of risk, and (2) it will make possible an estimation of the potential success of treatment, allowing for the planned application of resources. It is not within the range of this work to capture the full spectrum of child maltreatment theory in a single presentation. This theory is little more than the application of some practical elements of child and family research to the world of the clinician. In this sense, Family Resource Theory is a *clinical theory* of child maltreatment.

Despite twenty years of research and study, the search for a clinical theory of child maltreatment has been frustrating. A large measure of the clinician's frustration flows from that small number of families who seem impervious to change regardless of the time, energy, or resources applied. These are the families who repetitively engage in violent acts across all generations. For these families, violence seems a legacy from the past and a promise for the future. Identifying these highest-risk parent-child relationships is the basic purpose of Family Resource Theory.

The focus on clinical aspects of child maltreatment does not negate the power of the broader perceptions of the development of this problem. It must be recognized that culture and society are the ultimate "gatekeepers" (Gelles, 1979) of violence toward family members. However, these concepts are somewhat difficult to apply to a narrow clinical perspective such as this. The absence of direct discussion of broadly based contributions to maltreatment does not deny their value in bringing understanding. This is more a statement of the necessary narrowness of a clinical theory. Family Resource Theory is similarly restricted in its construction. It is also likely to be falsely interpreted as negative.

Most of the child maltreatment research and theory of the past twenty years has had an optimistic bent. There has been an unspoken sense that a continued attack on isolated variables would eventually uncover the key for bringing the problem closer to resolution. Amid this forward-moving sense, there was one description that did not promise change. Some of that thinking is reflected in Family Resource Theory.

Canadian psychiatrist David Bakan provided the child maltreatment world with a 1971 book entitled *Slaughter of the Innocents*. This work had an unfamiliar ring. Bakan suggested that violence against children might be a "natural" element of the human family. As such, child maltreatment was said to be an element of the human being's basic "evolutionary equipment" as well as a necessary mechanism for controlling resources. This view cannot be accepted in its entirety, but the time has come to consider the possibilities it presents to the clinician's theory.

The decade since Bakan's work has brought forth a behavior theory that complements his thinking: sociobiology. Its framework is "psychobiological" in the same manner as Bakan's description of child maltreatment. As with all theories that attempt to explain the panorama of behavior, sociobiology has as many enemies as it has friends. *It is not the purpose of this work to put those friends and enemies at peace.*

In this book, I do not utilize or attempt to support sociobiology as a global construct. Rather, elements of sociobiology, as well as attachment theory and child maltreatment theory, have been chosen to construct Family Resource Theory. The theory may enable us to distinguish families who find maltreatment to be "natural" from those who are responding to "unnatural" events in their world. The decline in resources for dealing with violent families in today's world demands a growing ability to achieve that level of discrimination.

The discussion of families that will not change should not steal hope from the optimistic stance of previous child maltreatment theory. A reduction in child maltreatment can still be hoped for, and Family Resource Theory is presented to accelerate that reduction. This decline can occur only through greater efficiency in applying the limited resources clinicians have for dealing with the maltreatment problem.

The time has come to relieve the clinician and child protection specialist from the burden of expecting that all families can change. The time has come to relieve the child protection "system" of the burden of families who consume disproportionate amounts of energy and resources, often while families who could be helped become more entrapped by their errors. The time has come to seek to identify maltreatment risk prior to an act of maltreatment. Finally, the time has come to make choices and plan for the application of our limited treatment resources. It is hoped that Family Resource Theory, as presented in this work, will begin to allow application of solid knowledge to all those imposing tasks.

The Animal in Us All:
Violence Potential Between
Parent and Child

As a group, we human beings are selective in the admission of the "animal" origins of some of our behaviors. As a rule, the animal nature of our more complex behaviors is denied. It seems more comfortable for us to assume that our animal origins have been wrestled into control through language capacity and intelligence. While it is true that we have more behavioral choices than less complex animals, even now we cannot forget that some of our behavioral choices grow out of the animal history living within us.

The past ten years have seen a growing interest in the animal origins of human social behavior. This interest is embodied in *sociobiology.* At its heart, sociobiology is an application of biological and evolutionary knowledge to the social behaviors of the human animal as well as other members of the animal kingdom. Family Resource Theory utilizes that knowledge, in part, to describe the mechanisms by which parents may engage in what is generally considered an "animal" act: violence against their children.

This is not a book about sociobiology. This work uses sociobiological principles, along with those of *attachment theory* and the *child maltreatment* literature, to structure a theoretical procedure for identifying the risk of violence between parents and children. Psychological field theorist Kurt Lewin once noted that "nothing is as practical as a good theory." This work attempts to live up to that axiom, combining these three collections of theoretical knowledge into a practical scheme for those who make decisions for and about violent families.

The application of sociobiological principles to social behavior in humans is mildly threatening to some behavioral scientists. The "father" of sociobiological study, E. O. Wilson (1979: 14), finds the origin of this threat in the reductionistic style of sociobiology. After all, if strict sociobiological theory can reduce our behaviors to a prescribed set of laws and reactions, the human seems less unique and in control. David Barash, zoologist/psychologist and another leading sociobiological thinker, offers two additional sources of discomfort.

Barash (1978: 19) feels that social scientific anxiety is raised through the use of natural selection as a guiding principle and the seeking of distal rather than proximal causes of behavior. As sociobiology is applied within this theoretical model of parent-child violence, literal interpretations of natural selection have no place. On the other hand, it *is* occasionally asked that the individual who would apply this model move from proximal to distal thinking. For example, it will be asked that the clinician or researcher remove himself or herself from immediate causes of violence and consider the possibility that violence is an adaptive response to the history of parent or child. That is a type of negative adaptiveness most of us find unfamiliar.

As evolution is understood by most, elements that become adaptive over time are assumed to be positive. Adaptations that occur as a result of evolution are presumed to be positive for the species as a whole. Sociobiological thinking postulates that change does not occur at the group level, as is commonly assumed, but at the level of the individual and his or her gene pool.

Assumption of group benefit through evolutionary change prevents adequate consideration of the culture and environment in which the individual must live and adapt. Also, the individual may find the need to act in ways contrary to acceptable group behavior in order to meet his or her own individual needs. A loose definition of the individual's need to act in ways that maximize his own survival, and the survival of his genes, is the sociobiological application of the term "fitness." An individual's "fitness" within a particular environment refers to an ability to survive and produce offspring who can also survive and prosper.

Sociobiology offers to its students the mechanisms by which we meet the challenges of survival and procreation. There is no attempt in this science to minimize the complexity of the human being. There is a clear message that an adaptive function lies behind our commonly shared behavior. One of those shared behaviors is violence. An understanding of the individual's perception of the adaptive needs behind a behavior, even violent behavior, will provide us reasonable clues to the whys of its occurrence.

In brief, sociobiology posits that behavior in humans originates in an interaction between the "instruction encoded" within our evolutionary history and the "environmental realities" we confront, which maximize the fitness of ourselves and our offspring (Barash, 1979: 27). These contributors to behavior are uniformly required, hold equal power, and hold an equal capacity for failure and distortion.

Foundations: Child Maltreatment Theory, Attachment Theory, and Sociobiology

Sociobiology is not the sole foundation on which the model presented in this book is based. Twenty years of child maltreatment research have produced a multitude of explanations for why maltreatment occurs. These descriptions cover diverse and familiar areas: crisis, environmental stress, psychopathology, economic stress, and numerous other demographic and dynamic factors that influence family "fitness" (Bolton, 1980: 150-156). Despite this research and theory, a mystery remains: Why do some families engage in violence when confronted with these stresses while others do not?

The presumption of the model presented here is that sociobiological theory can describe the mechanisms that drive humans and their offspring toward survival, attachment theory describes those mechanisms that work against destruction and ensure survival of the parent-child partnership, and child maltreatment theories describe how the "natural" drive toward survival and protection can become distorted or destroyed.

The use of these three theoretical structures demands acceptance of some basic assumptions. Above all, there must be an acceptance of the assumption that child maltreatment is a shared potential rather than an aberration that afflicts only certain "sick" individuals. This assumption is in accord with recent conclusions drawn by family violence researchers Robert L. Burgess and Rand Conger. These sociologists have observed that the frequency, history, and generalizability of family violence across species and cultures remove the sense of abnormality and pathology from it as a behavioral choice (Burgess et al., 1980). Violence, then, is seen in this work as an option for all families.

A second assumption is that individuals will behave in ways that maximize their fitness (Barash, 1979: 25). The individual will seek to maximize his or her own survival, increase the likelihood of offspring production and survival, support kin over others, and seek adaptation to their environment. This is a balancing act of choices that grows out of individual predispositions and environmental reality. Within this structure, the human is not empty at birth, awaiting the shaping of his or her environment. Humans are equipped at birth with a set of basic skills (attachment behaviors) that can influence the environments in which they are born. In a complementary way, their environments can also influence the demonstration of these basic skills (child maltreatment theory).

In the study of adaptive behaviors (fitness), bringing such elements together has come to be called the "interaction principle" (Barash, 1979: 24). Through this interaction, either the individual's predisposition or the environment can limit and direct that person's behavioral choices as he or she seeks survival. Violence is among those choices.

A third assumption of this model is that *all behavior is adaptive.* There is a purposefulness behind behaviors that directs their selection. The purpose of a unique behavior selection may not be in our conscious awareness; nevertheless, purpose is inherent. We can make choices, select from the environment available to us, and think independently. However, our choices of behaviors will lean toward those most beneficial to ourselves first, our kin second, and all others third. This is a selection process directed by two principles necessary for survival: altrusim and reciprocity.

Altruism relates to the cost-benefit ratio in survival. Generally, due to limitations in resources, giving benefits of any kind to another involves a cost to us. Some relationships are presumed to provide this giving no matter the cost. The human parent-child pair is an example of a relationship in which this is assumed. We are shocked when parents favor themselves over their children. When altruism toward kin fails, we find it difficult to understand. The key to understanding is the knowledge that altruism is maintained only through some level of reciprocity.

Seeking a general theory of behavior, Richard Alexander (1975) refers to a reciprocity model developed by Sahlins to describe parental behaviors. The Sahlins model divides reciprocity into three distinct types: generalized, balanced, and negative. Generalized reciprocity is that type expected of parents. It is a one-way flow that demands nothing from the child in order to continue. The person providing the altruistic behavior here must find a reciprocal reward in his own thinking about the beneficiary of his generosity. Balanced reciprocity, as anticipated by its name, is a direct and real exchange. This occurs between parent and child as the child becomes older and can actually reciprocate with the parent. Negative reciprocity is an attempt to get something for nothing (Alexander, 1975: 92). Although these principles will be explored in depth later, a simplified application may be seen in the following.

There are obvious costs in helping children grow and develop. We have come to expect an innate altruism in parents that minimizes this cost for them. The child reciprocates the parent's giving by growing and developing. For the adequate parent, this is sufficient reward in itself. However, when circumstances alter that capacity for altruistic feeling, or when the parent expects immediate and obvious reciprocity from the child, the form and substance of the parent-child relationship are substantially altered. Altruism and appropriate reciprocity in the parent-child relationship are resources for survival in the same way food or shelter would be seen as a resource. If these elements are distorted through parental inadequacy or environmental pressures, protection of that child's survival is decreased.

This theoretical perspective is based on the assumption that violence is an element of the "natural course" of things, even among families. The "adaptive" and "natural" elements of family violence are not those typically associated with today's positive sense of "natural" things. This simply respects the fact that *families can be driven to internal violence through a perception of threatened survival.* Violence in families is mediated by the fact that individuals will seek to sustain themselves. In some cases, the needs of an individual out-weigh that individual's need for the other family members. When the altruism and reciprocity that ordinarily direct behavior in families become distorted in this way, that family becomes vulnerable to environmental pressures, which can lead to violence. It is the prediction of distortion that is sought through this model.

WHAT SHIFTED IN SOCIETY THAT SOCIETAl mESSAGE is NOT To SACRifice AND NOT To HAVE CHiLDREN?

Parenthood:
The Promise of Protection

We are, as animals, constructed to promote the birth and survival of children. As David Barash (1979: 25) reminds his readers, "A genetic basis for intentional childlessness would have a dim evolutionary future." The parent also has the capacity to behave in ways that increase the likelihood that the child will be protected and prosper. Most human parents happily allow themselves to be drawn into that sacrificial role. Some parents do not. Those who do not seem to be able to give are prime candidates for violence against their children.

?

Robert L. Trivers (1974) has examined the costs of parenthood in great detail. He describes the parent-child partnership as a conflictual one balanced on a tenuous series of cost-benefit calculations. The key feature of the partnership is what Trivers (1974: 249) refers to as "parental investment." The parent in Trivers's model is required to sacrifice for the child in order to maximize the child's opportunities for growth and survival. Since the energy and resources surrounding the parent are limited, this expenditure must be taken from another area of the parent's life and becomes an investment. These are resources or energy that the parent could have devoted to himself. As the child develops from a helpless being to one more independent, the amount of the investment required of the parent will decline, at least in terms of energy expenditure. This allows for attention to be directed toward additional offspring.

our mothers HAVE Limited Resources to draw from.

For the human parent, this period of initial high investment of energy and resources is lengthy. This is a period that places limits on the number of children we can expect to produce. Because the number of total children is smaller, the human parent's investment in the quality of each child is very high, which means that parent will make huge investments of energy and resources in a small number of important parent-child relationships. The pressure within that relationship to meet the needs of both partners, as a result of the small number of relationships that are expected, can be overwhelming. ➔

Many reject the cost-benefit perspective on parenthood. Unable to find such thinking in their own consciousness, they reject it for all other parent-child pairings. It is difficult to accept the possibility of a parent rejecting a child as a result of the "costs" of parenthood, yet it does occur. Two major factors make it possible: (1) *The rejection is not often conscious.* (2) *The rejection is not a direct rejection of the child but of the controls that militate against violence and rejection in the parent.* These naturally occurring controls against parental rejection and violence are the bonding and attachment mechanisms built into all animal parent-child relationships.

Studies of animal parent-child relationships (Kennell et al., 1976: 26) as well as human pairings provide a dramatic demonstration that specific attachment mechanisms exist between parent and child. This capacity for attachment has been designed to maximize the child's opportunities for survival and growth. This is possible because attachment directs some measure of the parental investment to be applied automatically; cost-benefit considerations do not come into play.

Attachment and bonding between parent and child are sometimes spoken of as elements that enhance the relationship. They are, in reality, much more basic. The heart of attachment between parent and child is survival. This is a protective mechanism that aids the child in its struggle to survive as he or she conducts the difficult and consuming tasks of development. This layer of protection helps not only to balance the competitors in the child's external world, but also to offset some of the costs the parent might otherwise consider to be too great.

When the attachment mechanisms are functional, the parent is able to focus on the benefits of parenthood. Should they be dysfunctional, the parent will focus on the costs. From a sociobiological perspective, if the attachment mechanisms between parent and child are adequate, the dyad will follow culturally acceptable rules regarding the costs and benefits of parenting. Should the attachment relationship be impaired, the controls against parental aberration, ordinarily applied by cultural norms, no longer apply. By way of warning, however, even in the parent who has average attachment capacity, the costs of parenting a particular child or parenting within a particular environment may be too great.

COST of pg + child birth

Seeking Partnership in Survival:
Contributions of the Child

Anthropologist Robin Fox has described the parent-child bond as *the* basic social relationship. This is the one relationship that comes to us directly from nature. In fact, Fox (1973: 98) suggests that the parent-child bond and "considerable imagination" are all that nature really gives us to aid in survival. Should the bond prove successful, this imagination can be devoted to commitment and positive experience. Should the bond prove weak, the imagination is often devoted to more negative activity. While this entire process is often thought to be limited to the parent, that is untrue.

The child walks a precarious line with respect to parental investment. Somehow, the child must seek to acquire and consume all the parent has to give while letting the parent know that his or her investment is worth while. During this entire sequence, the child is working with an individual who clearly holds the *real* power in the relationship. If the child is to be successful, two elements must be present: (1) The capacity for altruistic behavior must exist in the parent. (2) The parent must have the capacity to understand the reciprocal nature of what the child has to offer, as opposed to a conscious awareness of what it takes from the parent. These two capacities cannot be assumed to be present in all parents.

When the capacity for the child to elicit parental investment is matched with the parent's ability to invest, there is a "reciprocal altruism" in the relationship (Shapiro, 1978: 35). The parent and child are cooperating. The child is consuming massive amounts of energy and parental resources but is successful in providing the parent the message that he or she will benefit from the child's successful growth and development. If this cooperation changes to the point that a scarcity of resources begins to threaten the parent's survival, competition between parent and child develops quickly. Given the domination of the parent in this pair, competition can only predict loss for the child.

Both parent and child are provided with some degree of the emotional strength it takes to weather competition between them. Competition will occur between them from time to time, and assessment of their ability to elicit cooperation during these competitive periods is helpful in understanding the partnership. In effect, the ability of parent and child to cooperate during stress-free times is important, but their ability to cooperate during stressful times is vital if violent behavior is to be avoided.

Nature has provided children with the capacity to attract parents toward them in a manner that evokes investment in their survival. The cooperative parent will be altruistic and reciprocate the child's giving if he or she is capable of appreciating the rewards the child's growth has to offer. This requires an ability to accept the social message that being a parent and having a child are rewarding in themselves. Should this message be distorted by unreasonable parental expectations, an underestimation of the costs of parenting, or an environmental factor which makes the child a competitor for scarce physical or emotional resources, the collapse of this "natural" relationship may occur.

Society changed message [handwritten marginal note]

The parent-child relationship can not be presumed to be a naturally safe environment. To the contrary, the family is a natural breeding ground for conflict and competition. When the controls against competition are minimal and the physical or emotional resources scarce, violence may occur.

A House of Cards: Physical and Emotional Resource Limitations in the Maltreating Family

Literally hundreds of professional studies and empirical research works have illuminated the limitations in resources faced by violent families (Bolton et al., 1981). The unpredictable availability of necessary physical and emotional resources is a characteristic risk factor to be considered in the assessment of violence potential in any family.

Since the reader of this work is likely to be familiar with the child maltreatment literature, it will be given only brief review. The purpose of this review is simply to establish the capacity held by this deprived environment to interact with impaired attachment capacity, reduce the natural protections within the family, and increase violent risk in the family.

Early surveys of maltreating family environments pointed toward a marked scarcity of physical resources. Basically, there appeared to be an overrepresentation of lower socioeconomic (SES) status families in this group (Gil, 1970). That is a characteristic finding, sustained in more recent work (Pelton, 1978). This general deprivation is exacerbated by continuing resource inhibitors, such as low educational and

Does EARLY pg. serve same function, even if terminated?

occupational levels (Holmes, 1978) and high rates of unemployment (Young, 1964). These predictors of failure to compete in the outside world are joined by similar factors in the family.

Parents engaging in maltreatment appear to be younger at the birth of the first child than nonmaltreating parents (Holmes, 1978). This raises the potential for a longer childbearing career, during which a large number of children are born in close succession (Light, 1973). The threat in this situation, of course, is the dispersion of parental investment. An additional threat is found in the fact that these parents do not possess the personal emotional strengths necessary to carry the relationship through the stresses of the environmental deprivation.

PARENTAL LOVE DEPRIVATION

According to the literature, maltreating parents have quite often experienced deprivation in physical and emotional resources in their own childhood (Kempe & Helfer, 1972). This background frequently leads to aberrant emotional needs in them as parents (Steele, 1975), which contribute to a perception of the child as a competitor even when he or she was not (Martin, 1976). These are parents who were isolated from predictable sources of physical and emotional support (Helfer, 1975). Not surprisingly, these parents turn to their children with the expectation that parenthood would enhance their own impoverished emotional resources. The parenting skills that might have compensated for their great needs are largely unavailable (Fontana, 1973). The net effect is an alteration in the child's role in the family from that of consumer of resources to one of provider. This new role is unfamiliar to the child, and failure in it often leads to frustration and aggression from the parent, who expects and needs more.

As indicated earlier, while this struggle for internal and external resources has proven a difficult one for maltreating families, it does not sufficiently explain the generation of a violent event. It does not account for similarly struggling families who do not fall victim to violence. In the theoretical model proposed by this work, there is a struggle that begins long before resource scarcity pushes that relationship into violence: the struggle of the parent and child to seek a bond that will promote altruism, reciprocity, and partnership. Not incidentally, this is the same bond that prevents violence. When this initial struggle becomes too great for the parent and child, the secondary struggle for resources leads directly to a failed partnership.

Graduated Resource Assessment:
Evaluating Early Suggestions
of Violence Potential

In order to survive, the parent-child partnership must strike a more delicate balance than often assumed. Somehow our society has assumed that, if parents are left to their own devices, their inherent strengths will anchor the operations of this relationship properly. This is untrue. The relationship between the parent, the child, and the environment in which they live is a tenuous one, which presents new stressors on a daily basis. A model for assessing this balance, the stressors, and the parent and child's level of partnership is the goal of Family Resource Theory.

The "graduated" nature of this model grows out of the necessity to consider the elements of this assessment in a stepwise and orderly fashion. If the first factor within the relationship under study (attachment) is distorted, it can be assumed that elements which follow will also be distorted in some manner. Since all of the factors under study within this model actually pertain to a physical, social, or emotional resource, it is also termed a "resource" assessment. The theoretical foundations for this model, and the measurements that stand as benchmarks for assessment, are drawn from the three knowledge bases described earlier: sociobiology, attachment theory, and child maltreatment theory. Before going ahead with a fuller description of this model, a word of warning is necessary.

The presentation of this theoretical model, at this point, provides a strategy that is simple enough to be deceptive. The complexity of the factors it describes is enormous. This complexity will be understood only through the detail of the chapters to follow. Consider what is presented in this chapter nothing more than a depiction of the skeleton of this model. The flesh that will operationalize it will be added as the work progresses.

The application of the three theoretical frameworks discussed early in this chapter can be evidenced through the basic operating assumptions of this model. These assumptions are: (1) *There is a basic structure necessary for successful parent-child partnerships.* This structure is, in part, naturally imparted through our natural heritage rather than learned. It is visible through the bonding and attachment capacity of parent and child. (2) *There is a balance between competition and cooperation in the successful parent-child partnership.* (3) *The emotional and physical resources necessary for partnership survival are finite in all parent-child relationships.* (4) *The human parent is able to use intelligent decision making to compensate for and adapt to resource limitations.* Within the model, these assumptions are interdependent.

Within the model, should the necessary attachment capacity and mechanisms be unavailable to parent or child, the remaining factors will not compensate for their absence. Should competition be distorted, resources will be misused. Should emotional or physical resources be too limited, intelligent choice by the parent may not provide adequate compensation for the stresses in the environment. Ultimately, each of these operational assumptions can serve to maximize the potential of the parent-child partnership—or to destroy it. The potential of the individual partnership can be collapsed into two major assessment themes.

The Relationship Assessment Continuum: Attachment Relations/Rejection Capacity

The first element of the parent-child relationship to be assessed within this model, is the attachment capacity of both parent and child. This assessment is conducted, as will be described in detail, through an examination of historical and behavioral observations surrounding pregnancy, bonding at birth, and the progressive expansion or destruction of the parent-child partnership. Attachment capacity must be present if the minimal standards for growth are to be met. Similarly, a gross absence in this attachment capacity is predictive of a high-risk situation in which the parent will reject the child and which will culminate in the destruction of the relationship. *Attachment capacity must be present to some degree* in both parent and child.

Discussing attachment as a range of capacities is necessary. It is not a single, self-contained relationship element that is either present or not. The range of attachment capacities to be seen will vary from the parent totally unable to attach to that parent seemingly attached even before the birth of the child. Most parent-child relationships fall between these two extremes. Even when functioning at the highest level, however, attachment capacity is predictive of only the parent-child partnership's potential to expand in the right direction. This is not a prediction of success. The presence of attachment only guards against immediate failure and satisfies the basic requirements for initiating growth between parent and child. Those elements that will maximize or inhibit the solid start offered by adequate attachment capacity are the substance of the second level of assessment.

The Resource Assessment Continuum:
Emotional, Environmental, and Educational Factors

Once the attachment potential of the parent-child partnership has been established, assessment of the resources available to this partnership must be undertaken. It is the presence or absence of these necessary resources, and their appropriate use, that predict maximization or inhibition of the capacity for positive partnership between parent and child.

Within this assessment procedure, *the physical resource limitations impinging on parent and child draw first attention.* This includes physical limitations of the parent and child themselves as well as those limitations that occur in their environment. It is assumed here that the inhibition of physical means to survival may prohibit necessary adjustment to social or emotional problems. Physical capabilities and requirements must reach some minimal level before social or emotional issues can be rationally addressed. For example, the pain of hunger or of caring for a congenitally handicapped child will be of more immediate importance to the overstressed parent than will emotional relationships with others in the environment.

Upon completion of a physical resource inventory, the examination of the family turns toward social elements within their world. The major reference point here would be an examination of the social support systems available to this parent and child, both currently and throughout their past. This examination is completed with an exploration of community resources as well as neighborhood and extended family supports. This may be considered an examination of all formal and informal mechanisms of support and of the parent's or child's use of these supports. The general question here is: *Who or what is here to help this parent and child survive the stresses they face?*

As a third element of this continuum, an assessment of the emotional resources present in both parent and child becomes necessary. This resource pool may grow out of the parent's childhood, the parent's or child's personality characteristics, or factors present in the current relationship between parent and child. There may also be huge gaps in emotional resources as a result of these historical and relationship factors. In their presence or absence, these emotional elements of the parent and child have far-ranging expression in the conduct of their responsibilities toward each other. The final elements of this continuum are the educational variables that play into success or failure between parent and child.

Human and animal parents differ dramatically when the issue of choice of parental behaviors is raised. The human parent, alone, is able to acquire vast amounts of new learning and information that expand the alternatives he or she holds in the parenting of offspring. In fact, the acquisition of this knowledge is almost vital to successful parenting. Should this information be unavailable to the parent, or should it be distorted, the alternative chosen may be inappropriate.

The knowledge factors under study in this category of assessment appear in two distinct areas. *The first of these assessment points is that of the parent's intellectual ability to acquire parenting concepts and the child's intellectual capacity to respond to them.* Should intellectual capacity be deeply impaired, the ability to adapt to the parent-child relationship will also be impaired.

A second point of assessment is that of the fund of parenting alternatives available to a given parent. Critical to this assessment is knowledge of the origin of those parenting alternatives known to the parent. It is important to understand not only what is known, but also how it came to be known. Should this fund of knowledge be adequate, adjustments can occur in the face of resource limitations. If absent or distorted, this aspect of parental inability can destroy an otherwise functional relationship.

This resource assessment procedure is intended to predict means by which the environment, emotional capacity, or educational factors can enhance or inhibit potential success or failure. The utility of the model at this point is in the identification of points of relief or stress.

Thus, while the initial relationship assessment is predictive of potential for success or failure generally, this second level of resource assessment predicts the direction of this success or failure.

Graduated Resource Assessment: A Summary

The assessment model proposed here asks the clinician or researcher to view the potentially violent family systematically. The "system" can be found in the application of two theoretical continuums of interdependent and progressive family operation. The first of these operational continua seeks to assess the relationship variables between parent and child and is made up of a balance of reciprocal behaviors that set the stage for parent-child attachment. The second continuum views resource variables available to parent and child that will maximize or inhibit physical, social, emotional, or knowledge growth in the parntership. Both of these assessment points seek to establish the parent or child's ability to use or misuse the resources and capacities each possesses. Finally, this is a graduated system, in which failure at early points is predictive of failure in subsequent areas.

The Graduated Resource Assessment model recognizes the animal origins of many parenting behaviors as well as the uniquely human ability to adjust and make choices. The natural elements of the parent-child relationship (attachment behaviors) are seen as providing the canvas on which the relationship takes form. The necessary dependence on a minimal level of resource availability in the environment is recognized. Finally, parental knowledge is called upon to provide for flexibility needed in the successful parent-child relationship. Graphically, this model would appear as in Table 1.1.

Taken as an interdependent group, these are the building blocks of a parent-child relationship, which can secure partnership or promise failure. The mechanisms by which the clinician or researcher can observe and identify the positive or negative aspects of each of these assessment points are offered in the chapters to follow.

TABLE 1.1   The Graduated Resource Assessment Model

I. *Relationship Assessment Continuum:*
   Assessment Element   *Assessment Procedure*

   1. Parental childhood attachments   Retrospective report

   2. Pregnancy (all children)   Retrospective report/
                                                 observation

   3. Delivery experience (all   Retrospective report
      children)

   4. Postpartum experience   Retrospective report/
      (All children)   observation

   5. Early bonding (all children)   Observation/parental
                                                 report

   6. Attachment prior to 1 year   Observation/parental
      (all children)   report

   7. Attachment prior to 3   Observation/parental
      years (all children)   report

   8. Ongoing attachment (all   Parent and child report/
      children   observation

II. *Resource Assessment Continuum:*

   1. Physical limitations of   Observation/parental
      the parent   report

   2. Physical limitations of   Observation/parental
      the child   report/child report

   3. Physical limitations of   Observation/parental
      the environment   report/child report

   4. Social support limitations   Parental report/child
      in the environment   report/Extended family

   5. Emotional limitations of   Parental report/child
      the parent   report/other professional
                                                 report/observation

TABLE 1.1 (Continued)

6. Emotional limitations of the child	Parental report/child report/other professional report/observation
7. Intellectual limitations of the child; intellectual capacity	Observation/parental report/other professional report
8. Intellectual limitations of Parent; intellectual capacity	Observation/other professional report
9. Intellectual limitations of the parent; fund of knowledge	Observation/child report/parent report/other professional report
10. Other limitations	Observation

PART II

BEHAVIORAL OBSERVATION OF ATTACHMENT CAPACITY

Chapter 2

IN THE BEGINNING
Initial Bonding and
Attachment Behaviors

As has been noted, we *Homo sapiens* can become mildly defensive
when similarities are drawn between human and animal behaviors.
This makes sense; the human animal is proud and lives a lifetime
packed with behavioral options. However, this blanket rejection of
the natural origins of some of our animal behaviors may be short-
sighted. A series of reductionistic maneuvers that bring behavior
down to its most basic elements may well be our best hope for early
identification of potentially faulty behavior selection. This is
particularly applicable to parents who seem to make inappropriate
decisions about their behavior with their children from the beginning—
parents who engage in maltreatment.

It is one premise of the model presented in this book that maltreating parents face child-rearing careers with fewer options than other
parents. The options are limited because their parenting capacity is
inadequate from the beginning. This inadequacy is most evident in
maltreating parent's impaired capacity to share a bonding and attachment experience with their children.

Bonding and attachment are the two most basic parenting abilities.
These abilities come to use in the same manner they come to all other
members of the animal kingdom—naturally. When there is an impairment or incapacity in these abilities, there will be something
"unnatural" about the parent-child relationship. A parent-child relationship without adequate attachment has a basic, and perhaps
fatal, flaw.

To the extent that a parent-child relationship is flawed by distortions in attachment capacity, there will be an increased susceptibility
to poor decision making, particularly in the face of physical or emotional
resource limitations. Should stress occur, such a fundamentally

41

impaired partnership is more likely to collapse under its own weight than is the soundly attached parent-child pair. It is the goal of the first assessment procedure in this model to gain some impression of the degree of impairment facing the parent-child pair that is thought to be at risk for maltreatment. This model examines those elements that hold the capacity to satisfy and those that hold an equal capacity to destroy the attachment. Unlike animal relationships, which display uniformity in attachment behaviors between parent and offspring, the human parent-child relationship eludes this uniformity and is therefore difficult to assess.

Attachment activities occurring between animal parent and offspring are geared toward maximizing opportunities for survival. This goal is not as clearly articulated in attachment between the human parent and child. In fact, there are wide variations in the way individual human parents relate to their children. These differences demonstrate our ability to bring our own uniqueness into all of our relationships. There are wide differences in the outcomes as well. The animal infant not given systematic attachment may die. The human infant is unlikely to die, but his life will travel a very different path from what it would have had the attachment experience been adequate.

The demand for caretaking follows immediately upon the birth of either the animal or the human infant. This demand requires a special synchrony between parent and infant. It is only through these "special unions" that the parent and infant are able to communicate caretaking requirements (Schaffer, 1977d: 292; Hersh & Levin, 1979a: 29). The organization and development before birth, at birth, and immediately following birth have come to be referred to as *bonding*.

Bonding, as opposed to attachment, typically refers to a unidirectional (from parent toward infant) process that begins during pregnancy and peaks in the first hours or days after birth. Although thought to be primarily facilitated by bodily contact between parent and child, eye contact, fondling, and some elements of the feeding process contribute to its development.

The bonding process does not differ in any major way according to the number of children the parent has previously borne (Klaus et al., 1970: 190). However, some parents seem to be immediately prepared for bonding with a given child, while others may require as long as six weeks to feel they are "in sync" with the child (Robson & Moss, 1970: 980). *It is the eventual establishment of the bond that is more critical than the length of time taken to establish it;* although this length of time should be noted as a possible factor in later behaviors. It is only with the successful bond in place that the parent and child can begin to move forward toward a more permanent attachment (Lozoff et al., 1977: 190).

Note that the *presence* of a satisfactory bonding experience in the history of a given parent-child pair does not remove all possibility of violence between them. Similarly, the *absence* of such a bonding experience does not guarantee violence between them. The assessment of the presence or absence of the bond has twofold value: (1) The absence of a bonding experience is predictive of an inability to respond to instinctive controls against violence in the parent-child relationship. (2) The quality of the early bonding experience is assumed to be predictive of the quality of the later attachment relationship. It will be the combined flaws of a weakened attachment and an inability to control against violence that place the parent-child relationship at risk for future maltreatment. The completion of the evaluation of the *bond* between parent and child leads to the second assessment point in this model, the *attachment capacity* held by the members of this pair.

Attachment, as it is currently understood, is a process that develops over the course of the first year of the child's life. This process reflects the growing trust and security the child finds in his parents. Additionally, the level of attachment is reflective of the sense held by the child that his parent is *the single individual,* at that time, suitable to facilitate his survival and development.

To avoid confusion at a later point, please note that subsequent gender references to parents and children, unless exclusively to the mother, will be masculine. Let it also be known, however, that under most circumstances the attachment relationship is first constructed between mother and child.

The attachment relationship is a reciprocal one in the best sense of the word. The giving within this relationship moves back and forth between parent and child; little consideration given to the costs of parenting or the requirements for reciprocation. Within this framework the parent simply provides for the child and is rewarded internally through some small action undertaken by the child. When functional, this relationship is so finely orchestrated that the independent observer may not perceive the reward provided to the parent by the child. Importantly, the rewards of and for attachment can be shared with persons other than the natural parent (Ainsworth, 1967).

[handwritten margin note: Do children today have alternative attachment figures today?]

The assessment of attachment as it is spoken of here implies the study of each attachment in the child's life. Entering an attachment relationship is the most selective measure of giving to another person that the human holds. These relationships develop only with persons who are extraordinarily useful in fulfilling the multiple needs of the child's developmental life (Ainsworth, 1979: 936). Each attachment relationship is worthy of note for that reason alone. An assessment of the value of each attachment will lead to a better understanding of the total world as the child perceives it.

[handwritten margin note: ? HAS A highly mobile society made this difficult beyond immediate family.]

The message to the person seeking to understand the role(s) of attachment in a child's life is a simple one: *Look beyond the initial attachment with the mother. Look to the attachments, or their absence, with all other family members.* Klaus and Kennell (1976) estimate that the human child will develop an average of ten major attachments in his life. These are the ten most important partnerships the child will ever hold, and they must be given the attention they are due.

The child's willingness to redirect his attachment behavior away from an inadequate parent is indicative of the pressing need felt by the child for an attachment of some description. It is difficult to over-estimate the importance of that need. If attachment is successful, the child has an opportunity to become secure in his exploration of the physical and emotional aspects of his development. The attachment is not only a base from which to explore developmental curiosities, but one to return to if stressed. The absence of such a relationship in the young child's life is synonymous with the absence of the possibility of security and comfort. An assessment of the degree of security and comfort felt by the child, then, will provide some measure of the sense of being attached available to him.

Ground Zero:
Building for Tomorrow

Perhaps more than any other theorist, psychiatrist John Bowlby (1969) has convincingly demonstrated that the infant requires a solid attachment with a caregiver if stability and predictability are to be found. In fact, Bowlby has made an eloquent statement, through his many writings that all human behavioral organizations, throughout life, have their origins in this childhood attachment and its related experiences (Bowlby, 1969, 1973, 1980).

Early childhood development rests with the secure provision of physical needs. The establishment of a sense of security regarding these physical needs provides the child with the opportunity for developmental risk taking. This risk taking is best described as a movement from a secure base of physical satisfaction to the insecure world of behavioral options. No child will emerge from the first phase of attachment until certain that physiological requirements will continue to be met. Similarly, the child will not emerge from the parent's direction of behavioral options and into his own testing of behaviors until he knows he can return to the safety of the parent's control at any time. *Should the child demonstrate an unwillingness to move along developmentally for too long a period of time, the message that physical security is uncertain may be assumed.*

Stuck?

From this perspective, the first "phase" of attachment is one in which the child tests the parent to determine whether the parent will provide for his physical requirements. If successful, a second phase will find the child testing himself and his parent to determine whether he has the ability to motivate the parent to meet those needs on demand. The child, in this way, begins to learn that he, as an individual, can demonstrate some control over another individual. Once secure in this ability (power), the child widens his testing of the parent by including other options. The same sequence of seeking power over the parent and then testing it will be replicated in the area of emotional needs. It is only with the successful exertion of power over the parent that the child will perceive himself strong enough to venture into relationships with persons other than this primary attachment figure.

The information gathered by the child through these long testing periods is vital. Successful conduct of this testing will be carried with the child as an expression of self-confidence throughout his life. The lack of self-esteem and confidence often seen in maltreated children may flow from early failures in the achievement of personal power over the attachment figure. The failure of the maltreated child to experience success in these activities may be a result of the parent's unwillingness to allow domination by a child.

our people have low self-esteem

In many ways, the child's early "job description" is mastery of the parent. This is a practice experience for later mastery of the world. Additionally, it is a confidence builder, for power over that "big person" in the child's world allows the world outside to be a bit less frightening. Should the child be successful in this "job," the strength and confidence necessary to sally forth into the world will be his. This success will be found only in a relationship in which the parent sufficiently "invested" to allow the child to control some of his activities. *The parental ability to submit to control from the child as well as the child's ability to take advantage of this opportunity are critical points of assessment.* If both are present, the growth of the child and parent will be facilitated. If one or both are missing, there is a problem.

Attachment may be best perceived as a system of interlocking relationship activities that help the child maintain his stability amid a constantly changing environment (Bowlby, 1973: 149-150). Each day in the child's short life brings myriad new pieces of information and requirements for the child. The parent exists as the one stable and predictable element in the middle of this constant flux. Not only is the external world held steady through this relationship with the parent; it also allows the child to express himself. This expression originates in the newfound power to motivate behaviors in the parent (for example, by requesting a drink of water in the middle of the night). A successful attachment at this point will move the child toward more exploration and control activities in his world. There will be no success unless the parent can find some reward in allowing this domination. The possibility of reward rests not only within the parent, but also within the specific child.

Individual differences in the child contribute directly to the success or failure of the attachment relationship. These same individual child differences must be assessed in exploring the potential for maltreatment. The child will contribute a huge inventory of differences to which the parent must adjust. These differences may be seen in such factors as activity levels, developmental sequencing, self-regulation, and flexibility in response to change (Murphy & Moriarity, 1976).

Should the parent be capable of responding to these individual differences in the child, he will be capable of finding reciprocal rewards and will continue the parental investment. This process will be evidenced through the observation that behaviors that appear to be a burden (such as sitting up all night with the child) are experienced as a mutually rewarding accomplishment shared by parent and child (Goldstein et al., 1979:8). If the parent falters under the child's unique demands, the requirements of the attachment will be experienced as a burden and the attachment will fail.

While assessing the factors that maximize or inhibit the growth of a parent-child relationship, it must be remembered that both parent and child enter this relationship with different levels of competence, activity needs, and sociability (Bell & Harper, 1977: 61). The very young child is biologically primed for communication that facilitates attachment (Newson, 1977: 49), but as this communication becomes more abstract, individual differences between parent and child play a more imposing role.

The beginning of communication within the attachment relationship is demonstrated through the child's innate social capacities, such as rooting, sucking, grasping, crying, and postural adjustments (Grey et al., 1976: 390). These actions are rewarding to the functional parent and stimulate movement toward the smiling and shared vocalizations that are signals that all is well between the parent and child. Rewarding the parent is easy at this point. The child can foster continued parental investment through the simple process of growing and developing. Once the child and parent progress beyond the provision of physical requirements as the basic function of attachment, communication demands change.

During the "doll" period of parent-child relationships, the parental responsibilities are most clear. The results of meeting these responsibilities are also immediately obvious. There is a period when communication of physical requirements is basic. Hunger in the child brings messages to the parent that result in feeding the child and the pleasure of watching him grow. As time goes on, the parent must allow not only this physical dominance but a matching emotional dominance from the child. The reward for the parent in this is more difficult for the child to communicate.

As has been noted, once the child is physically stable, he will initiate behavior that tests himself, his parent, and his environment (Condon, 1977: 61). Implied in this testing is the willingness of the parent to sublimate his needs and "go along" with the child. The child makes a face; the parent makes the same face. A sound comes from the child; the parent mimics that sound. These are the superficially silly activities that allow children to understand that they initiate behavior in themselves and others. These behaviors are at the core of their understanding that they are individuals. The demands on the parent at this time are tedious and extreme. The demands of physical care have not lightened, only become more familiar. Now these physical demands are joined by the demand for learning from the child. Should some characteristic of parent or child impair their willingness or ability to engage in this expanded communication process, the attachment relationship will fix itself at this point.

The atmosphere in which the attachment relationship will flourish is a narrow one for both parent and child. This partnership must contain a variety of stimuli; the opportunity for exploration and discovery; respect for individual differences, needs, and preferences; feedback; and the ability to make an obvious change in the partner (Murphy & Moriarity, 1976: 45). All of these activities must be balanced by costs and benefits for both partners if reciprocal activities and investment are to continue. The child is invested for his survival. The parent who does not share this investment (giving too much attention or too little attention) destroys the equilibrium of the relationship, and it will falter. The demand is for a balanced attachment partnership that continues through the parent and child's life together. This balance must be struck if the poor decision making that increases the risk of violence is to be avoided.

Biology and Bonding

It is one assumption of the assessment theory put forth in this work that bonding and attachment across all animal parents and offspring serve a natural function. That natural function is protection against danger and insurance of survival. The animal infant finds this protection necessary because of dangers in the external world. The human offspring also requires such protection from internal sources of danger in its family.

The preparation for and commitment to survival demonstrated by the human infant are unmatched at other stages of life. This survival effort uses organized and predictable behavior from the very beginning of the infant's life (Schaffer, 1977a: 5). Not only is the infant programmed for survival tasks immediately following birth; he also is capable of drawing the adult caregiver into a partnership that will maximize the survival value of these preadapted behaviors. This is an intriguing partnership; as Bell (1979: 824) point out, this is one of the few partnerships in which there is such a wide discrepancy between the relative size of the two participants and, at the same time, a lack of discrepancy in the power that each holds. In assessing this power, however, it must be remembered that it is the infant who is equipped to evoke survival mechanisms from this pairing. Should the parent enter this partnership unprepared for any reason, or to any degree, the survival of the partnership is threatened. This potential lack of preparedness in the parent is of major importance in predicting violence in the family unit.

No phase is more familiar to the professional working with mal-treating families as is the outsider's observation, "How can they do that to those helpless children?" This image of the child as helpless and the stereotypical response to it are not accidental.

The image of the helpless and passive infant is a survival mechanism in itself. Were the infant perceived to be more competent and in control, the adult caretaker would be less inclined to play the complementary roles necessary for the child's ultimate survival. This helplessness is real, of course, but the child is far from powerless. Rather, this small creature holds the ability to educate the parent about his needs and to play a responsible role in the development of the attachment between himself and his parent (Grey et al., 1976: 390). The infant, through these capacities, is not only a consumer but also a producer of social interactions. This is a source of power that allows the infant to participate in bringing order to what, at first, appears to him to be chaos.

The child's biological systems are thrown into disarray by movement from the womb to our world. The predictability and stability offered by the shared prenancy experience is suddenly shattered and must be reestablished through predictable parental responses to basic physiological maintenance. It is only after the physiological balance has been achieved that the child can turn his attention to the stimuli of his new environment—stimuli that hold the secret to his individual role in this new world (Gorski et al., 1980: 282).

The behaviorial organization capacities of the infant do not negate those of the parent. It is mandatory that the parent accept the organization partnership with the child from birth forward. This initial partnership is almost a mechanical response to physical need rather than the affectionate interchange it may be perceived as by the parent (Parens, 1972: 601). However, the mechanistic nature of this initial parental response does not minimize its importance. *It is the automatic nature of the early partnership that provides the infant the security and predictability from which the affective elements of the partnership can be generated.*

The physiological basis of early attachment behaviors takes on great importance in assessing the attachment. If the parent in the partnership is unable to respond correctly to the most basic of physical mechanisms or perceives the child to be more competent than reasonably expected, a fundamental flaw in the parent's attachment ability may be in evidence.

Basic attachment behaviors do exist to provide the child a sense of security and protectedness. It is this same basic sense of security that he will seek from the parent again and again when stressed. He will also not venture forth into the world until he has found some similar measure of security in his own actions.

What appears to be critical in the successful establishment of the feeling of security is the sameness of behaviors between parent and child. The child is being assaulted by multiple external variables, but the repetitive nature of the behaviors between himself and his parent seems to lend some sense of order to that bombardment. This relationship unrolls as a carpet would, constantly covering more ground yet retaining a sameness. Through this routine behavioral sameness in the face of constantly changing external demands, physiological needs, instinctive reactions, and somatic sensations are met with regularity and predictability (Brazelton, 1963: 933). The attachment relationship is, in this sense, a peaceful oasis for the child to hide within when the demands of development become overwhelming.

The regularity of the successful attachment partnership not only assures life support and protection, but also helps to maintain and expand the relationship between parent and child. Once the regulation of the infant's rhythms is no longer a prime issue, the relationship circumstantially developed serves to foster more sophisticated developmental progress (Sander, 1962: 135). By the third month of life, the predictable sharing has provided a mechanism through which the partnership comes to be understood as a reciprocally rewarding arrangement (Murphy & Moriarity, 1976: 81). All developmental tasks that follow come to be understood as goals that are intended to be accomplished together (Brazelton et al., 1974: 56). The child who attempts to attach with a parent at high risk for maltreatment finds this sense of sharing with the parent to be a goal sought but never reached.

Playing the Role:
Parent and Child Behaviors
in the Partnership

Opportunities for shared activities between parent and child can be loosely ordered into two types: functional and structural (Schaffer, 1977a: 8-9). The *functional* activities are those related to the timing and rhythm of events (such as sleeping). *Structural* elements are those largely outside the control of either parent or child (congenital limitations, for example).

Under ordinary circumstances, the functional elements of the child's early life were first regulated internally, during pregnancy, and soon come to be regulated by the child's external world (for example, in learning to sleep at night). The child matches his rhythms to those of the parent through a process referred to as "entrainment" (Schaffer, 1944b, 1977d). The sharing of these rhythms brings a sense of union to the parent-child partnership and provides for increasing harmony. While these functional changes play a positive role, structural elements may interfere with this harmony and may lead more or less directly to a dysfunctional parent-child relationship. The most basic structural aspect of the parent-child relationship is also one of the most commonly overlooked. This basic element is the *appearance of the child*.

The human infant is more helpless than most within the animal kingdom. It cannot feed itself, move itself, or express itself to non-parental caregivers in its struggle for survival. The human infant must, as a result, be provided with mechanisms to demonstrate this helplessness, secure aid, and maintain the proximity of the person able to provide this aid. The initial expression of this helplessness is the child's appearance. The survival mechanism implied is the parent's response to that appearance.

The helpless appearance of the infant is inherently appealing to the functional adult (Emde, 1980: 89). This appearance secures the parent's aid and proximity. Evidence of this response can be found at any nursery or pet store window. In fact, noted animal behaviorist Konrad Lorenz (1966) has identified this character in infants of all types (human and other animals) and has given it the wonderfully understandable name, "babyness."

When confronted by a small creature with a disproportionately large head, large eyes, a round forehead, puffy cheeks, and a round soft body with short, thick limbs, the functional adult is not only disarmed but finds protective instincts aroused. This helpless appearance draws the functional adult to the child and provides a sense of urgency and necessity to the demands made on the adult by the child. Once capturing this attention, the child accelerates his use of protectiveness through a series of ritualized behavioral "runs" likely to include smiling, random eye contact, thrashing of arms and legs, and noisemaking. Through the judicious use of these "cuteness" behaviors (Bell, 1974: 3) the child can also reduce parental frustrations over the endless demands of child care and lower the potential for aggression toward him from the overtaxed adult (Robson & Moss, 1970: 980).

All who work with parents and children understand the statement, "but when he smiled at me it was all worth it!" This is a clear expression that babyness is working for both parent and child. *This phase is equally important to the assessment of the parent-child pair when it is never heard.*

Appearance factors and babyness hold still another developmental function. There is a value in the progressive disappearance of this behavior. The movement away from helpless behavior over time is rewarding to the parent, for it allows the parent to know that demands for care will not always be so high. It also serves as a reward, since it confirms to the parent that the child is making progress in development thorugh his (the parent's) efforts (Solnit & Provence, 1979). Tragically, when the parent is unable to respond to the helplessness of the child, the task of child-rearing presents itself as an endless series of demands with no rewards to accompany them—a clear signal of the heightened potential for violence.

Pediatrician T. Berry Brazelton and his colleagues (1974: 57-66) have observed thousands of parents and children in interaction and find the infant's arsenal of proximity-inducing and behavioral maintenance weapons to reach far beyond simple appearance factors. Importantly, however, the child's innate relationship skills presume the presence of a functional parent as well as the absence of a structural impairment in the child. Should these two major elements be absent, the relationship activities are unpredictable. This pattern of unpredictability should be noted in the assessment of the parent-infant relationship.

Initially, the child will look at the parent in a slow, relaxed manner. Once certain that he has the recognition and attention of the parent, the child begins a series of actions (thrashing, smiling, and vocalizations), which steadily accelerate. During this active stage, the parent works continuously to help the interactive flow by focusing all attention on the child and demonstrating a readiness to participate in any activity the child might direct. This is an intertwined series of behaviors, each participant systematically rewarding the other and allowing the other opportunities for reacting to, or initiating, new behaviors. This is a reciprocal demonstration of the contact made within the relationship generally. It is a "conversation" (Brazelton et al., 1974) that communicates many positive messages to both partners.

Through this interaction, the child is told that the parent is available and alert to his needs. The parent is informed, through this same interaction, that he is individually important to the child and that his behaviors influence the child's behaviors. This reciprocal process allows both participants to understand that they can influence each other. The message of individual importance and ability to influence one's world is of critical value to both parent and child. Should there be an imbalance in these messages, the security and development of the relationship is jeopardized. Structural elements of the parent-child pair may also predict jeopardy.

Congenital problems in the child can contribute important difficulties to the development of the parent-child relationship (Bell & Haper, 1977: 61). These congenital aspects are not always seen as negative by outside observers, but they represent differences between parental expectations and the realities of the child asking for a relationship.

It is quite common that "differences" in children reported by parents are related to neurological or hormonal construction which differs from that of their parent(s) (Hersh & Levin, 1979a: 32). These differences can contribute to mismatching in perceptual thresholds, behavioral capacities, levels of arousal, and sense of security (Sroufe, 1979: 836). Should the child's organization differ vastly from that of the parent or from that the parent expected, this parent is called upon to develop individualized patterns of meeting the needs of this child (Korner, 1973: 51). *It should not be assumed that any parent is capable of making this adjustment.* In those pairs where such an adjustment is insurmountable, dysfunction in the relationship between parent and child is easily predicted. Two extreme examples of this mismatching are common.

Consider first the child who is very quiet and in need of increased stimulation. Unfortunately, this child receives less stimulation due to his low responsiveness to his parent, and becomes even more quiet and unstimulated. A second example is found in the extremely irritable child. This child may drive the parent away through increasing the parent's guilt in being unable to comfort and quiet the child's constant seeking of stimulation. In either case, the child does not receive the attention he is seeking. Both of these examples demonstrate the possibility of a parent who was initially willing to cooperate and a child who was "uncooperative" in his behavior due to a mismatch in activity levels. The children do not control these characteristics, of course, but this type of mismatch must been seen as "high-risk" (Gorski et al., 1980: 284).

The assessment of matching structural levels in parents and children begins with two warning signals. The first is any structural element that may eliminate the reciprocal nature of the giving between parent and child. The second is any structural element that prohibits the establishment of predictability and regularity in behavioral exchanges. The loss of this form of routinized communication between parent and child can have a devastating developmental impact in the best of parent-child pairings. Should the parent also have inherent difficulty in forming attachments, this impasse could predict future violence due to the child's continuously "failing" to match the parent's inappropriate expectations.

The question that is not asked frequently enough by clinicians and researchers alike is, "Where did this parent learn appropriate expectations for a child's behavior?" That is a pivotal questions. Child care is not as familiar as it once was to the adolescent soon-to-be parent. Persons becoming parents today are frequently unprepared for the tasks to come. Fortunately, the child arrives prepared to teach them a great deal about himself—if they are prepared to listen.

The World's Smallest Ringmaster: The Power of the Child

The child is not a random contributor to the relationship between himself and his parent. He does not await an action by the parent and only then reinforce or reward (Dunn & Richards, 1977: 449). The child is an active participant from the beginning (Sroufe, 1979: 836). The child actively seeks to direct behaviors and, given a functional partner, can elicit support, protection, and equilibrium (Bell, 1974: 14). Success in these endeavors does demand an adaptable parent, but the child himself and the environment in which the relationship exists also restrict or facilitate success.

A functional child will seek to teach his parent about his limits and preferences (Bell & Harper, 1977: 131). For some children, innate constitutional differences and temperamental characteristics (Thomas & Chess, 1977) interfere with that teaching process. These children, as a result of mismatching with their parent, have delayed behavioral development, fail to get any message across, or become a burden to the parent (David & Appell, 1969: 181). The result is a frustrating interaction that clouds the parent's ability to "read" the child (Bell, 1974: 6). *An inability to "read" your child's message is threatening to all parents.* It is most anxiety provoking for those parents least prepared to cope with any anxiety in parenting—those with maltreatment potential.

A difficult-to-read child is an anxiety-producing experience for all parents. Many external observers view this inability as the parent's "fault." Competent parents may feel guilt over this apparent inability and accept the "blame" for not understanding the child's cues. Still other parents, those having difficulty with all parenting, turn against the child and place the blame for the problem on the child rather than accepting it as their own. In the worst cases, such a parent may begin to believe that the child is being purposeful in its lack of communication. The imagined goal of that child, in the distorted thinking of this parent, is to reveal to the whole world just how inadequate his parent is as a parent. This is a critically dangerous juncture in the attachment relationship. It is by means of these expectations that parental fears, child anxieties, and external judgments impinge on this relationship and distort its ability to right itself (David & Appell, 1969: 181). The delicate balance of reciprocal behaviors, which is designed to maintain parental investment, may be suddenly lost due to the unrealistic expectations of the parents. The inadequate parent has asked for attachment from the child but has given none in return. This parent has asked the child to allow him the appearance of being a "good parent" when he has not been. This is the child's first double-bind in this family; the parent has not done his job and sees that failure as the fault of the child.

It must be remembered that the appropriate attachment relationship is an interactional system in which the actions and responses of either partner develop a level of reward value over time (Bell, 1974: 7). This maintains altruistic and reciprocal behavior as well as keeping the parental investment high enough to allow the parent to continue in this difficult job. Each participant learns that the other has a reward value through long periods of trial-and-error social learning. Children will approach this learning from multiple angles, but most children tend to become more like their parents in their communication styles over time (Bell, 1974: 11). *It is those children who are temperamentally difficult, constitutionally misdirected, or different from their parents in disposition or expectation that are predictive of problems* in this matching reward system (Schwarzbeck, 1979: 107).

When the majority of the reciprocal interactions in the attachment relationship occur as rewarding experiences, the child will learn to give and become a source of reward himself. This positive learning allows him to feel in control of himself and provides a sense of trust through the predictability of his environment (Emde, 1980: 94). Should this reciprocally altruistic investment system fail, the result is a child who does not give, does not trust, and is not predictable himself. Maintaining sufficient investment to provide care for this frustrating, unpredictable, and demanding infant can become too much for any parent—especially the parent who struggles with his capacity to attach generally. Again, however, these problems do not reside solely on the parent's side of the relationship.

As difficult as it may be, it must be accepted that there are parent-child relationships that are continuously unsatisfactory for both members. There are those in which frustration is the only feeling the parent and child have in common (David & Appell, 1969: 180). Many persons reject this possibility. However, to the extent that a parent cannot subvert his own needs, in the circumstances in which the child has no other attachment figure, and in the event that the lack of reciprocal reward has led to "uncontrollable deceleration and turning off" of the relationship (Schwarzbeck, 1979: 108), this parent-child relationship has failed.

The determination that a parent-child relationship is wide open for failure is a difficult one. Obviously, should the parent demonstrate no ability to invest in the child; give no reciprocal rewards, and have no altruistic impulse for giving in the absence of reward, this relationship will fail. However, there is one other pattern which is predictive of failure in more subtle ways.

Should the parent have come into this relationship with an intergenerational and interactive (attachment) history that forged absolute feelings of inadequacy (Emde, 1980: 94-95), should the parent's guilt over not being able to deal with the child maintain these feelings of inadequacy, and should the parent's inability to deal with the child cause him to blame the child for the full measure of his inadequacy, the relationship between parent and child will not work. This is particularly true of the parent who remains unable to accept the fact that his own parents were incompetent in their attachment relationship with him (Fraiberg, 1980). If the dysfunctional attachment history of the parent is less intense, or should he recognize that his own parents are inadequate, these problems may respond to help. Similarly, not all problems in the child are closed to positive change.

It is obvious that interacting with a child who is unhampered by temperamental or constitutional differences and who communicates well is preferable to interacting with one who has impairments in these areas (Ainsworth & Bell, 1969: 160). However, it is not impossible to compensate for inadequacies in these areas. This compensation demands a parent with extraordinary sensitivity and investment, but it can be achieved.

Recall that reciprocity begins as a unidirectional dialogue in which the parent reacts to the child "as if" his actions had direct communication value even before they take on true meaning (Schaffer, 1977a, 1977d: 10). These pseudo-dialogues provide the child with a sense of control (intentionality) by the end of the first year of life, as he comes to understand that he is actually directing the actions of others to various degrees. This entire process is dependent upon the parent's ability to read the child's cues with what Ainsworth (1979) terms "sensitive responsiveness." When the relationship decays due to child-centered variables, it is frequently this sensitive responsiveness that is lost from the parent. This loss contributes to the further decline of the reciprocity between parent and child. If this loss can be avoided early in the relationship, compensating mechanisms can be developed.

Reading the cues in the human parent-child pair is more complex than in other animals. Less complex species find successful cue reading to be necessary, for it allows the parent to gratify the infant's needs. For the human pair, each successfully read cue provides a reciprocal interaction that serves as a "platform" on which future interactions will be developed (Bell, 1979: 823). Thus, *the attachment relationship in which cue sensitivity has not developed between its members has no point from which to grow.* The task is to enable the parent to sustain a high investment in this sensitivity to the child's cues until the child reaches an age at which more obvious (and understandable) communication can take place. If the parent finds this impossible, even with support, the reciprocity in the relationship is in jeopardy.

The parent-child relationship lacking in sensitive responsiveness has no rules and, subsequently, no mechanisms for guiding the actions of either member. The lack of sensitive responsiveness is also evidence of the parent's low level of investment in the child. Should this element be missing, predictability for either member will also be absent (David & Appell, 1969: 181). Also absent will be a framework that allows for not only interaction but also withdrawal by either member (Brazelton et al., 1974: 59). This responsiveness, then, requires that the parent adjust his needs and rhythms to those of the child rather than (a) imposing his requirements on the child or (b) not responding to the child's requirements by continuing the demand for interaction when the child seeks rest (Brazelton et al., 1974:64). *When this rhythmic behavior is evidenced through the finding that only one of the partners' needs are respected, it can be assumed that the attachment relationship is handicapped.*

The second point of recognizing poor communication between parent and child also involves cues, but in a different sense. The attention provided to sensitive responsiveness initially pertained to the parent's ability to recognize that *the child's cue was telling him something.* The next level of communication rests with that parent's ability to interpret the cues in order to *understand what it is that the child is attempting to communicate.* In many ways these are overlapping abilities in the well-prepared and highly invested parent, but it is important to be alert to a common form of distortion. *Too often in the failing attachment relationship, only the negative messages or cues receive attention and recognition.* The parent, out of guilt or a pattern of consistently negative interactions in his own life, may have trained himself to recognize negative messages while ignoring others (Pawlby, 1977: 220). Through this mechanism the parent with low investment due to fear of failure can convince himself that he does not want to deal with this small being, because children are not very nice anyway. It is completely possible for the parent to ignore the smiles, the reaching out, and all of the natural proximity-inducing behaviors of the child. This is usually supplemented by tallying the minutes of crying, counting the diapers, and totaling the daily cost of nutritional supplements. The net message is a negative one to the parent. He is, in effect, unconsciously missing all of the rewards of parenting. Ultimately, as they are left unrecognized, they will decrease and eventually disappear through a lack of being rewarded.

The decline in proximity seeking from the child is indicative of a general decline in the possibility of successful attachment. When this decline occurs through fear or a lack of knowledge, a concerted program of pointing out the child's rewards to the parent should take the edge off the problem. When it is a true rejection, even this studied approach will not gain the recognition of rewards adequate to build the necessary reciprocity between parent and child.

In assessing the parent-child partnership at different points, it must be understood that the parent is going through a developmental process similar to the child's (Emde, 1980: 95). Parenting styles and knowledge change, as does a child's knowledge of his world. It is unlikely that either parent or child will ever come to know all things necessary for a perfect relationship. But just as the child is respected for what he has yet to learn, so should the parent be afforded the same respect. This respect must be tempered by the understanding that he cannot be allowed to ignore the needs of the child completely for the sake of his own. What requires assessment beyond this basic knowledge is the parent's attitude toward the acquisition and application of this vital knowledge.

The parent's attitude toward the child and child rearing is equal to, if not more important than, the specific actions taken on the child's behalf (Ainsworth & Bell, 1969: 161). It is the attitude held by the parent that leads to the selection and conduct of activities in the relationship. The promising find is the parent who does things "with" rather than "to" the child (Rutter, 1979: 286). This is a parent who provides appropriate responses to the child's actions, receives pleasure from the child's responses, and initiates new interactions when the child is ready (Rutter, 1979: 286). This is anything but a static individual with low investment in the progress of the relationship.

Attached parents are constantly learning new elements of their children's communication systems. They are also learning new things about themselves and the value of what they have to offer in this reciprocal investment. This knowledge about themselves and their own children may be more vital to the progress of the relationship than any abstract "parenting" knowledge that they held in a general fund of information (Newson, 1977: 59).

Even a solid and experienced parent can misread a child's cues from time to time. Even the experienced parent has some new developing to do with each new child. These factors can generate periods of frustration and weakened communication in all attachment relationships (Schwarzbeck, 1979: 108). The major assessment variable remains *the parent's ability to place himself in the role of the child and see things from that child's perspective* (Ainsworth & Bell, 1969: 160). This ability is the return on a solid parental investment, one offered only by the parent who is able to attach.

Capturing the Attachment Potential

To this point, the balance mechanisms between parent and child have been discussed in general terms. Points of success or failure have been sought in such diverse areas as sensory differences, activity level differences, appearance, developmental pace, and attempts to manage the environment containing the relationship. These are all elements of what Murphy and Moriarity (1976) have called "issues in coping." This is appropriate, for the development of attachment is a massive, shared coping effort.

Child rearing can be a positive experience, but it is also a job— perhaps the most difficult in the world. Understood as a job (or career), it can be accepted as something that may not be the most desirable for every person, despite the protests of our pronatalist society.

Broussard (1980: 262-266) has categorized the "job" of child rearing and notes that each point offers the potential for placing the relationship at risk. The pivotal points are (a) anticipation and fulfillment of the child's needs, (b) anticipation of threat or danger, (3) establishment of appropriate limits, (d) play, (e) effective training and mirroring, (f) coping with stress, and (g) body management. Attachment must be captured within each of these shared activities, and captured through the demonstration of the parent's investment in the success of the child. The investment in the child held by the parent is vital. This investment is evidenced through the parent's belief that what he is developing with the child (and the child as an individual) is valuable. This belief should be sought. Maintaining this investment in the face of attachment demands depends on the parent's view of himself.

Child rearing, according to Bettleheim (1971: 23-24), requires an "integrated" adult. This individual must be in conflict about neither his adulthood nor his childhood. He must also be aware of those areas with which he is still not comfortable in his own life. Seeking this perfect adult is futile; some element demanding change will always be present.

What is more realistically sought in the assessment of the successful attachment partnership is that adult with healthy goals for himself and his child (Murphy & Moriarity, 1976: 62). This is an adult who holds a reasonable level of personal adjustment and a degree of acceptance for the child. This acceptance of the child as an individual frees the attachment partnership from always conforming to the adult's needs and preferences only. This relationship focuses on reciprocal interactions and behavioral organization within both adult and child.

The attachment partnership can be assessed on such objective criteria as quantity of behaviors, frequency of behaviors, point of initiation of behaviors, point of termination of behaviors, and actual behaviors chosen (David & Appell, 1969: 172). On the other hand, the attachment partnership can be assessed using a subjective criterion such as Ainsworth's scales of acceptance-rejection, cooperation-interference, accessibility-ignoring, or sensitivity to signals (Bowlby, 1973: 357). In either style, all parent-child interactions exist well beyond those that can be taught in a child development or parenting class (Joy et al., 1980). What is being assessed is the presence or absence of a natural gift—the ability to attach.

Basic assessment of attachment begins by watching. What is being "watched" are the natural animal behaviors of all parents with their young. It is body contact, eye contact, and fondling, but it is an aura surrounding these activities that indicates comfort in their demands. The attached parent reciprocates without sense of cost or reward. The attached child returns with a sense of security and comfort. Together, this parent and child move through developmental tasks, each learning something about the other, and himself, at every point. The parent is willing to submit to control from the child and to appear a bit silly to outsiders in the submissive behavior. The child revels in the power over the parent and expresses his delight freely. Both parent and child recognize each other as an individual and see individual differences as important rather than inhibiting. Mere growth and change reward the parents and keeps them invested; they ask for no more. Through these behaviors, in their natural progression early in the child's life, comes the promise of all possiblities. Their absence, or distortion, promises troubled times.

Chapter 3

FUNDAMENTAL BEHAVIORAL PATTERNS

Building Bridges:
The Natural Origins of
Reciprocal Communication

The suggestion that failed attachments may lead to inappropriate parent-child relationships is not revolutionary. Most clinicians have been confronted with a parent-child pair that "just makes me uncomfortable." That same parent-child pair is often described by the statement, "There just seems to be something missing." What is missing in these vaguely inappropriate relationships is a competent attachment. The mechanisms for early identification of this "absence" are the routine child-care behaviors of this pair.

The previous chapter provided evidence that the parent-child relationship is a partnership from its very beginning. Despite the fact that the child is more dependent on the parent than the parent on the child (Mahler et al., 1975: 44), the power of the child and the maleability of the parent mold this sharing into a partnership (Bell, 1974: 14).

When the parent is able to feel that the child occupies an essential place in this life (Robson & Moss, 1970: 977-978) and the child feels that the parent is "not interchangeable" with any other adult (Ainsworth, 1979), the partnership moves into an attachment.

The clinician who observes this completed attachment will identify love, a sense of possession, devotion, protectiveness, concern for the other's well-being, and the driving need for continuing interactions (Robson & Moss, 1970: 977-978). These effective contributions come about only if three requirements are met: (1) This must occur through a process which is reciprocal; (2) this must occur in a framework that is mutually satisfying; and (3) this demands a relationship in which both members gain competence in dealing with each other constantly (Bromwich, 1976: 440). This effective growth will be present only if the basic communication patterns necessary have been firmly established.

The earliest parent-child communications are, in comparing across parents and children, more alike than different. This lends credence to the biological origins of the basic units of parent-child communication. The human newborn does not respond to the parent with psychological mechanisms built on love and affection (as so often assumed by high-risk parents). The neonate responds to the parent and builds a communication system with that parent through a series of behaviors that are physiologically based and reflexively conducted (Parens, 1972: 601). This reflexive communication process permits the organization and shaping of the relationship through a rhythmic pattern of attentiveness and withdrawal (Brazelton et al., 1974: 55). *It is this pattern of instinctively patterned behavior sharing that becomes the earliest target for assessing this relationship.*

While most inborn communication patterns are demonstrated *actively*, through such behaviors as eye contact, relaxation from soothing, orienting to the parent's face, or responding positively to being held (Brazelton et al., 1974: 68), others are *passive.* For example, the infant may initiate interaction simply by remaining quiet (Jones & Moss, 1971; Bell, 1974: 9). The parent, curious about the silence, comes to the child and begins the interaction initially desired by the child. Whether the communication is active or passive, understanding the need for its regularity provides greater understanding of why the shared learning of these patterns progresses most rapidly when the child interacts with a single caregiver on a regular basis (Lozoff et al., 1977: 3). *It is only with the establishment of these basic patterned interactions between them that the parent and child will move toward the more complex, unpatterned interactions of later childhood* (Levine, 1969: 66).

Those who have sought to assess parent-child relationships through observation of these basic behaviors have likened the process to a "conversation" between parent and child. This is a conversation in which the two partners use basic "communication gestures" to direct each other's activities (Pawlby, 1977: 204). The active "director" role alternates in this partnership, with turn-taking and appropriate attentiveness teaching active responsibilities in this and all other social relationships (Bell, 1974). *Failure to observe a "conversational" nature in these interactions is a warning.*

Under most conditions, except those of resource scarcity, which makes parent and child competitors, parents and children are prepared to conduct basic communications and develop a sound interactional pattern (Stern, 1977). In the event that one or both members of this partnership are unable to perceive the other's communication accurately, the entire foundation of the relationship is weakened. However, the observer of this pattern must temper their expectations with reasonable expectations.

A reciprocal relationship between parent and child implies the potential for bidirectional systems in which each partner influences the actions of the other (Bell, 1979: 882). The continuation of this relationship implies that both partners find it rewarding and therefore generate new experiences to share on a regular basis (David & Appel, 1969: 179). The expectation that all areas of the child's or parent's life will be of interest to the other is unreasonable. Additionally, some areas of both parental and child performance will always be substantially less than ideal (David & Appel, 1969: 180). The fact is that no single person (for example, the mother) can be expected to share every developmental task with the child. That is why the child is instinctively prepared to form multiple attachments. *What is critical here is whether or not the child is permitted to form these multiple attachment.*

In the past, the successful accomplishment of all developmental tasks was thought to be a reflection of the mother's competence. That is an unnecessary weight for mothers, or any parent, to carry. Unfortunately, that is a weight that is borne heavily in the hearts and expectations of marginal parents and those with difficulty in attachment.

As has been reflected upon earlier, parents with high maltreatment potential hold *unrealistic expectations* for their child. They also hold similarly unrealistic expectations for themselves and the parental role that they plan to undertake. The expectation of being what must be seen by outside observers as the "best parent in the world" is a short-lived one. The flexible parent allows this fantasy to die its richly deserved death in the face of realistic parenting demands. The marginal parent struggles mightily to hang on to that image. These unnecessary and unrealistic expectations for parents can have the same contributory effect to the development of the violent family, as do unreasonable expectations for the children in these families. When they are voiced to the clinician, they must be heard.

Evidence introduced in the previous chapter points toward the fact that neither the parent nor the child holds exclusive governance over the initiation of interactions (Bell & Harper, 1977: 64). *A non-stimulating and deprived environment,* however, will lower the personal interaction rate for both parent and child (Rutter, 1972: 100). This can also be observed in the environment in which the response to needs is approached in a routine fashion or one in which there are multiple caretakers, none having regular interaction with the child over a period of time (Rutter, 1972). Even mothers not only react to the environment in which care is to be provided, but also have personal limits on their ability to interact cheerfully with a demanding child.

Both members of the parent-child partnership have upper and lower *limits of tolerance* regarding the other's behavior (Bell & Harper, 1977: 65). These limits are often more easily determined by an objective third party than a member of the family and should be considered an elementary point of assessment. They may break down the relationship in two directions.

The first example of mismatching of limits may be seen in the child whose need for activity exceeds the parent's limit for providing such activity. As the parent withdraws, the child increases his "engaging" behaviors to encourage continued interaction from the parent. This constant demand is a continuing source of overload for the parent, and an explosive outcome is sometimes the result.

The opposite mismtaching can be seen in the example of the premature child. Here the parent tends to overstimulate the child through constant ministrations. The child withdraws, and the parent, as the child in the first example did, increases his attentions and overloads the infant (Bell, 1974: 5).

These two situations are predictive of a circular mismatch that keeps parent and child at constant odds with one another. Using more scientific terminology, both of these examples demonstrate a failure of the reciprocal relationship to maintain organized behavior in the face of excitation (Sroufe, 1979: 837). Either expression of the problem is predictive of ongoing communication failure.

Another expression of individual differences, touched on previously, is that of *constitutional differences* presented by individual infants. It is quite possible that temperament and developmental delays may present themselves in a manner that prohibits matching between parent and child (Schwarzbeck, 1979: 106). Should the parent's constitutional factors and expectations exist at variance with those presented by the child, a violent outcome may result. In fact, Schwarzbeck uses the example of the violent parent in describing this situation.

Consider the parent who does not understand his lack of ability to read his child's cues. This expresses to the parent rejection by the child and his own personal inadequacy and stupidity. Holding the expectation that he *should* be able to care for his child, the resultant frustration is manifested through a violent act against this child (Schwarzbec, 1979: 106). Again, the observation of differences in temperamental characteristics and the information to the parent that this is understandable and natural come best from the outside observer.

The observer of a parent-child relationship must come to this task with the understanding that *the parenting role can reach a point at which the frustration involved prohibits effective communication, and the results can be total dysfunction.* This failure may grow out of environmental, educational, or constitutional problems in parent or child and can lead to real danger. On the other hand, the challenge and frustration within the reciprocal relationship between parent and child can serve as a motivator (Murphy & Moriarity, 1976: 71). The difference is often found in the manner in which outside persons view and handle this parent-child pair.

What must be clear from the beginning of the assessment is that the reciprocal relationship between parent and child is not rigid with respect to substance, format, or timing. The clinician must be flexible. *Almost all of us expect too much of the person in the role of parent.* This level of expectation is most easily seen in our failure to provide the parent blanket permission to admit mistakes (Bettleheim, 1950: 28). What must be understood is that each parental role player in the family must be given permission to fail in occasional small tasks if he is to be successful in the larger mandates of parenting.

Snowballing: Communication Events Between Parent and Child

It is obvious that *the functional parent-child pair tends to demonstrate orderly and predictable patterns of communication.* These patterns are learned during interactions and take on a shape that is nonrandom, organized into repetitive "runs" and demanding the willing give-and-take of each partner. This pattern of shared learning is enhanced through limiting the number of partners the child must instruct in his own unique communication style.

The infant is structurally and functionally organized to secure the proximity and protection of a primary caregiver. This does not eliminate his capacity to engage more than one caregiver for purposes of survival, but it does state the biologically ideal case. The child runs the risk of being overstimulated and confused if the messages he receives in return for his communications flow from several adults. An examination of newborn propensities reveals the strength of this link with a primary caregiver.

Lazoff and colleagues (1977: 4) have observed the newborn to be responsive to the smell, voice, and appearance of his mother within a week of birth. The newborn, if the bonding is adequate, will allow this parent to soothe it, imitate the parent's gestures, and move in synchrony with the parent's voice. This communication match, or "synchrony," is rewarding to the functional parent and provides cues from which the parent can direct his own interaction with the child. Not incidentally, this synchrony provides information to the outside observer that this parent-child pair has the basic requirements for a positive relationship.

These are instinctive communication tools. They will be active in the child if the parent is at all willing to accept them. These actions take on greater meaning for parents who work hard to receive these responses from their child. These communications are interpreted by the parent as having emotional overtones. They become emotionally significant to the parent (for example, "Just look at the love in those little eyes"; Levine, 1969: 5). Because of this importance and emotional overlay from the parent, the clinician must be aware of two elements: (1) *the absence of these early communication links* and (2) *the inadequate parent's capacity to misinterpret these messages.*

Absence of communication as the parent expects it or distorted interpretations can lead to negative emotional assumptions by the parent of the child (for example, "He doesn't love me!"). *The parent's interpretation of these basic interactions during the provision of care contributes directly to the success or failure of the parent-child partnership.* These interpretations occur during each of the fundamental child-care acts. The clinician must assess the success of the communication between parent and child at each of these times.

Those who have previously sought to assess parent-child relationship potential at early stages have found the following to describe the critical points of assessment.

FEEDING

The most familiar and easily observed synchrony between parent and child is in the act of feeding. The feeding process is a satisfying one to the good parent and even brings smiles to those who watch the process occur. Unfortunately, a polarity exists between proponents of feeding styles that may detract from the pleasures available in the feeding act itself.

Proponents of breast-feeding seem to exaggerate the importance of the feeding act in the developing parent-child relationship. Those in opposition to bread-feeding tend to underrate the importance of this shared time between parent and child. Terminating this argument is not the purpose of this work. However, some comment does seem to be necessary.

Child development researchers Mary Salter-Ainsworth and Richard Bell (1969: 133) studied breast- or bottle-feeding, schedule or demand feeding, and early or late weaning. The conclusion of their study was simply that no single technique affects development to the exclusion of the other. Murphy and Moriarity (1976: 49) found breast-feeding to be important, but not necessarily a direct contributor to optimal closeness between parent and child. This author's research with young mothers has found neither bottle- nor breast-feeding to be a significant variable in the potential maltreatment of the child. The study of mothers using either method would find a normal distribution of attachment successes and failures. The differential in feeding styles seems to be that *both parent and child must be comfortable with any feeding method selected, or it will not enhance the relationship.* Parent-child synchrony is possible in the presence of breast-feeding or in its absence. Each pair has unique needs. The focus of parent-child communication cannot be captured in a single act between parent and child.

Any work dealing with "natural" aspects of parenting would be remiss if it ignored the natural contributions of being fed at the breast. The anatomical evolution of protuberant breasts in the human female does indicate the importance of eye contact during feeding, but that can be achieved through other methods. Additionally, the transfer of protection from infection through the transmission of antibodies, lymphocytes, and microphages in the nutritious mother's milk speaks well of the physiological aspects of breast-feeding (Lozoff et al., 1977: 4). However, those protective mechanisms have become less significant in the face of modern medical progress. The critical point is that neither social nor physiological aspects of breast-feeding provide a mandate for its use by the human parent-child pair. *It is not the act of feeding itself that contributes to the development of the parent-child partnership but elements hidden within this act that provide the substance of synchrony.*

Prediatrician and child maltreatment authority R. E. Helfer (1978) of the Michigan State University School of Medicine finds many affective clues to failure in the feeding relationship between parent and child. The clinician must note whether or not the parent wishes to feed the child, how the child is held, what is said, and how the demands of feeding are perceived. Again, breast-feeding has many advantages and not too many disadvantages, but it is not mandatory.

The University of Washington School of Nursing provides a very specific training program in assessing feeding behaviors between parent and child. This program encourages the observer to note bodily contact, smiles from the parent, verbal stimulation, touch during the feeding process, movement during the feeding process, and, most important, the parent's ability to be sensitive to the child's cues about his feeding needs. When appropriate, the parent and child move into a process of feeding that has a pace directed by the child's needs.

A closer look at negative synchrony in the feeding process is provided through some unpublished research by J. Funke and M. Irby (1973) of the University of Colorado. These researchers alert clinicians to watch for forced and disrupted feeding, during which the food is offered and withdrawn sporadically. This is often done by a parent who feeds the child only after long perids of crying and hurries the child through the process. Ultimately, this parent is neutral or negative toward the child being fed but quite interested in talking with the observer about herself. Clearly, the focus of attention is far from the child.

A specific method of assessment is not required. The clinician will feel uncomfortable about the process he or she is watching. The parent does not relate, care, become excited, or appear pleased with the process. This is another burden of the parenting task. It should be noted that feeding problems frequently grow out of parental misunderstanding about the needs of the child. However, *when the problem is not educational, a strong warning should be offered to the clinician.* Failure at the act of feeding is not immediately predictive of continuing problems. *The clinician's role is that of making absolutely certain that the problem is affective rather than educational,* then considering other points of interaction between parent and child for confirmation of the problems.

MOVEMENT

A major source of expression available to the parent and newborn is frequently overlooked in child-care interactions: movement. The motor and kinesthetic senses have been described by Mahler and her colleagues (1975: 15) as the major expressive pathways available to the newborn. The expressive function of rocking, gestures, and general affectomotor behavior has long been recognized but only recently measured. The result has been that the influence of the vestibular system on development has been underestimated as an observational point.

Impairments in the vestibular sense have been traced to a variety of learning disorders, even childhood schizophrenia. Additionally, the Harlow studies with rhesus monkeys deprived of vestibular stimulation provide evidence that this absence contributes to unalterable developmental disabilities (Korner et al., 1975: 362). Without vestibular stimulation, the child is simply unprepared to respond to his caregivers or his environment.

Vestibular stimulation brings the child to an alert state. This alertness is mandatory if learning between parent and child is to occur (Lozoff et al., 1977: 2). Not only is the alert child more prepared to engage in synchronous behavior; the parent sees himself and is seen by others as more effective (Parke et al., 1980: 129). This is a part of all parent-child interactions, but has been overlooked in assessment in that its effects are difficult to perceive objectively (Korner, 1973: 58). Observers have tended to focus on obvious social events between parent and child (such as feeding) and have ignored the more basic components of the act, which may actually influence the developing relationship directly.

The successful parent-child partnership demands that the parent facilitate movement for the child. In the beginning, the movement depends on the parent's willingness to handle the child. As time progresses, the sense changes to that of a parent who is willing to facilitate exploration and provide movement opportunities for the mobile child. *The functional parent should be observed to rock, cuddle, and move the child a great deal.* This should be smooth movement that reorients the child to the parent in several different ways. The child should neither be rigidly held nor ignored. There should be touch, holding, frequent change of position, and interaction with toys and objects held by the parent. An understimulated child is a child who will have difficulty in initiating basic communication links with his parent. This successful movement relationship is dependent on one even more basic, the simple pleasures of tactile and bodily contact.

BODILY CONTACT

The early Harlow studies with rhesus monkeys (Harlow and Zimmerman, 1959) leave little doubt as to the critical nature of parent-child contact. This contact was shown to be vital to the very survival of the infant (Ainsworth, 1979: 933). Human parents demonstrate the same pattern of contact with their children (Klaus et al., 1970: 188).

Bodily contact is an extension of rhythmic communication between parent and child. As intended, the successful maintenance of this contact provides a sense of security for both parent and child. An important focus of study that has been missed, however, is that group of parents and children who find bodily contact and tactile stimulation to be unpleasant.

Helfer (1978) has speculated that many parents who developed within an inadequate parent-child relationship have not developed the capacity to relate touch to a pleasurable sensation. This includes those parents who were physically abused and accustomed to touch as being painful, but it also includes a group who simply never learned of touch as a communication mechanism. Murphy and Moriarity (1976: 83) have found infants who seem to experience contact as unpleasant. This is a terrible message of rejection to the parent who seeks to establish bodily contact. Most critical is the information that, irrespective of origins, those sensitive to touch in early life or those who missed touching opportunities appear to have difficulty in touching later in life.

The cuddling, rubbing, stroking, kissing, and snuggling that are indicative of a positive parent-infant partnership are not accidental. Bodily contact is a method of communication as well as a movement stimulator and a bonding-enchancement process. Some children, or parents, are neurologically mismatched and have differing tolerances for this communication system. Some never learned it as a device to transmit feelings. There is speculation that maltreating parents may experience more failure in this sharing than others. On the whole, the reason for this failure in some persons remains a mystery. Two factors lessen the problem: (1) It is easily observed in the parent and often amenable to change. (2) The child is provided with many compensatory mechanisms for relating to the adult who fails in one communication area. A major compensatory ability in the child is his visual ability.

SIGHT/EYE CONTACT

Beginning his life without any real ability to interpret what he hears and with a mechanistic response to tactile stimulation, the newborn relies heavily on his visual ability. Contrary to what is often assumed, the newborn is prepared for visual tasks at birth. Even complex abilities such as focusing, following, and the selection of visual preferences are his to employ (Brazelton, 1944; Franz et al., 1975; Lozoff et al., 1977). This is one of the neonatal capacities that does not wane with time and that reaches a relatively early maturation, at about two months (Grey et al., 1976: 390). The early maturation of the visual capacity is indicative of the important role visual abilities play in the early partnership between parent and child.

Although the child is prepared at birth to employ unifying perceptual abilities (Restak, 1979: 105), the majority of the visual perceptions are wrapped up in watching the parent. The child uses his visual familiarity with the parent to aid in most of their shared interactions. The most obvious mechanism for this sharing is the eye contact made between parent and child.

The eye contact pattern established between child and parent is one of the earliest "mediators" of the relationship between them (Grey et al., 1976: 390). The parent who seeks visual contact with the child is rewarded when the child follows his movements with his eyes (Robson, 1967; Klaus et a., 1970). This visual interchange between parent and child has been described as the "heart" of the social relationship between them, due to its ability to allow the parent to feel "close" to the child as a result (Kalus et al., 1970: 190). There is a special quality to this visual contact between parent and child that motivates other "closeness" reactions between them, such as causing the infant to smile or motivating the parent to reach out and cuddle the child. Eye contact between parent and child motivates other relationship actions as a result of the reward that eye contact holds for both partners (Bell, 1974: 9). The observer should seek to find this reward for both partners.

At the level of basically rewarding actions and points of contact, *the shared interactions that describe the positive parent-child relationship* (feeding, movement, holding, touching, and eye contact) *are interdependent.* Each behavior can, and should, motivate another. Each of these behaviors can compensate for the absence of another. Each behavior has a specific reward value for the parent and the child. To the extent that this recognition of reward is impaired in either partner, the future of that relationship can also be assumed to face obstacles. One of the most obvious rewards for the parent is his child's smile.

SMILING

Even the most strongly attached parents demand some small reward for their ministration on behalf of the child. Asking that the child recognize their caring and level of effort is normal. One great reward available within the child's array of behaviors is the smile. Attached parents will find that this smile from their child is all the reward necessary for the hard work and care given (Klaus et al., 1970: 191).

The interaction that results in a smile frequently begins with the eye contact generated through time spent in a face-to-face orientation. When it occurs, not only does the parent feel that the child recognizes his presence, but it generates a smile on the parent's face (Robson & Moss, 1970: 980). As the parent smiles, the child smiles again, and a reciprocal reward system is generated that says to both partners, "You make me happy" (Lewis, 1972). This pattern of visual following, fixation on one another, smiling, laughting, and continued eye contact is the initial demonstration of attachment behaviors. This sequence is the first of many through which the parent and child will learn to relate to each other (Robson & Moss, 1970: 979). Should this pattern be unavailable to the parent and child, all relating that should follow may also be missed. This interaction, in this way, is the cornerstone to all future sharing. The only communication ability of the child with a power equal to that of the smile is the cry.

CRYING

Just as the parent is drawn to visual contact with the child, it is the rare individual who can ignore a crying child. This does not suggest that the response is always positive; one of the leading motivators of a parent's hitting a child is the child's crying. However, the child's cry does bring a strong response from almost all adults.

The initial utility of the cry in nature is to bring the parent to the child (Bell, 1974: 4). Once this contact has been established, the child's other communication mechanisms (such as eyes or touch) can deliver supplemental messages. In this way, the earliest utility of crying is as a "signal" communication that brings the parent into close enough contact to use the "executive" (clinging, vocalization, and touch) behaviors available to the child (Bell, 1974: 9). It is only with time and experience that crying takes on meanings such as hunger, anger, frustration, and pain (Wolfe, 1969), It is much later still that crying becomes a mechanism for emotional communication (Hersh & Levin, 1979a: 29). As with all other early survival/relationship mechanisms, the parent's willingness to respond is the pivotal variable on which the utility of carying balances.

The observation of the parental response to the child's cry is a vital point of study. Not only does this cry stimulate action; it provides parents an opportunity to demonstrate their ability to soothe the child as well as their understanding of the child's needs. *The inadequate parent may well be seen as overly responsive and anxious about the child's cry or underresponsive and inappropriately unconcerned.* Should the parent and child be mismatched in either the parent's ability to respond and soothe or the parent's understanding of the meaning of the cry, a prolonged lack of understanding between this pair is predictable.

SUMMARY VIEW

This review of the instinctive communication mechanisms provided the child through inborn capacities makes it clear that the child is built for survival. In fact, all the sensory modalities of the infant are attuned to aid in his early survival.

The natural framework for survival in the human, as well as the less complex animal, infant begins with the use of behaviors that first bring the parent into contact. This contact is then maintained and caregiving stimulated through complementary actions that are rewarding to both parent and child. The efficiency of this balanced system is lost to the child if the parent is impaired in his ability to respond to these instinctive communications. The earliest parental role, and that which must be available to the observer, is a willingness to recognize and respond to biologically induced behavioral patterns (Barnett et al., 1970: 198). This is the "natural order" of attachment. Most humans have this capacity and use it successfully to satisfy the basic relationship needs. Some parents do not have this capacity, and the potential for destruction of offspring, as a result of its absence, is great. Before leaving this area, however, one absence that is often assumed must be corrected—that of the father in the caregiving relationship.

May I Please Be Excused?
The Father's Role in the
Parent-Infant Partnership

Traditionally, the father has been excused from a mandatory role in the parent-child relationship on cultural or sex-role grounds (Klaus & Kennell, 1976). The father can no longer be relieved of this responsibility. The other members of the partnership (mother and child) require his presence. The child requires the father's attachment for some aspects of his growth, and the mother requires the father's participation to allow for her own human frailties and limitations.

Parke and his colleagues (1980) have studied the relative importance of mother and father in the child's early life. Contrary to common assumptions regarding the mother's primary role in early life, this work suggests that to ignore the father is to neglect a critical element in the infant's development. Parke cites studies by Michael Lamb (1977) as support for the notion that infants show no consistent preference for either parent during the first year of life. Additionally, there is evidence that the presence of another adult in the caregiving relationship (presumably the father) has a positive effect. The effect noted is one of an increase in positive affect for all members of the relationship and higher levels of exploration on the part of the child (Parke et al., 1980: 128). At the opposite extreme from this positive information is the Pedersen and Robson (1969) research indicating that the father can play a direct role in the development of maladjustment of the child. Such maladjustment grows out of distorted early relationships with the child. The father, then, is a prime target for the outside observer's assessment.

The human offspring, as contrasted with some other animal off-spring, makes a strong impression on the adequate father from the beginning. "Engrossment" is the term used by Greenberg and Morris (1974) to describe the father's immense reaction to the newborn. This reaction is characterized by total preoccupation with and absorption in the infant. Just as he will with the mother's bonding, the infant will capitalize on this absorption and use it to initiate attachment behaviors between himself and his father.

The assessment of this early bonding in the father, probably through the relative lack of research in this area, seems more basic than with the mother. A description of the early bond finds the father moving through a series of visual and tactile exchanges with the child until his exploration has convinced him that the child is "perfect." At this conclusion, the father demonstrates a sense of elation and an almost visible growth in his self-esteem (Greenberg & Morris, 1974: 522-525). The pride is obvious. It is not difficult to imagine how this sense of pride and perception can lead to a protective relationship for the child. The observer must be wary of those circumstances in which this pride is not evident.

Beyond these global descriptions of the father's reactions to the child's bonding attempts, the knowledge begins to weaken. The literature dealing with the father's attachment is not wide. There are some general points of reference for the observer, offered by Belsky (1981: 4), that provide some direction. Belsky has captured the essence of the father-child attachment in the following broad concepts:

(1) *The infant does develop a relationship with his father but when stressed may seek out his mother.* This is in keeping with earlier comments describing different attachment for different purposes and the likelihood that the primary caregiver is the person most useful in reducing stress.

(2) *The father's role leans toward play, while the mother's role focuses on caretaking.* This is a fact echoed in other reviews (Parke et al., 1980) and reflective of the father's spending less time in feeding and caretaking activities. The consequence is that the father spends a greater percentage of his time in play activities. The style of play is different as well. Fathers tend to touch and lift during play, while mothers tend to talk or play with the children through the use of their toys (Lamb, 1977b).

(3) *There is a marked difference in mothers' and fathers' reactions to infants of different sexes* (Parke et al., 1980: 123; Belsky, 1981: 8).

Not unexpectedly, the influence of the father on the son may exceed his influence on the daugher.

A final point, outside the Belsky review, bears mention. Pedersen and Robson (1969) report that the father's attachment will proceed more slowly than the mother's. This, in itself, is of little note. However, in those circumstances in which the birth did not occur as the father had hoped, or in which the child was different from what was expected, this reluctance in attachment is magnified. This signals a need, according to Robson and Moss (1970) to *explore the father's sense of the pregnancy and delivery in the course of assessing the father's capacity for attaching to a given child*. In addition, the observer must ask if there are any discrepancies between the father's expectations of the child and the child's actual performance.

Although a growing body of knowledge, the research in father-child attachment is sparse, burdened with methodological difficulties, and very traditional (Parke et al., 1980; Belsky, 1981). That does not minimize the importance of observing the father in the potentially violent family. *We have been too forgiving of fathers in their relationships with their children.* A father should be as accountable for his caring for and caregiving to his children as a mother, despite the fact that his parental investment would be predicted to be lower than that of the mother. This point bears brief discussion.

Sociobiological theory is accused of sexism in its view of mothers versus fathers. This is a charge that is probably accurate in a theoretical sense but one that is of little practical significance in discussing human parenting. Recall that the key to sociobiological thinking is the individual's striving to maximize his "fitness" through the survival of his genes through the offspring. The female of the species, tied to the long gestation and early caregiving role, will have many fewer opportunities for this maximization of fitness than the male. The male's early role is limited to that of fertilization. Once joining with a female in order to conceive, the male is assumed to be free to move on to another female and replicate his genes again. While this is, of course, theoretically possible, it is not common practice among human parents. Therefore, for the sake of assessment in the human couple, it should be assumed that the investments of both parents in the child are equal. The equality demands complementary performance by each parent to ensure the child's survival. There is one exception to this rule—a dangerous one.

Family sociologists Robert Burgess and Rand Conger have discovered what they have termed the "Cinderella Effect" in some
maltreating families. This term describes the situation in which a hus-
band and wife are living with their own children as well as a child from
a previous relationship. Typically, this is a child of the mother. That
child, living now without the support and protection of a biological
father, appears to be at some increased risk for maltreatment (Burgess
et al., 1981). This child is not only a living manifestation of a sexual
act between the stepfather's wife and another man, but also one in
whom the parent is less invested than those who carry his own potential fitness. While not an absolute, the risk is significant enough for
the observer to note. The mandate here is for a very *intensive assessment of the attachment between that child and the nonbiological
father.*

*The assessment of the father's relationship with the child should
be conducted in the same manner and be held up to the same standards as was the observation of the maternal-child attachment.* It is
likely that the expectations of the father may be less within a given
family. But that should not be permitted to influence the observer's
expectations. The male may well be less knowledgeable of and less
competent at basic attachment tasks, but the desire for attachment
should remain a constant. If this child's life is to be one with a solid
beginning, it will be one in which both parents find reward and
investment.

The Outer Limits:
Boundaries of Behavioral Demand

Bruno Bettleheim (1950: 40) has suggested that it is only reasonable to expect a child to control his behavior if he has experienced the
world as a "satisfying place" in which to grow. This "satisfaction"
can be found in positive attachment experiences between parent and
child. A developmental tracing of how this satisfaction develops has
been provided by Sroufe (1979: 837, Table 1).

According to Sroufe, the first year of the child's life must be
responded to with predictable, responsive, and sensitive interactions.
It is through experiencing these interactions that the child begins to
learn the management and regulation of the physical equilibrium he
seeks in this new world. These early interactions have been described
in this chapter and form the basis of attachment.

From one year to thirty months, Sroufe describes the parental function as that of serving as a foundation from which the child can explore and achieve some sense of autonomy. Over time, the clear communication, predictability, and flexibility demonstrated by the parent allow the child to achieve a sense of his own powers of self-management, control, and identification. These activities are predicated by the prior existence of "permission" to move ahead—a positive attachment. This is the process by which movement toward a competent child and family is assured.

The study of development as it flows from a positive attachment between parent and child demands recognition of the increasing "intentionality" of the child's behavior. Intentionality develops as the child comes to understand that his own behavior has meaning and can be used to manipulate other persons in his world (Schaffer, 1977c: 10). *Positively attached parents will be observed willingly to subject themselves to manipulations of the child to a degree that would be thought ludicrous in an interaction between two adults.* This acceptance of manipulation on the part of the parent provides the child a measure of self-reliance and trust (Bowlby, 1973: 358-359). Conversely, the parent unwilling to accept this "supervisee" role provides little of that trust and self-reliance for the child.

The competence of the child is directly related to his attachment figure's willingness to allow him to demonstrate this competence. The child, in this way, uses the parent to learn that he is competent. The parent's availability for this learning contributes to a stronger child and a stronger relationship than would otherwise be possible (Sroufe, 1979: 837). The child who lives without this opportunity to learn is placed in a constant double bind of being fearful of his own behavioral competence and fearful of his parent's lack of competence as well. These are common anxieties among children in maltreating and poorly attached families and are the antithesis of the security necessary for positive growth and development (Bowlby, 1973: 313). In this way, attachment is a necessity for appropriate development. The observer seeking this attachment must be cautious, however.

A cursory reading of attachment descriptions would suggest that parent and child exist at polarized points. They are either attached or they are not. If attached, things will be positive. If not attached, things will be negative. That is not true. The world is not populated with parents and children who either match completely or not at all. Additionally, all attachment functions are not carried on by a single individual in his relationship with the child. Finally, children who are positively attached are fully capable of demonstrating the dysfunctional behaviors of those who are not securely attached. The difference in relationships rests with the ability of the partners to involve each other in their needs and overcome the obstacles provided by the environment in which the attachment must develop (Sroufe, 1979: 838). There will be variability in the child and in the parent.

The observation of attachment behaviors is rarely absolute. The clinician must infer a great deal through the style of behavior. For example, the attached parent may not be overwhelmingly affectionate with the child, but may almost never reject the child's wish for contact (Murphy & Moriarity, 1976: 43). The attached parent will also be appropriately responsive to the infant's signals in any context (Ainsworth, 1979: 934). This is important for the child, for he requires the knowledge that his behavioral skills will generalize across new situations (Sroufe, 1979: 837). The important point to be made to the individual assessing the relationship is that *specific behaviors and levels of responsivity will vary a great deal within a given parent-child partnership and across all partnerships being observed.* The parents' willingness to accept these differences in the child and themselves is more important than differences in psychological functioning or temperament in the members of the partnership (Ainsworth, 1979: 933). Recognizing these differences is vital in assessing the potential for violence, for the violent parent may be no more than an inadequate individual who held unreasonable standards of perfection for himself and his child. The frustration such parents realize when these goals become unreachable motivates them toward aggression. This acceptance of parental individuality does not suggest that characteristics of the individual parent are unimportant. There are specific demands on the qualities present in the attached parent.

The attachment serves the child as a haven when confronted by stress. The individual with the greatest stress reduction capacity for the child will earn the primary attachment relationship (Rutter, 1972: 39). As noted earlier, this person does not have to be a mother, or even a female. In fact, optimal development can be achieved through multiple attachments with a small number of individuals of both sexes (Rutter, 1976: 106). The critical requirements for attached parents here is their *willingness to accept and respond to the role demanded by the child.* The manner in which this role is played out also does not change.

Reciprocity between parent and child signifies the beginning of the attachment and continues as a measure of its maintenance. This reciprocity is demonstrated through a pattern of connection, relaxation, and reconnection between parent and child—a pattern dictated by appropriate sensitivity to the child's cues (Brazelton et al., 1974). The willingness of the attached parent to connect or withdraw on the basis of the child's needs is a source of comfort to the child. Through this pattern there is a "dialogue" built, in which the effect of taking turns in responding instills the understanding that communication can lead to control (Schaffer, 1977c: 12). The series of these reciprocal experiences linked across early childhood provides the "units of communication" (Watzlawick et al., 1967: 50) that are necessary stimulants to human development. The attached parent must reveal a willingness to take part in this reciprocal process.

The observer of the attachment partnership should first see an action from the parent motivated by cues in the child's behavior. The reaction of the child to the parent's initial behavior should stimulate still another action from the parent, and through this process a social exchange takes place that stimulates learning (Bell, 1974: 8). The positive attachment relationship, in this observational scheme, can be seen as a human environment (Eisenberg, 1969) in which positive growth mechanisms and social experiences can be played out. The positiveness of this environment is related to the parents' awareness of the child's needs, the parents' willingness to convert their own immediate needs to allow the child to express his, the parents' mechanical skill in dealing with the child's needs, and positive goals for the child and family (Murphy & Moriarity, 1976). Should these elements be present, a partnership that satisfies the basic requirements for growth and development can be assumed.

There is no isolated path to the development of an attachment relationship that is superior to all others. In every parent-child partnership that is functional, new behaviors are constantly being added, old behaviors constantly refined, and all behavior becomes more complex as the parent and child mature together and encounter new situations (Epstein, 1979; Sroufe, 1979). What can be isolated as a constant in this ever-changing process is the reciprocal relating and sensitivity to the partner's needs that begins with the bonding process. These consistent requirements appear slightly different at each stage of development. Clues to their observation are given in the chapters that follow.

Chapter 4

ASSESSING THE PARENT'S INTERNAL INSTRUCTIONS
Developing Attachment During Pregnancy

Any observer, pronatalist or not, must consider the process of pregnancy and childbirth as something of a miracle. The most obvious result of this miracle is the development of a functional, highly complex human infant. Less obvious is the *emotional change* in the pregnant woman that prepares her for the tasks ahead as a parent. The physiological elements of the miracle tend to move forward automatically; the emotional progress may travel a rougher road.

A traditional response to pregnancy within our society is to tout it as "the most natural thing in the world," claim, "Isn't it wonderful!" and, upon viewing the pregnant woman, state, "Doesn't she look radiant!" Obviously, these are intended to be supportive statements. They can also be very confusing and frustrating attitudes to the woman who does not feel "natural," "radiant," or "wonderful" during pregnancy, either physically or emotionally. Unfortunately, this confused woman is not likely to confess her true feelings amidst this pervasive optimism. She is more likely to hold these feelings within and suspect that something is "wrong" with her. This is isolating. It is also possible that she may withdraw and await the child's presence before pouring out her resentment and confusion. This is dangerous.

Generally, the pregnant woman who is not at peace with the pregnancy experience prepares herself to receive any blame for problems. She does not know where to turn to discuss her fears. If the assessment is being conducted retrospectively, through a discussion of "how you felt when you were pregnant," the clinician may find that she has never admitted these fears to anyone. The critical piece of information is that *her ambivalence about the pregnancy experience either does not or did not match the "wonderfulness" or "joy" people tell her she is supposed to feel.*

Ambivalence about pregnancy is natural and to be expected. When out of control or hidden, it becomes destructive. The woman confused or angered by pregnancy presents an early failure potential that may influence the remainder of the parent-child relationship negatively. Ultimately, whether the pregnancy was planned and conducted smoothly or fraught with problems, pregnancy is a crisis for all concerned (Pohlman, 1969). Assessment of this phase of parent-child relating, whether current or retrospective, should be conducted with an awareness of this potential for crisis and continuing problems.

A great deal is asked of the pregnant woman, not only through external reactions to her pregnancy, but through internal mandates as well. The pregnant woman must work through a microcosm of parenting itself in her preparation for birth. She must first accept the fetus as one with her, to stimulate parental investment, and later grow to understand that the fetus is a separate individual (Klaus & Kennell, 1976). This process, conducted during pregnancy, prepares the woman to repeat the process in the later parent-child relationship (Bell, 1974: 2). Should this be observed as a difficult process for the woman during pregnancy, it will be a difficult process for her in the parent-child partnership.

The conflicts of pregnancy and the ambivalence present during this period allows reflection on these concerns during a time still free from the most immediate caretaking demands of the child. In effect, this is a practice period. It is imperative that the observer of the pregnancy recognize this and make room for the emotional changes and variable reactions that accompany this time. If this assessment is conducted retrospectively, the clinician must assure the parent of the "natural" origins of this confusion. This holds true for work with a currently pregnant woman as well, for the "isn't it wonderful!" attitude pervading her world will deny her the opportunity to work through ambivalence and concern, resulting in a less well-prepared mother at birth. From this background, the two major observational tasks can be described.

Whether conducting the assessment during pregnancy or at a later point, two global emotional elements in the parent's life merit attention. *The first task is the assessment of any situational or personal factors in her life that inhibited her ability to work through ambiva-*

lence about becoming a parent. The second is recognition of how this unresolved conflict has, or will, influence the child in his effort to attach with this individual. The child will come prepared for attachment through the physical miracles of the pregnancy process. The parent may not meet the child with attachment capacity, due to a failure in the emotional miracles that should have taken place.

Emotional Miracles: Becoming Someone's Mother

It is doubtful that any one person has studied the emotional aspects of pregnancy as thoroughly as T. Berry Brazelton of Harvard Medical School. His earliest explorations of the topic proposed the pregnancy process as a "challenge" (1963: 131) to the mother, and this is a notion that has remained consistent throughout his work.

Brazelton (1963: 931-932) sees the newly pregnant woman as entering the process with "mixed emotions" that call out all of the anxieties and defenses that have been within her for a long period. Cohen (1980: 53) describes this same effect as an attempt to find a balance between all past and present "stresses and supports." *This series of defenses and supports becomes the substance of an assessment of this mother.* A minimal array of influences over this process would include the mother's past history, her own parental relationships, the culture in which she lives, the values she holds, those who will share the parental role, and her own personality (David & Appell, 1969: 182). These elements come into play again and again during the development of the attachment relationship.

Pregnancy, under normal circumstances, is a period of hoping and fantasizing; it is also a time of being afraid. The absence of either positive or negative emotions is a warning signal to the clinician.

Pregnancy is a time when the woman draws into herself somewhat to examine her own strengths and inadequacies (Brazelton, 1963: 932). This is the beginning of the parental investment and the recognition that fitness is going to be increased with the successful parenting of the child. This process is necessary if the mother is to be able to surrender herself to the demands for protection made by child's "babyness." It is also necessary to generate sufficient parental investment to tolerate the near-total dependency of the infant about to enter her life. This withdrawal should result in an altered frame of reference in the mother's thinking. This movement in thought goes from self to

self → fetus

fetus as the pregnancy progresses. Should this movement not occur, the promise of early relationship stress has then been made.

As the clinician seeks to discover the movement of thought from mother to fetus during pregnancy, the aura of sacrifice should be present in the mother. This sacrifice can be seen in her moving away from immediate physical concerns and toward marshaling resources for the parenting tasks ahead. This is not so much the giving up of oneself as it is the gathering of all energies to focus on the protective caring tasks soon to capture the majority of the parent's time. *Functional parents should be concerned at this point.* This is not just a concern about childbirth. This is a real concern about whether they will be equal to the child-care and protection task.

Given the normal ambivalence of the pregnant woman, her fears, concerns, and anxieties should be anticipated (Klaus & Kennell, 1976: 28; Osofsky & Osofsky, 1980: 39). "Normal" worrying during this time tends to gravitate toward such issues as changes in body structure, feelings or symptoms, psychological shifts, relationships with the mate (including sexual relationships) and, most important, *a pervasive concern about parental abilities* (Osofsky & Osofsky, 1980: 39). The intensity of these worries will be tempered by situational variables such as whether the pregnancy was planned, her relationship with the child's father, other children, work or professional plans, and the woman's own experiences in childhood (Klaus & Kennell, 1976: 28). Each of these circumstantial variables should be explored by the clinician, but the critical factor is anxiety over the impending child-care tasks. Needless to say, the experienced parent may frame this anxiety differently but it will be present in any parent capable of attachment. Other factors in the pregnancy process also serve as satisfiers or destructors of the budding attachment partnership.

Each of the critical incidents associated with a given pregnancy holds the capacity to be a facilitator or an inhibitor of the attachment process. Physicians Marshall Klaus and John Kennell (1976: 39) of the Case Western Reserve Medical School have described these points of facilitation or inhibition as the following: (a) planning the pregnancy—making it a desired part of the woman's world; (b) confirming the pregnancy—recognizing that a child will be produced and her fitness maximized; (c) accepting the pregnancy—demonstrating a willingness to undertake the sacrifice necessary for a positive prenatal and birth experience, and understanding that this experience is being shared with another being (the child); (d) accepting fetal movement at the "quickening"—acquiring the understanding that this

DETERMINE

experience is being shared with an individual who has his own needs and reactions. This is a sequential process that is nearly mandatory for successful attachment. Each point must be explored by the clinician and the woman's full range of feelings must be sought. This is the process of accepting the parent role; without this acceptance no parental investment will develop, and attachment will be unavailable.

The process described here is a progressive one that allows the parent to accept the fetus as an individual and begin the process of investment. The marshaling of resources, examination of past experience, introspective analysis, and preoccupation with parenting abilities set the stage for a willing attachment.

Early Warnings:
Rejection of Attachment Mandates
During Pregnancy

Rejection of the attachment process can be identified even at the earliest point in the parent-child partnership: pregnancy. The causal factors leading to this rejection are innumerable, but an examination of the mother's readiness for pregnancy, general emotional stability, childhood experiences, social/environmental resources, and physical status should provide the clinician with some clues to the basis for this early attachment failure (Osofsky & Osofsky, 1980: 29).

Cohen (1980: 61-62) suggests the possibility that two distinct rejection responses distort attachment capacity during pregnancy. *The first response of the woman undergoing a stressful pregnancy might be rejection of the pregnancy itself. A separate response might be found in the rejection of the emotional attachments that are demanded of the parent during pregnancy.*

The woman rejecting the pregnancy presents a different picture from the woman rejecting attachment mandates. Generally, the woman rejecting pregnancy will present the observer with a concentrated concern over issues related to herself. This woman is likely to deny changes in physical appearance through maintenance of normal dress, for example, and she probably takes part in activities not compatible with pregnancy. She is also very likely to be preoccupied with diffuse physical complaints about her body for which neither cause nor solution is available (Cohen, 1980: 61).

The woman who is rejecting emotional attachment demonstrates her disturbance through the absence of anticipated behaviors. The clinician is forewarned that problems will arise in attachment when

Article for medical prof:
screen aborted women
88 carefully   BEHAVIORAL OBSERVATION

this woman does not respond to the quickening (first movement of the fetus). Should there be a response to the quickening, it is frequently a distorted one rather than the typical excitement engendered. Perhaps more dangerous, this woman does not seem to generate the positive fantasies of the child soon to be born that characterize the mother who accepts attachment responsibilities (Cohen, 1980: 61-62). Regardless of the clinician's sense that it is the pregnancy or the attachment that is being rejected, either problem is predictive of an impaired parent-child attachment.

Rather than constantly approaching the relationship between mother and child as a search for negative aspects, the clinician should begin the assessment process with some sense of the structure of a positive pregnancy experience. He should accept the fact that there is a shared life between mother and fetus and that the emotional responses of the mother have an immediate impact on that developing child (Verny, 1981). A positive emotional response would be similar to that described by Klaus and Kennell (1976: 29).

Klaus and Kennell suggest that under positive conditions the pregnant woman will fantasize about the baby, attribute personality variables to it (a clear measure of attachment and valuing), develop a detailed mental picture of the infant, respond favorably to fetal movement, and begin to prepare her environment (physical and emotional) for the presence of the child. Should these responses and preparation go unobserved beyond the first trimester, should the mother become preoccupied with her physical appearance, or should the mother withdraw and become extremely moody, difficulty with the pregnancy and subsequent attachment can be predicted. Unfortunately, not all warning signals in pregnancy are this easily observed.

Anticipated behaviors during pregnancy that are easily observed may be considered the "hard" signs of the assessment process. These are vital elements, to be sure, but "soft" signs also contribute to an assessment of the attachment potential during pregnancy.

Grey and her colleagues from the University of Colorado Medical School (1976: 378) have found that the best time for an examination of the softer signals of distress in pregnancy is the third trimester. It is at this point that the "hidden" factors of childhood relationships, present relationships, and preparation for or knowledge of the parenting task reveal their influence (Sugarman, 1977: 408). Also, by this point, decisions have been made between the parents about the child, preferences for sex or name have been settled, and the "nesting"

behaviors indicative of acceptance should have begun. The presence
or absence of these decisions and behaviors must be examined. Also
at particular risk at this time is the woman who has recently relocated, *have women*
is wholly inexperienced in child care, or is isolated and in conflict
about her pregnancy (Cohen, 1980: 56). All of these "soft" stresses
must be assessed, irrespective of their seeming triviality. As the
woman's emotional resiliency and defenses begin to weaken in the
face of these stresses, the behaviors symptomatic of rejection will
slowly surface (Cohen, 1980: 60-61). It is at this point of failure that
the harder signs of rejection will be available to the clinician.

The message to the clinician attempting to conduct an assessment
of a pregnancy experience, either current or retrospective, is a basic
one. *Early distortions of the attachment capacity do not flow during
pregnancy, only from observable elements in that pregnancy* (Klaus
& Kennell, 1976: 42). *An equal degree of stress and reactivity will
originate in the hidden and unobservable elements of the woman's
life.* The only mechanism for capturing this sense is to seek information regarding family background and experience, educational
history, childbirth and child-rearing knowledge, occupational and
marital relationship histories, and fears and concerns about the
present and the future (Klaus & Kennell, 1976: 47). Without this in-
depth exploration, the information in the assessment is superficial to
a point that risks error. Early distortions in the attachment capacity
stem from multiple points in the parent's past and present history. To
ignore exploration of any one point risks failure to observe a potential
distortion. These distortions in the parenting elements of the pregnancy process are transmitted directly to the parent-child partnership
after birth unless immediately corrected.

The assessment of the world of a parent experiencing a difficult
pregnancy, rejecting a pregnancy, or rejecting the attachment mandatory for successful parent-child partnerships demands more than a
simple observation of the pregnant woman. True assessment demands
exploration of all aspects of the family's environment.

*Primary Prevention:
The Earliest Possible Identification
of Problems*

Most pregnancies pass through the difficult times mentioned in
previous sections of this chapter without great upheaval. It is obvious

that nature has provided some built-in mechanisms to cope with the problems of pregnancy (Kramer, 1978). However, the increased rates of younger, poorer, and less well-prepared women giving birth today contribute to a realistic fear that the "average" mother of the 1980s may be less prepared than parents of any previous generation (Bolton, 1980).

A common assumption regarding pregnancy is that the female of the species is programmed with "instinctive" mechanisms sufficient to allow her to cope with the stresses of pregnancy. It is also assumed that, in those circumstances in which this programming has not had time to form (in the adolescent mother, for example), an educational program can compensate. Neither assumption is valid.

In the first place, there is as much "instinct" for the rejection of a pregnancy that is troubled as there is the capacity to overcome the ordinary stresses of pregnancy. Although it will not be discussed in depth here, recent research evidence suggests that the spontaneous abortion may be, in part, triggered by the "instinctive" message in the mother to reject this pregnancy and try again when circumstances are more favorable (Verny, 1981). *If we are to contribute a positive "instinct" to the pregnant woman, we must be ready to accept her "instinctive" abilities to reject the pregnancy process.*

A second point to be made is that *the complexity of the human parent's life is sufficient to outweigh most of what can be provided through a simple educational process.* The information already presented in this chapter revealed personality, social, and environmental aspects of a woman's life that not only distort "instinctive" coping mechanisms, but also prevent the learning or practice of new coping skills. Unfortunately, the positive outcomes of most pregnancies have led many persons to the conclusion that one pregnancy runs a parallel course to all others. This is untrue. Those that are atypical must be identified early if the parent-child relationship that is their consequence is to avoid dangerous distorting.

The labor and delivery nurse who experiences two to four deliveries each shift, the obstetrician hearing vague complaints from thirty women during one day's office hours, and the mental health professional dealing with the same child-care problems day after day share a common risk: boredom, complacency, and the perception of some problems and their solutions as routine (Grey et al., 1976: 382). The family members experiencing this problem, since they do not travel the pregnancy and child-care path too many times in their history, perceive any problem as absolutely unique to them in substance and intensity. This is the family that falls between the run-of-the-mill and the hysterical. Such families require the extra attention, for they truly do not have the coping mechanisms to deal with pregnancy issues. Specific warning signals in these families are readily identified.

As has been noted throughout this chapter, *evidence of the parent-child relationship should be present prior to actual birth.* That mother and fetus interact physiologically is obvious; less obvious is the behavioral interaction between them (Verny, 1981; Bell & Harper, 1977: 125). When it is the pregnant woman who is unable to recognize these behavioral demands, this may be a prediction of disturbances in the demand for synchronous relations between herself and her child at a later time. One simple indicator of this emotional sharing is the ability of fetal movement to simulate fantasy.

It has been noted that fantasy about the impending birth and the child himself is necessary for adequate adjustment to the pregnancy. The content of this fantasy must be considered in its assessment. The fantasy regarding this infant should be one of the "perfect" baby, of chosen sex, who will fulfll elements of the mother's life that she feels to be lacking (Brazelton, 1963: 932). Obviously, no single infant will fulfill all these requirements. However, if the parent is functional and the pregnancy an adaptive one, these fantasies will fall away in the presence of the actual child and adjustments will be made (Caplan, 1960a: 76). *If the parent cannot adjust to the differences between the fantasy and the infant himself, attachment problems can be predicted.*

Assessment of the presence of fantasies, as well as their rigidity, will provide the observer with solid information on the flexibility of the parent-child relationship to be established. Particularly valuable in this assessment are questions regarding the name (Klaus & Kennell, 1976: 186) or preferred sex (Grey et al., 1976: 379) of the child. Other "commonsense" questions regarding these fantasies should provide additional opportunity to become aware of impending difficulty.

Practically speaking, one of the most basic measures of the parent's reaction to the pregnancy may be seen in the willingness to make and keep appointments for prenatal care (Grey et al., 1976: 379). The implication of repetitively missed appointments is obvious; however, maternal age and socioeconomic status may play a role in the interpretation of this observation.

Younger mothers and mothers from lower socioeconomic status environments will have lowered rates of prenatal care (Bolton, 1980: 119-123). Medical care within these populations is for illness and emergency, not for a "wellness" such as pregnancy (Osofsky, 1968). Realistically, such everyday problems as transportation, child care, work hours, loss of income, long clinic waits, and the attitudes of some clinic personnel (Herzog, 1966: 29) bear on this mother's reluctance to seek prenatal care. If these practical hinderances do not apply, the reluctance to seek prenatal care may well be a direct statement of rejection. This statement must be explored with the mother, father, and all available members of the extended family if its meaning is to be assessed.

Considering the assessment of the father more closely, it must be remembered that a pregnancy in a relationship has the potential to solidify or destroy it (Klaus & Kennell, 1976: 46). A large number of parents find the impending birth of a child to be an expression of the reasons they elected to spend their lives together. An alarming number of parents, however, stumble into pregnancy accidentally or with a grossly exaggerated sense of their preparation for the task. This could be a promise of incapacitation in the face of the real demands of child rearing. When this lack of preparation for child rearing affects the relationship between the parents and between the parents and their offspring, these persons are said to be "asynchronous" (Klaus & Kennell, 1976: 46).

Asynchrony is the absence of the same ability to relate that builds an attachment between parent and child. When the relationship between the parents is asynchronous, they will be observed to be increasingly isolated from each other, losing the capacity to share feelings, and failing in their ability to respond cooperatively to the child's needs. This decline is directed beyond the parents during pregnancy and into the relationship with the child after birth (Bell, 1974: 3; Belsky, 1981).

Pregnancy is far from the "perfect" experience it is often thought to be by those who have experienced it positively. It is a "natural" process that includes both positives and negatives. It is a difficult physical and emotional process that requires constant attention from all of its participants, mother and father alike. Even the most wanted child can distort family relationships when the parents discover that pregnancy and the prospect of child rearing are not "the most natural thing in the world." The alert clinician has the opportunity to assess symptoms of "unnatural" pregnancy early on, in most cases. Once assessed, preventive measures can be initiated. Periodically, distortions in attachment capacity do not reveal themselves until the point of delivery, however, as will be shown in the next chapter.

Chapter 5

MAKING THE INTRODUCTIONS
Labor, Delivery, and
In-Hospital Concerns

The description of pregnancy and childbirth as "the most natural thing in the world" is based on the experiences of persons who have found it to be nondisruptive. These persons probably found the affective elements of attachment and rewards from the child almost immediately available. This provides the promise of a strong relationship. It does not always work out that way.

Using terminology that is easily understood, Hurd (1975) has reviewed the elements of attachment described by Robson and Moss (1970) and encourages clinicians to seek evidence of the "soft signs" of attachment (discussed in Chapter 4) immediately at birth. These soft indications include evidence of warmth, love, devotion, protectiveness, concern, and positive anticipation of being together. These affective elements have come to be considered the basic requirements of "mothering" and signify a building attachment. Most people feel these affective elements to be an automatic outcome of the pregnancy and delivery experience. They are wrong. *Some parents find these affective drives and rewards unreachable in any form.* Fortunately, the presence, absence, or distortion of these affective elements can be determined at this early point.

Pregnancy, Labor, and Delivery

Experiences in labor and delivery *can* be indicative of the potential relationship between parent and child. Dunn and Richards (1977: 448) have examined the effects of labor and delivery and have determined that this experience can alter the behavior of the mother, the child, or both. Any change in either partner may contribute to an alteration in interaction style that is enduring. Also helpful to the clinician is the fact that experiences in labor and delivery may activate a previously unobserved behavior (such as loss of control) that warns of similar behavior between parent and child under stressful conditions later.

The observation of the mother in labor, delivery, and early child care can provide a clue to previous experiences that may influence behavior with the child. Specifically, the mother's own child-rearing experience, or experience with earlier pregnancies, may be reflected in unusual behaviors at this time (Klaus & Kennell, 1976: 42). It must be warned, however, that these behaviors must be assessed in light of existing hospital programming, policy, and staff behavior.

A schism exists between those who would seek to impose medical supervision over each stage of the labor and delivery process and those who prefer a more "natural" approach (Kramer, 1978). This gap extends beyond control to such issues as the effects of drugs, the role of the parents in the delivery process, and the lasting impact on the parent-child relationship. These arguments will not be resolved here, but they do merit discussion.

The ultimate "natural" experience in delivery is to deliver in the child's home. Klaus and Kennell (1976: 46) illustrate that even physicians can understand the attraction to this natural experience. Klaus and Kennell note that the home-delivering mother not only appears to be in control of the process but also moves into a joyful state they term "ekstasis" immediately after experiencing the birth. This ecstasy seems to spread to all involved in the process as they are captured by the wonders of the new being among them. This process gives *the appearance* of developing strong attachments between the child and those in attendance, as well as between the mother and all involved (1976: 53). Importantly, *there is nothing solid to suggest that this attachment is automatic or that it is unavailable in the hospital delivery.*

This joyous description stands in stark contrast to the opposite extreme, which can be found in Robson and Moss's (1970: 978) description of the hospital-based delivery, in which subjects were "preoccupied with completing the task at hand as quickly and painlessly as possible." Critically, and despite the coldness of the description, Robson and Moss relate that there was an immediate expression of interest at the point of birth even in the clinical setting. This interest moved through stages of concern and curiosity through which new mothers came to know their children in exactly the same manner as did the mothers who delivered at home.

The implication of both descriptions is that the mother who is relaxed, who is cooperative with, and who relates positively to those in attendance will find the labor and delivery experience more rewarding. Control during delivery is relative. Overall, those mothers who were allowed to participate in the process in the manner of their choosing seemed to be pleased with their infants and to demonstrate the immediate rapport sought by those hoping to observe attachment behaviors (Newton & Newton, 1962; Kramer, 1978). These effects were observed independently of where the labor and delivery experience took place.

The position taken here is that *attachment is possible in any labor and delivery setting.* That is a sweeping generalization, but one which is defensible given current knowledge. A critical determinant for the clinician, however, is learning what the mother believes. If she has been led to believe that the "natural" birth is the only road to "real" mothering, her anxiety may influence her immediate ability to attach. *The mother's expectation of her attachment capacity based on the type of birth experience cannot go unexplored.* Studies of drug effects at delivery are similarly cloudy.

Reviews of the effects of obstetric anesthetic and analgesic drugs on mother-child interactions indicate that the isolated impact of the drug(s) is difficult to assess (Aleksandrowicz, 1974). These drugs interact with the physiological, behavioral, and emotional status of the child and mother. Since these elements vary by situation, the effect of the drug(s) may be different in individual circumstances (Dunn & Richards, 1977: 430). The study of these drug effects, then, is limited by our inability to isolate effects as well as their lack of generalizability (Anonymous, 1974). Klaus and Kennell (1976) have summarized these research works by noting that studies of anesthesia and amnesic drugs have not reached a systematic and thus conclusive point. Some isolated effects do seem to be known, however.

A review of anesthetic effects (Dubignon et al., 1969) would find some laboratory studies and retrospective maternal self-reports (Brazelton, 1961) to connect anesthetics with feeding anomalies or depression of infant responsivity (Klaus & Kennell, 1976: 48). Other work finds the use of anesthesia to have no effect on the immediate postpartum period (Robson & Moss, 1970). Still other research on mothers requesting anesthesia (particularly lower socioeconomic status mothers) demonstrates that this period of reduced sensitivity is a functional mechanism for coping with the stresses of the labor and delivery experience (Kramer, 1978). This benign sense was corroborated by Klaus and Kennell's (1976: 46) finding that unconsciousness at birth does not lead to direct infant rejection, as it might in the animal parent.

Given a research path that is seemingly supportive of all arguments, the key for the clinician is to *determine whether or not the mother is comfortable with the need for drugs.* Should she be uncomfortable about the use of drugs, her behavior will reflect this. It is likely, however, that the mother with attachment capacity will not experience any prolonged impairment of her attachment capacity through this temporary inconvenience. It is probably more disappointment demonstrated by this mother than a disruption of the bonding process.

The behavior of mother and child in any delivery setting is an observational key. At the extremes, the mother and child are the "stars" of the home-centered birth and, potentially, mere "subjects" in hospital-centered birth. Most deliveries do not involve either of these extremes. In any setting, if this experience is frightening, conducted without cooperation or support, or extraordinarily difficult, it is likely to have some negative impact on the immediate parent-child relationship (Grey et al., 1976: 380).

As is true in the assessment of pregnancy, *the mother's preexisting knowledge and expectations are vital pieces of information.* Her fantasy of labor and delivery, as well as her expectations of her own performance during this process, must be known. Should any of the reality of the experience contradict fantasy and expectation, short-term problem behaviors may arise. Unless her preexisting capacity for attachment has been impaired, it is not likely that this behavioral effect will be anything but short-term.

Despite this limited view of delivery and early parenting experiences, the past fifteen years have seen a rapid growth in research and interest in the concept of early bonding. One of the major motivators in that series of examinations was the pioneering work of Klaus and Kennell.

The focal point of study for the work of Klaus and Kennell was the observation of mothers who were allowed prolonged contact with their child immediately after birth. These mothers were then compared to a group of mothers receiving routine hospital care not including this "extra contact." The extra-contact (first hour after birth plus five extra hours over the following three days) mothers demonstrated behaviors toward their childn that have been described in previous chapters as generally evidencing positive attachment. The implication is that the period immediately following birth holds some extra promise for the facilitation of attachment, if handled appropriately.

The facilitation of attachment immediately following birth has been variously referred to as "binding in," "bonding," or "early claiming" and progresses at an independent rate between individual mothers and children (Grey et al., 1976: 380). Studies of this early facilitation reached immediate acceptance and enthusiasm, in part due to the animal studies that tracked this immediate relating through a process termed "imprinting" (Lorenz, 1966). Recent work has questioned both the similarities between early human parent-child behavior and animal behavior (McCall, 1982) and the methodology of the Klaus and Kennell work (Taylor, 1980). The net effect has been to remove the magical or "necessary condition" properties of early contact between parent and child and view it as a "facilitator." That is the professional view. The clinician must note, as is critical in delivery expectations, that the parent may have a different view of early contact.

Professionals now view early contact as a facilitator of the attachment process, although not a necessity, as was first believed. Parents may continue to see it as necessity. The public acceptance (particularly the educated and reading public) of an early "sensitive period" has been sustained. Parents may see it as an absolute, and anything (hospital policy, necessary use of drugs, Cesarean sections) that interrupts it may predict doom to that parent. Once again, the parental expectations of this early period require note. Should the period of early contact be "stolen" from them for any medical reason, resentment, disappointment, and anger may play into all their actions. In the emotionally stable parent, this will not interfere with attachment capacity.

The concept of a sensitive period, despite its diminished status in the research and scientific world, has been found to have continuing utility in labor and delivery practice. The absence of this opportunity is not a precursor of failed attachment or emotional disturbance (Campbell & Taylor, 1980: 12), but its presence can maximize the warm experience of the immediate postpartum period. This is particularly true for parents who are aware of it and believe in the concept. Unfortunately, other aware parents worry about the lack of opportunity to share this early contact with their child.

Many parents, particularly adoptive parents, express concern over having missed this sensitive period with their children. It is now fair to inform those parents that this time together is not a necessity for attachment. Obviously, to suggest that early contact is mandatory denies the success of thousands of foster and adoptive parents; mothers who have been separated from their children as a result of illness, premature birth, or surgical procedures; and those who were simply not afforded early contact but experienced successful attachments with their children (Robson & Moss, 1970: 978; Klaus & Kennell, 1976: 39; Campbell & Taylor, 1980: 12). *All indications are that early contact facilitates attachment, but its absence can be compensated for in the later relationship.* This information should be freely offered the parent by the clinician if it is in question. It should also be reinforced that these early contact assessments and behaviors do extend beyond the mother to the father.

Early contact has been described as useful for facilitating attachment. This facilitation extends to all members of the family, father included. Specifically, the father's attendance at the birth, his immediate observation of the child, and immediate touching between father and child appear to provide a closer tie not only between father and child, but across the entire family as well (Hersh & Levin, 1979a: 31). This depends, of course, on the role the father is willing to play in the attachment process and how closely he wishes to become involved at this early point. Despite these personal choices, *there is mounting evidence that the father's participation during this early period is very helpful in the attachment process.*

A leader in the study of father-child interactions, Ross Parke (1978) of the University of Illinois has pointed out the benefits of a father's skill in handling a child in this early period. Parke speculates that this early paternal handling has a positive influence on the child's later ability to cope with stress. As has been noted, and as any tired, just-delivered mother will testify, the entire family benefits from this early mutual interaction. Both parents have an effect on the other's interactions with the child. These effects should be noted by the clinician.

When both parents are involved, the interactions seem to increase in intensity and frequency. When both parents are involved, the interactions tend to be more effective. When both parents are involved, the infant is able to maximize the impact of his instinctive proximity-inducing and "babyness" actions, for he is drawing two persons to his

UNMARRIED FATHERS in labor/del.

protection, not one. Most telling is the fact that opposite effects have been found within families who are experiencing marital or relationship strife (Bronfenbrenner, 1968: 846). The alert clinician will explore not only what is happening in front of his eyes but all aspects of the affective world of the individuals and partnerships under observation.

There are few elements in the labor and delivery process that fail to claim some short-term role in the impending parent-child partnership. Historical elements of both parents' lives, medical procedures or necessities such as anesthesia, the maternal behavior at delivery, and the behavior of all other family members play a role in the initial presentation of the child to his attachment partners. These relationship variables must be assessed in light of practical circumstances, such as initial separation of the parent and infant, the presence of a supportive person during labor, birth abnormalities or complications (such as prematurity or Cesarean section), or medical problems in the infant (Sugarman, 1977: 409-413). This series of behavioral, affective, and situational variables within the labor and delivery process sets the stage for the critical neonatal period to follow.

Progress or Duress?
Attachment During the Early Days Together

Observing a parent-child relationship at a single point in time does not absolutely predict that relationship at a later point in time (Dunn & Richards, 1977: 449). The human animal, in its complexity, has a broader capacity for adaptation than his animal brethren, and as a result early effects are not necessarily enduring (McCall, 1982). Despite those warnings, it is suggested here that the parent's recurring reactions to the child and his needs during the early relationship, as well as the parent's general emotional state during this time, provide some clues to the potential success of the attachment (Hurd, 1975: 38). Two mediating variables must be considered to be influential in this in-hospital assessment: *maternal parity* and the *hospital* practices that influence the immediate postpartum period.

There are positives associated with the fact that a woman has experienced a previous successful pregnancy. At a minimum, this is one positive indication that this woman can succeed in this endeavor. Even experience has its limits, however. Women who are in their fifth or later pregnancy place themselves at some increased risk for bearing a child with developmental problems (Osofsky, 1972: 42). On the other hand, the mother who has experienced an earlier successful pregnancy has been shown to be more sensitive to the cues of her infant (deChateau, 1980: 147).

The maternal skill of the experienced parent does not suggest that the clinician can relax in her presence. Every child is a new experience; ask any experienced parent. Neither does this suggest that parents of first children are less attentive to their child. That would be absolutely untrue. This information simply speaks to the benefits of having experienced the attachment process with another child and the ability to generalize this experience to the next.

The first-time parent may be as attentive, or even more attentive, but inexperience in reading a child's cues is often demonstrated. Most often, this inexperience reveals itself in the anxiety level of the parent and their reduced ability to quiet the infant in comparison with multiparous parents (deChateau, 1980: 147). Upon viewing this difficulty in soothing, the clinician may be observing nothing more than the fact that this new parent has a few things to learn. *All observation must reflect a healthy respect for just how much there is to learn in parenting a first child.* In addition to previous child-rearing experience, *hospital procedures* can influence the degree of difference between parents and their ability to relate to their child. Rooming-in is one major difference.

Whether the influential variable in rooming-in is the early contact previously discussed or some other aspect of the experience, behaviors of parents who do experience rooming-in and those who do not are remarkably different. There are multiple serendipitous effects of this procedure, a procedure originally initiated for children who had problems in the nursery and required the extra care of their mothers (deChateau, 1980: 68).

The clinician will find that the self-confidence of the first-child parent who has experienced rooming-in is higher than that of a comparable parent who has not. This is evidenced through the parents' feeling that they are competent in the care of their child and their perception that they will require only minimal help upon their return home (Greenberg et al., 1973: 788). These parents also appear better able to interpret children's clues (such as crying) than the parent who has not had the concentrated exposure to the child (deChateau, 1980: 148). Not incidentally, the rooming-in experience provides a much magnified opportunity for the other members of the child's family to join in the child-care and early attachment experiences (Kramer,

1978). This exposure and sharing would be predicted to benefit that attachment potential. In the absence of other pathological variables then, rooming-in appears to facilitate the attachment environment. This is a maximal attachment environment, because the attachment possibilities of all family members are enhanced. The presence of other forms of parental or child pathology, however, can eliminate any gains to be made through a program such as this.

Early separation is not the sole predictor of difficulty in forming attachments during the neonatal period. *Many parents who fail to form attachments simply view the child as an intruder in their established lifestyle.* The child is met with continuous messages from the parents that they cannot be bothered with him and that he is too demanding (Grey et al., 1976: 385). Rooming-in will not compensate for, and may even worsen, this situation.

The clinician must break loose from the traditional notion that all parents will compensate for selfishness and lack of caring when ultimately faced with a child to provide for. The child is prepared to overcome some obstacles in the inadequate parent, but some persons are simply too inadequate ever to function adequately as parents. We must begin to recognize this possibility instead of making excuses for these parents and relying on treatment or education to ameliorate essentially impenetrable problems. *A failure to view the child realistically* during this early period may be a warning to the observer that such a dysfunctional relationship is developing.

Should the parent demonstrate an inability to describe specific behavioral or appearance attributes of her child, or should the parent attribute distorted, noninfant characteristics ("He just won't listen to me," for example), this is a warning to the clinician. The implication of these actions may be that the parent is not capable of recognizing the helplessness and babyness of the neonate. The effect is that all instinctive mechanisms in the child provided to incur protection and work against violence are essentially removed.

Recall from earlier chapters that the role of babyness is to encourage proximity between parent and child, protection from outside threat, and the willing provision of needs. Should these normal neonatal abilities be ignored, the clinician must question the parent's ability to provide protection. Similarly, should meeting the neonate's ordinary needs (such as feeding or excretion) be seen as messy, upsetting, or too much to ask, the clinician must question the parent's willingness to participate in the sacrifices necessary to form an attachment.

Warning signs of threatened attachment may be extended to the clinician through the parent's inability or unwillingness to ask for help, inability to put useful suggestions and teaching into practice, and all behaviors that give the impression of ignoring the child-care task (Grey et al., 1976: 385). Other specific points of critical observation can be captured in the parent's responses to the child, such as positively anticipating continued contact, the ability to relate mechanically to the child (such as in manner of holding), and how the parent speaks to and about the child (Hurd, 1975: 38). A continual reference to the parent's own condition rather than the child's, hostility directed toward the child's father, disappointment over the sex of the child, or lack of support from a spouse or relative may also present themselves as danger signals (Grey et al., 1976).

Although some specific observational points are presented here and earlier in this work and the assessment guideline is presented later in the work, an exhaustive litany of warnings cannot be offered here. Published assessment tools are available from the University of Colorado Medical School, Michigan State University Medical School, and the University of Washington School of Nursing. The clinician seeking the comfort of a standardized assessment instrument should seek these sources out for that comfort. What is being offered here are some small clues to why the clinician will sense that "something is not right" between parent and child and a speculative sense of the outcome of that mismatch.

Pregnancy, labor and delivery, and the immediate postpartum, in-hospital period are all points of experience that can enhance or impair the attachment relationship. What must be avoided by the clinician is the assumption of inevitability or unalterability of the parent-child effects noted during this period.

Pregnancy and childbirth can be a strange and wonderful or a strange and awful experience. The experience can have lasting effects, no effects, or effects that are subject to change in either direction. The parent-child attachment relationship is a dynamic and continuous one, each developmental point holding a new meaning. The assessment of this relationship must share that dynamic character. How that sharing takes place in later periods of childhood is described in the next chapter.

Chapter 6

THE FIRST LINE OF DEFENSE
Attachment in the Neonatal Period

The attachment process has been shown to hold many roles in the development of the human parent-child partnership. Attachment motivates the parent to learn about the child and allows the child to learn about him. It encourages the parent to undertake the endless series of child-care tasks that are necessary to the child's survival. Most important, this relationship element provides protection for the child.

The protection provided by attachment serves to secure against not only external sources but also internal sources of violence in the family. *Attachment is the mediator that balances natural capacities for rejection.* The capacity to reject a child *is* present in the human parent. Unfortunately, isolating the evidence of this rejection after it has occurred is more easily accomplished than is the goal of this assessment model: predicting parental rejection prior to its occurrence. Each stage of the parent and child's life together provides different observational alarms.

The parent in the immediate postpartum period has been studied more closely in the past ten years than ever before. This is due in large measure to the interest generated in bonding through work in the early 1970s. As such, most of the work focuses on positive aspects of the parent's behavior. Fortunately, complementary study has also occurred, which relates warning signals in those parents who have difficulty with this early bond.

Cohen (1980: 63) has identified a "syndrome," or series of problems, that contribute to bonding failure in the parent during the child's early life. Individually, each of these problems has the capacity to hinder the partnership this assessment model seeks. A warning of such problems may be found in (a) loss of mother before puberty, (b)

103

chronic conflict with relatives, (c) previous birth of a damaged child (emotionally disturbed, physically handicapped, or behaviorally disordered), (d) marital strife, (e) lack of experience, (f) rejection of the pregnancy, or (g) an inability to view the infant as an individual. Many of these elements are points of concern that have been expressed as warnings in earlier stages of the parent-child relationship. As with earlier presentations of these symptoms, the clinician should seek the presence of any of these factors first and measure their importance in the life of that individual later. Each relationship will be judged in light of its unique needs.

Klaus and Kennell (1976) present a broader view of the syndrome and encourage the clinician to seek out problems in areas such as cultural variation, family and marital relationships, previous pregnancy history, style of care by the parent's own mother, planning for the events of pregnancy, experiences in the first days of life with the child, and the effects of the hospital staff and its policies. In both formulations, disturbances in any one or all of these areas are seen as holding the capacity to result in developmental problems, behavioral problems, failure-to-thrive children, and child maltreatment. Importantly, the offering of these formulations serves as confirmation that earlier suggestions for observation are valid at all points in the relationship. As always, the clinician must assess the importance of each element in light of the individual parent and family uniqueness.

All parents, as individuals, will respond to the stresses of childbirth and child rearing differently. A heavy contributor to these differences is the juxtaposition of the just-mentioned factors within parents' lives. Early warning of an impending rejection of the child is found in an examination of each potential stressor as well as the interaction between them. For example, if the parent is inexperienced and the product of a maltreating family, the clinician would do well to suspect that this parent is at high risk to replicate that problem. It is not the simple presence of stressors that contributes to an assessment of degree of risk. *The degree of risk in a given family is determined by an examination of how the stressful variables play off against each other as well as any compensating mechanisms that might be present.* The most obvious stressor, of course, is the child himself.

The student of child rearing is sometimes forced to wonder how the attachment process can ever succeed, given the numerous potential barriers to its development. For example, deChateau (1980: 139) has proposed no less than eighteen separate variables that influence the positive development of the newborn. These variables have been mentioned throughout previous chapters and include such things as nutrition, drugs, pregnancy history, cultural requirements, mother's relationship with her own parents, pariety, delivery process, infant sex, and immediate postpartum adaption—all elements with which the clinician should be intimately familiar through the assessment process. To the lasting credit of Nature, the child, and the parent (in that order) most parents and children rely on the attachment skills provided naturally, and all is well. The power of this natural gift cannot be overestimated, and its presence should be an imposing one to the clinician who is assessing a parent-and-child partnership in the neonatal period.

The behaviors presented earlier as somewhat isolated skills come together in a rhythmic pattern easily observed during the neonatal period. The helplessness of the child, described earlier as "babyness," captures the parent immediately through appearance factors. Moving instinctively, the infant makes random eye contact with the parent, makes noises that give the impression of efforts at communication, and spends the first hour after birth in a period of "quiet alertness," which provides an opportunity for sensory relating between the family and child (Bell & Harper, 1977: 129; Klaus & Kennell, 1976: 66, 78).

The parent responds automatically to these relationship invitations from the child. Upon seeing the child, parent will very likely count fingers and toes as a reassurance that all is well. It is also likely that the parent will want the child's entire body exposed as additional reassurance of the child's completeness. Touch will follow, moving from the child's extremities to the trunk with increasingly sure strokes. Just as he will in the days to follow, the parent will orient to the child and watch every move made toward him in the delivery room, regardless of who is talking or the other tasks at hand (Klaus & Kennell, 1976: 70-74). It is at this time that the strange set of behaviors we accept as completely normal between parents and children begins.

At this moment, the first alterations of speech (to a higher pitch), continuous eye contact, changes in vocal quality, and exaggerated facial expressions that are to be observed between parent and child begin. Were this same communication pattern to occur between two adults, it would appear incredibly strange; hence, this communication pattern is scientifically known as "infant-elicited variations" (Bell & Harper, 1977: 137). A nonscientific expression of the adult's willingness to engage in this behavior that the parent is "good with children." The crucial observational variable here is the demonstration of *the adult's willingness to be led by the child.*

Even at brith, the child has well-developed sensory channels and less well-developed motor abilities that allow the adult to communicate with the child and to interpret his actions and needs (Klaus & Kennell, 1976: 11). For example, the mother's voice serves as the first rhythmic pattern to which the child learns to respond as he moves in time to that voice (entrainment). This is but one of the early steps in reciprocity between himself and his attachment figure that will serve to retrain the child's timing and bodily systems. This vital training and matching process should be readily observable in the first few days following birth.

Since the child is no longer attuned to and balanced by the mother's internal state, the confusion of stimuli in the external environment impinges on the child's underdeveloped systems and overstimulates them. The parent should be observed to protect against this over-stimulation and aid the child in the retiming of his steady states. This allows the child to reach a point of homeostasis both internally and externally (Klaus & Kennell, 1976: 74-76). These early interactions are the precursors to the executive and signal behaviors that will define the parent-child relationship in the coming months. These signal behaviors will be observed to induce contact between parent and child, and the executive behaviors (less easily observed) will maintain this contact once it has occurred. These interactive behaviors in the first few days of life, then, are the first "tools" of reciprocity.

The first few weeks of life, if the attachment process is going well, may be the child's most self-centered period. He is slowly training his parents through a combinaton of executive and signal behaviors. His biorhythmicity is returning to some steady state after the dramatic change from being *in utero* to living in the outside world (Klaus & Kennell, 1976: 38). He is rapidly capturing the father's complete attention through engrossment. This mutual reward system between mother and child, the total absorption of the father, and the slow adaptation of the child's systems to the demands of the outside world become the foundation on which the successful family develops.

Shaping Things to Come:
Early Postpartum Experiences

Although the first few days of life can be critical in the development of the attachment between parent and child, the absence of this *shortened hospital stays —*

attachment opportunity does not preclude its development at some later point (Rutter, 1976: 152; McCall, 1982). This fact mandates flexibility in the clinician seeking to assess attachment during this period.

Animal studies of the immediate postpartum period provide firm evidence that there is a "critical period" immediately following birth during which the mother and infant must be responsive to one another if acceptance of the relationship between them is to occur (McCall, 1982). It must be remembered that the animal infant is less easily identified than the human infant. It must also be remembered that the animal infant is somewhat less helpless at birth, is more mobile, and has much less time with its parent to learn the tasks of survival than the human infant. The human mother has a great deal more time to acquire ownership of her infant than does the animal mother, as well as more time to impart survival lessons. Nevertheless, the human infant, being helpless, must secure the closeness of the parent during this time. Without immediate closeness, the human infant would not survive at all. Therefore, it is reasonable to seek to observe a heightened level of responsiveness on the part of the parent during this period (Barnett et al., 1970: 198), but not to that degree demonstrated by the animal parent. Whether the pair is animal or human, however, events leading to separation of parent and infant in the early days of life may stress the attachment potential in a manner that can influence its development (Lozoff et al., 1977: 8).

Those seeking to assess this relationship must be reminded that, while it is reasonable to observe relationship behaviors in the hospital, it cannot be forgotten that being in the hospital influences the behavior being observed. An example of this is the Robson and Moss (1970) work, (Rutter, 1971, 1976, 1979) in which mothers reported it much easier to feel warmly about their infants during the period they were getting help with them in the hospital. Compared to the work-filled weeks at home, the free time to develop the affective elements of the parent-child relationship was much more abundant in the hospital. In spite of this, neither home nor hospital has complete control over the success of the attachment; this is simply a warning to those observing in either setting.

Continuing with the experience gained from the Robson and Moss study, some of the mothers gave an immediate impression of attachment to observers during the postpartum period. These mothers were termed "early attachers" and were found not to require the normal reciprocal interactions assumed to be necessary to reach attachment. Some parents are, apparently, simply ready to attach at birth. It was speculated that the early attachers had developed the relationship between themselves and their children to such a degree that it had been virtually accomplished by the time of birth. The child's instinctive efforts at seeking the attachment were found to be nothing more than a wonderful confirmation and enhancement of what already existed (Robson & Moss, 1970: 980). This information should also serve as confirmation to those seeking to observe attachment development that exploration of the fantasy work accomplished during pregnancy is vital. Unfortunately, not all of the mothers found attachment so readily available.

Some of the mothers in the Robson and Moss work (1970: 978) found it difficult to describe their infants immediately and did not evidence attachment behaviors until several months later. As has been expressed, the ability to describe the child was a pivotal variable. Another warning to the clinician must be offered in that, despite this inability, attachment did develop over time. This speaks again to flexibility in assessing the anticipated results of a parent-child relationship that gets off to a slow start.

It is not appropriate to predict doom from observations during this period. The sense given by the work just described is that there are parents who will attach in any setting: those who find attachment behavior easier to demonstrate when someone else is attending to child-care details, and those who simply take longer to demonstrate attachment behaviors. *There must be room for all of these parental types in the clinician's assessment routine.* Beyond this perspective on "time," this is a topic that continues to be important in postpartum attachment, especially with regard to the anticipated duration of these early effects.

There are generally agreed-upon short-term benefits of a successful early contact period. Long-term effects are less certain. Follow-up work with the children in Klaus and Kennell's early contact group revealed higher intelligence levels in the children of the early contact group, for example (Kennell et al., 1979: 39; Kennell & Klaus, 1976). Campbell and Taylor (1980: 10), however, report that subsequent researchers have failed to find the maintenance of effects of early contact beyond the first year of life. These effects are not lost; it is just that other parents and children "catch up" to the behavioral and intelligence benefits shortly after they have been reached by the early contact group. Campbell and Taylor (1980: 10) suggest, from this type of data, that the presence of an early sensitive period and the benefits of early contact have been "overinterpreted." Striking a middle ground, British psychiatrist Michael Rutter (1976: 152) posits the presence of some "vulnerable" individuals (parents, children, or both) for whom the negative effect of lack of early contact could be long-term. Obviously, the synthesis of research on duration of effects provides mixed results.

The position taken here, with respect to the importance of this early contact, is a brief one. Scientific evidence is highly mixed, yet many of today's parents have come to accept the need for early contact in principle. *Although it may not be a direct effect, the denial of early contact within a family that sees it as important can have lasting impact.* Therefore, while science does not have sufficient evidence to confirm or deny lasting effects, many of the families being observed will feel as if they do. The assessment, then, must begin with and take into account the belief system of the family regarding this issue.

Ultimately, the work on the early period of attachment yields a blend of absolutes and cautions. While it is true that this period is vital and can enhance the attachment given the right family mind set, it can also be missed without eliminating the possibility of attachment. Several general categories of attachment behavior are found to be enhanced by a positive early experience, but specific behaviors may or may not be impacted (deChateau, 1980: 10). There may well be a link between this early time period and later attachment, but this link does not seem to be linear in the sense that one behavior can be traced to another. The best sense is given through the finding that *early behaviors are interactive at several points in time and the absence of, or distortion in, a given early experience can easily be compensated for at a later time.*

As this information is used by the clinician, a previous message returns. Some pattern may be observed in the conduct of these behaviors early on. The interpretation or assessment of the importance of this pattern, however, can be conducted only with strict attention to the historical and personality issues contributing to the child's and the parent's behavior during this time.

Rude Realities:
The First Months at Home

Contrary to some popular misconceptions, caring for a child in the first six months of life is not always enjoyable. At this time in the child's life, he is wholly dependent on the parent for every aspect of survival. He is not hesitant to make these needs known on a moment-by-moment basis, either (Elmer, 1960: 717). This demanding nature of the infant's early behaviors is one of the major reasons the parent's involvement capacity is immediately suspected if many of these needs are not being met. *What is often forgotten in this observational period is that the parent(s) have their own confusion to deal with during this time.* The clinician assessing this period cannot allow either parent to become a forgotten individual through this common lack of compassion and sensitivity.

The neonatal period is marked by constant adjustment for the parent (Brazelton, 1963). Realistically, the parent's relationships with every point and person in their environment will change as a result of the presence of this new family member. It is nearly axiomatic that the parent's anticipation of both his own and the child's behavior as "perfect" will not be met. When this realization is added to the physical and psychological depletion inherent in providing total care for the child, a mild depression may develop (Brazelton, 1963: 934). Unfortunately, neither the infant nor the persons in the parent's environment typically offer the "time" for these depressive feelings to work themselves through. This marching ahead in the face of these feelings has become the "right stuff" (Wolfe, 1979) of parenthood, and the parent is asked to perform despite internal fear, insecurity, and many questions. These issues must not escape the clinician if the assessment of risk is to be correct.

Despite the sensitivity to the parent's concerns, *the clinician should quickly determine that the parent's actions during this period are orchestrated by the child.* Bell (1979: 824) notes that, due to this control, the infant can often be seen as more competent than the parent, especially if this is the first infant this parent has attempted to raise. That is strong testimonial to the confidence the infant has in the "instinctive" mechanisms he has been provided. It is also a statement regarding the many questions most parents have but are too embarrassed to ask. *Asking questions is "not allowed" in parenting, because our world expects every parent to be better prepared than he really is.* Whether as a result of insecurity or as a result of the child's commands, this is a period of intense responding to survival needs by parent and child that is not likely to be suffused with warm feelings of attachment. Basically, the time for reflection and self-analysis is not available if the mundane, though necessary, tasks of child rearing are to be accomplished (Robson & Moss, 1970: 979).

The first six to eight weeks is a period of rapid change. The clinician is likely to see the first glow of attention and wonder at parenthood falling away in the face of the drudgery of child care. Ideally, by the end of the third month, some of this glow will be seen to return with the child's increasing responsiveness and adultlike behaviors, signifying positive responses to the hard work just completed by the parent (Robson & Moss, 1970: 979-982). Despite the low period represented by this heavy child-care demand, several attachment tasks must be accomplished while conquering this period.

The early tasks of parenthood are sensitive to disruption from many sectors. These disruptive influences may be as obvious as disappointment over the sex of the child (deChateau, 1980: 155), age of the mother (Lynch & Roberts, 1977: 624), or size, shape, or maturity of the infant (Tanner, 1974: 99). On the other hand, these disruptions may stem from something as diffuse as the mother's self-image (Brazelton, 1963: 933). Fortunately for the clinician seeking to assess these problems, they are observable at many points. Two quick and reliable performance indicators are the processes of *feeding* and *soothing*.

Feeding and soothing the infant are two of the earliest parental mandates. This work has taken the position that breast-feeding is positive if both mother and child are comfortable with it. It is not seen as necessary for a successful bonding experience. Breast-feeding does hold a nutritional superiority over many supplemental feeding practices, particularly if the supplement's directions are not followed exactly. However, it must be recognized that a breast-feeding schedule not only intrudes on daily living; there is also an emotional risk implied.

The breast-feeding mother has been described by Brazelton (1963: 933) as testing her maternal and feminine abilities to their maximum. Failure in breast-feeding is rarely blamed on the infant. However, a difficult-to-feed child presents immediate problems to the most well-intentioned mother, contributes to increased irritability on the part of parent and child, and leads to further difficulty in feeding (Murphy & Moriarity, 1976: 67). The sensitive clinician will not only identify the child's contribution to this problem, but also will sympathize with the struggling parent. Most frequently, when this sensory reactivity in the child leads to failed breast-feeding, the mother blames herself. Unthinking outsiders can also find fault with the mother in this failure. A similar experience can be met in the most frequent parental task: soothing the infant.

Beyond feeding, much of the time parent and infant spend together in the early weeks of life is devoted to soothing the child (Korner, 1974: 105). It is natural that the infant turns to the primary caregiver to reduce the myriad stresses he feels. The parent's ability to soothe the upset infant is frequently but mistakenly interpreted as an indication of the parent's ability in all parenting tasks. The sensitive clinician should be very flexible in this determination. As with the observed feeding behaviors, this determination of "poor parenting" is made by the parent and unthinking outsiders without regard to the infant's behavioral contribution or sensory threshold.

A third major early task of parenting, one that frequently leads to violence with the parent-child pair, is the *tolerance of crying*. Crying is a form of communication and stimulation that quickly reaches the average parent's upper limits of tolerance. In fact, should crying behavior not decrease over the first month of the child's life, there is likely to be a demonstrable decrease in feelings of attachment to the child (Bell, 1974: 5). This is particularly true for the 18 percent of infants who have colic. This is a situation in which physical irritation leads to increased demand for attention but makes for an inability to respond to efforts at soothing when they are offered (Bell, 1974: 8). This is a terribly frustrating and negative situation for the parent. Support and empathy are needed here, not an assessment of parental inabilities. Two interrelated factors come into play in the parent's tolerance of crying: the *frequency and length of crying* and the *soothability of the child*. Both of these elements define the assessment of how the parent handles the problem.

Crying is a vehicle for multiple messages. At its heart, it is an attachment behavior that tends to bring the parent into contact with the child (Bell & Harper, 1977: 131), but one that is stressful for most parents during the first few months at home with the child.

Bell and Harper (1977: 135) report that the mean duration of crying ranges from 7.7 minutes to 21 minutes per hour until sometime between the sixth and sixteenth week of life. Many infants will exceed this. Should the infant with the high crying rate also be difficult to soothe due to his general arousal levels, the effect on the caregiver can be devastating (Murphy & Moriarity, 1976: 60).

When observing a parent or having a child's infancy described in retrospect, the clinician must understand that the ability to soothe the child and help him stop his crying and distressed behavior is the sine qua non of parenthood. The absence of this ability provides parents with a significantly negative message regarding their effectiveness and competency (Korner, 1974: 108). Such parents feel hopeless and helpless and often feel like crying themselves (Grey et al., 1976: 385-386). These feelings are familiar to all parents, but reaching this level of frustration too frequently can mark the origins of a dangerous relationship between parent and child.

Obviously, not all parents who experience this stage of what might be called "normal parental helplessness" will fail to work through it. *A fixation at this stage, however, must be considered a warning to the clinician.* Robson and Moss (1970: 979) reported that the model mother first expressed love for her child when he was about three weeks of age. This feeling developed gradually, growing out of the ups and downs of the relationship between the two. It is important that these fluctuations in the relationship be recognized and allowed by the clinician. *It is more important that the parent understand that these fluctuations will occur.*

The parent's understanding that there will be both good and bad times with the child is a vital observation. Both the constant expression of loving and its total absence should be considered extremes, perhaps offered for the clinician's benefit. Remember that the parent receives messages of "love" and attachment from the child through such ordinary behaviors as smiling, eye contact, the cessation of crying upon parental soothing, and differential reactions to other adults. Parents will vary in their ability to pick up such communication and reward (Robson & Moss, 1970: 980). Regardless of parental sensitivity (unless deeply impaired), the parent should be responding to behaviors of the child that are also visible to the clinician. Should the parent's expression of affection be mismatched with, or present in the absence of, complementary behaviors in the child, the messages of attachment may be less than genuine. The failing parent is quite capable of letting the clinician hear what he "wants to hear." Also, despite the presence of attachment *behaviors* in this early period, true attachment may not be in evidence until somewhat later in the child's development.

Bowlby (1969) has found little attachment affect demonstrated prior to the seventh month of life. The differential, or behavior discriminator, is a strong protest from the child when the attached parent leaves him for even a short period (Ainsworth, 1979: 935). Most parents would not agree that no attachment can be seen prior to the sixteenth week of life. In fairness to parents, Bowlby's pronouncement (1973: 53-54) may be the victim of a lack of sensitivity in the observational tools used. Let it certainly be noted that attachment behaviors increase markedly between sixteen and twenty-six weeks of life if the relationship is a sound one. This is primarily an increase in the observed reciprocity between parent and child.

Still another acceleration takes place between twenty-four and thirty weeks, in which the infant begins to make preferential statements about the primary caregiver through his clinging to them. By the age of six or seven months, the differential behaviors demonstrated toward and in the primary caregiver's presence are predictable elements of the successfully attached partnership. This is an observable signal of stability and a mark of the child's readiness to learn of his own influence on the world in which he lives. The parent should be observed to offer complementary attachment signals to those of the child.

Observing the parental attachment at this point is a relatively easy process. Bromwich (1976: 440-441) has offered a description of attachment signals to seek at this time which are long on common sense and easily observed. These behaviors sought include the parent's enjoyment in being with the child, a parental sensitivity to the child's cues, a mutually satisfying quantity and quality of interaction, parental awareness of the child's developmental limits and capacities, the provision of appropriate activities and experiences for the child, and parentally generated experiences and situations that stimulate and capture the infant's interest. *The clinician at this time should find himself in the presence of a partnership that gives the sense that almost any demand from either member of the pair would be acceptable to the partner.*

Almost No Past at All; Looking Back at Neonatal Attachment

Despite the triumphal seven-month achievement of the positive attachment relationship, this is but the beginning of a process that must be lifelong if protection of the child is to be ensured. This is as positive a promise, when it works, as its obverse (the continuation of a dysfunctional or empty attachment relationship) is negative.

The continued development of the child and his ongoing safety depend on the progress of the attachment relationship. Progress in this relationship will be observed through caring behaviors and parental availability in the time to come (Kennell et al., 1976: 51). The child has been shown to be structured for shared activity with this partner throughout life. This structuring of an instinctive partnership will enable the child to grow within himself, his family, and his environment (Bell & Harper, 1977: 123). The lack of observed cooperation from the adult partner from this point forward will signal a reduction in this capacity for continued growth and safety.

The clinician seeking to assess the parent-child partnership should not interpret the information presented in this chapter as indicating that parent and child must be in constant interaction. The demands of the child are such that the parents will have little enough time to themselves. What little time is available should be gratefully enjoyed. In fact, parents who feel the need to be constantly in touch with their child may be displaying some distortion in their attachment needs. What should be sought in a general sense is a partnership arrangement in which the activity-reactivity sequence can take place between parent and child in the reciprocal manner for which it was designed. This is vital, for should this pattern of reciprocal behavior be disrupted for any reason, negative results may occur in three areas. Initially, the *parental attachment or commitment to the child may be reduced*. Secondarily, *the child's security* in the ability of the parents to protect and care for him *may be weakend*. Finally, the establishment of *predictable and regular interaction patterns* between parent and child *may fail* (Barnett et al., 1970: 202). Under these conditions, the growth of the child, parent, and family is threatened. It is this threat that the early assessment model seeks to identify and work toward removing. What remains is the development of an observational scheme for the parent and child's early years together. That scheme will be presented in the following chapter.

Chapter 7

ATTACHMENT AND EXPLORATION
The Movement into Independent Childhood

The clinician seeking to assess attachment relations within a given family must accept the fact that variations in conduct of attachment behaviors, differences in intensity of these behaviors, and the distribution of attachments will vary within the same family as the child grows older. *Attachment is a continuous process within the functional family, but one that is extraordinarily flexible* (Rutter, 1972).

The need for flexibility in the conduct of attachment behaviors is based on the fact that the full attachment role is beyond the capacity of any one individual, no matter how loving. Sugarman (1977) has described these multiple functions as (a) drawing the parent to the child, (b) directing the parent to sacrifice for the child, (c) providing protection and nurturance for the child, (d) enabling the parent to recognize the child's signals and needs, and (e) providing the parent with resistance to separation from the child. The process, with its multiple elements, has come to be assumed as one automatically available in the natural family.

The natural family has been given too much responsibility in today's world of child-rearing expectations. Many assume that all natural families will fit the mold necessary to form attachment if simply left alone. In an attempt to identify what these "natural family" characteristics are that would aid in attachment, Grey and colleagues (1976: 378) have identified "best of all possible worlds" family characteristics. These ideal characteristics include the ability to view the child as an individual with likable attributes; the presence of a healthy child who does not disrupt the family; a stable marriage in which either parent can aid the other, a solid coping system that has persons on the outside to turn to in times of need; intelligent and healthy parents who had solid relationships in their own childhood; and a family that provides a stable home, economic, and occupational life. If these characteristics were automatically available, even in part, the need for the attachment assessment would be absent. Fortunately, the forgiving nature of the attachment process provides for its successful operation even when the observer is able to identify great gaps between this "ideal" family and the family being assessed.

Mothers and Others:
The War Between the Caretakers

Those devoted to the earliest writing on attachment have tended to interpret this work as mandating maternal care on a twenty-four-hour basis if attachment is to be accomplished (Rutter, 1972: 15). This perspective is not only rigid but dangerously underresponsive to the available compensation mechanisms in the family. *The clinician who finds a family subscribing to the belief that "good parents never leave their children" should be forewarned.* No one, not even the most strongly attached parent, can give his entire identity over to caring for a child and not experience some undesirable effects. Attachment development does not demand this level of rigidity, and it should be seen as an overinvestment. Sound attachment is perfectly available to parents who remain somewhat flexible and aware of their own needs as well as those of the child.

Among those presenting this flexible view of attachment, Michael Rutter is probably best known. Rutter (1972: 17) argues that not only is the "monotrophic" (attachment only with a single figure) theory in error, but all attachment requirements can be met through interactions with different persons. These attachment relationships can also vary in their intensity. Rutter (1972: 125) does concede that there is likely to be a "chief bond," but this attachment is not necessarily made only with a female or a biological parent. It is this chief bond that the clinician has been asked to seek thus far in this work, but by this stage of child and family development, the focus changes somewhat.

Although the attachment between parent and child is still critical at this point, the child's exploration and reaching out to other individuals should become obvious after the first year of life. The instinctive *alternative attachments*

mechanisms used to draw the parent into a protective stance generalize to other adults. Unfortunately, knowledge of how these multiple
attachments influence the child's growth is currently inadequate. It
does seem logical to assume, however, that these extraparental attachments can help compensate for weaknesses in the parent's attachment capacity. The clinician should seek to determine whether
alternative attachments are available to the child. Persons other than
the mother hold great importance in the course of his development
(Ainsworth, 1979: 936).

Rutter (1972: 49), has concluded that a "mother's care" requires
neither a mother nor someone with a biological relationship to the
child. Significantly, it is not the early protective mechanisms that are
being discussed here. "Mother's care" refers to a later caregiving role
that is supportive of adequate growth and development. In addition,
the utility of the "substitute" relationship is significantly altered if
there is a necessity for multiple persons to perform these functions.

The essence of Rutter's (1972, 1976, 1979) study of multiple caretakers lies in the suggestion that if several parent figures dealing with
the child's needs remain the same persons, if they provide good-
quality care, and if environmental variables are held relatively constant, there need not be a major upheaval in the child's life. Should
these conditions be present, the child's capacity for attachment and
development should be unimpaired. Ultimately, *if the child has the
opportunity to attach to a predictable number of caretakers in a
stable environment, the negative impacts anticipated through the
absence of a single maternal caretaker can be minimized.*

In a variation of this theme, the clinician may find that the mother
may be the attachment in the child's life that accounts for caretaking
activities, and that still other attachments exist for other purposes
(Rutter, 1972: 125). It is far too easy to accept the mother as the
primary attachment and, subsequently, the major influence on the
child (Lamb, 1979: 938). This is not necessarily accurate: Attachments can and should exist between brother and sister, father and
child, or with persons outside the biological family. The clinician
should find such extramaternal attachments available to the child
each time a role for such an attachment arises in the child's life. As is
the primary function of all attachments, this flexibility maximizes the
possibilities of survival.

During this, the child's period of most rapid development, the clinician will find frankly dysfunctional families that prohibit any internal
or external attachments. There will also be families whose internal

attachments appear solid but in which external attachments are disallowed. This second family is equal in dysfunction to the first.

Should the assessment find a family in which the attachment needs of the parent are so strong as to prohibit the child's seeking extrafamilial attachments, problems in the child's development are predictable. Even in families that face relatively serious human and environmental inadequacies, the child can compensate if allowed to reach beyond that family to meet his attachment needs. Should the family be found to be both inadequate and prohibitive of this reaching out, this rigidity will stifle the child's progress.

The willingness of the family to allow outside relationships for the child must always be assessed. This willingness to allow the child's affective exploration is a measure of family adaptiveness. This adaptiveness is available in the functional family, for the massive number of roles required across a child's development are more than can be asked of one family. Successful child rearing requires all the strength and innovation available to even the most functional family.

The Child as Taskmaster:
The Never-Ending Work
of the Attached Parent

Child development specialists Richard Bell and Lawrence Harper (1977: 148) have aggregated the first year of development into three stages. These stage descriptions give an approximation of what the clinician will view in watching the attached parent conduct his felt responsibilities. The first (birth to two months) is termed the stage of "primary caregiving," during which the helplessness and high demand level of the child keep the caregiver busy in meeting the primary needs of protection, soothing, and feeding. The second stage has been termed "social interaction" and occurs between the third and sixth months of life. The signals of the child, during this stage, take on meaning, allowing social interactions to be modified through the actions of either the caregiver or the child. The final stage (seven to twelve months) is that of "attachment," during which a specific attachment figure will be seen to take on increased importance to the child. This attachment figure must not only respond to increasing responsibility for the child's exploratory activities, but also be available during times of stress and strangeness.

Playing the role of an attached parent during this time is a mixed blessing. It is a pleasant sensation, or should be to the functional parent, to increase in importance to the child daily. However, there is an accompanying increase in the magnitude and number of responsibilities associated with the child's care. Acceptance of the rewards demands acceptance of the costs. As the promise of independence for the child is met in one area of his life, another, new activity quickly appears to take its place and demands more from the parent. This is a constant weight carried by the attached parent across all childhood development. *The assessment of the parent's capacity to carry that weight is the key to predicting success or failure.*

The best attachment relationships observed will be predictive of the most work for that parent. When a sensitive parent responds quickly and regularly to the child, the attachment is strengthened (Ainsworth & Bill, 1969). The best attachments are also predictive of the most playful, exploring, and curious children (Bowlby, 1973: 358). Basically, the child is not free to explore unless he has reached the security of a positive attachment. The more secure the child, the more he will explore. In this sense, the clinician may view the active and curious child as a positive signal of the attachment he feels. The point here is that the high intensity and frequent attachment interchanges that characterize early childhood do not signal the end of the attachment partnership between parent and child. To the contrary, this pressure on the parent is continuous, if only through a protective awareness of the child's explorations. *The clinician should find room for thoughts of the child in the attached parent's mind, irrespective of the other activities in which the parent might be engaged.* The fact is, the better the parent, the more intense the parenting experience. This "work begets work" phenomenon might be seen as the paradox of parenting.

A point of warning must be offered here. The child is a taking animal. He is not the giving animal that some unprepared parents expect him to be. When the clinician finds a parent who resents the child because he does not "give" as anticipated, an exploration of that parent's past is mandated. This type of expectation can destroy what was a positive attachment relationship during their early time together. Remember, while early attachment behavior is critical for future development, a positive early attachment does not insulate the parent-child partnership against all future failure.

While it has been previously determined that the true attachment relationship begins at about seven months, just how long the child will survive in the absence of that relationship is less certain. Survival in this sense is not physical, but social and emotional. In his early work, Bowlby surmised that the clinician should find the child to be attached to at least one individual prior to the age of two and one-half years if the attachment was to achieve its intended effects. Most children, according to Bowlby, would suffer some detriment if this relationship were not established prior to one year of age (Rutter, 1972: 75). This two-year critical period is generally agreed upon by most writers in the area (Barnett et al., 1970), although most do not consider attachment at a later date an impossibility. It seems safe to say that *the child must reach some level of attachment prior to his third year or some negative result will be present.* Despite this somewhat depressing notion, recent works suggest that compensation can be a reality to some degree.

Working from the perspective of correcting attachment deficiencies, Rutter (1979) suggests that both social and intellectual deficits can be compensated for if the child has an attachment experience by age four. Intellectual deficits can be controlled even for a child as old as eight years, but social inadequacies will tend to persist if an attachment experience is unavailable until this time. Placing this in line with the earlier research, a general perspective on the outer margins of the attachment relationship finds the development of attachment behaviors to become increasingly less likely after the third year of life—not impossible, less likely (Rutter, 1972: 104). As should be anticipated, *the earlier the attachment is formed, the sooner the child will organize his own behavior, become more discriminating about stimuli, and the more confidence he will have in the attachment figure* (Bowlby, 1973: 51-52, 99).

The child whose needs are met in a responsive manner and who develops a solid attachment relationship is capable of developing secure feelings toward the parent and the environment. Typically, his behavior with the parent will be predictive of his approach to others in his environment (Ainsworth, 1979: 936). The importance to the clinician is that if the child's attachment is unstable, he will be seen to approach all other tasks in a tentative and fearful manner.

The observer of the securely attached child will enjoy watching him. These secure children, knowing that they do not have to fight to gain attention or play a low-key role to avoid angering the parent, approach life confidently and with great curiosity. These children are enthusiastic and persistent, and they reveal coping skills that are even and predictable (Ainsworth, 1979). The child who has not experienced this security will be the antithesis.

This work is predicated on the assumption that attachment dysfunction can have a negative impact on the family. This begins with the early dysfunction that impairment in this process brings to the child (Brazelton, 1963: 931; Robson & Moss, 1970: 976). The exact areas of disturbance for the child and their specific outcomes are not easily predicted. What is known is that these areas of distortion will affect the entire family's relationship with this child in the beginning and for the remainder of the child's life with them.

Parting's Sweet Sorrow: The Effect of Separation

The clinician engaged in the assessment of the violence potential of a family will frequently come into contact with children who have been or will be separated from their families. Some mention of the results of that parting are merited.

Family sociologist Urie Bronfenbrenner (1968: 845) describes two environmental contexts necessary for the growth and development of a child. The first is one in which the child takes part in increasingly complex activities that are shared with a person holding a reciprocal attachment to the child. The second is an experimental one, in which the child is encouraged to take his newly learned skills out into the "real" world and attempt to put them to use. The requirements for this pair of contexts are that the first precede the second and that the attachment figure be available for teaching skill development in the first. The absence of the attachment figure, either physically or emotionally, promises a retardation in this growth process. It is the absence, and subsequent retardation in the child's ability to learn to cope, that is feared in the separation experience. *This fear has not stood the test of empirical examination.*

Years of study in the area of separation have led to a single conclusion: *Although traumatic for the child, separation does not automatically lead to attachment disruption in parent-child partnerships that have achieved some level of attachment prior to the separation,* (Rutter, 1972: 124). A blanket view of all separations as negative and that all are devastating to the attachment relationship does not provide adequate attention to differences within and among separation experiences.

Much of the early work in separation and deprivation was drawn from samples of children residing in institutions. Generalizing from institutionalized children to all children is questionable. Similar studies were conducted with children in hospitals. This environment *anxious attachment* (handwritten annotation)

strange setting (handwritten annotation in left margin)

is an unpleasant one for most people, and separation effects are magnified. This exaggeration of the effect can be attributed to a total separation from all persons the child knows, the strangeness of the physical environment, and a lack of opportunity to form compensating attachments as caretakers' faces change every eight hours (Rutter, 1976: 150). Predicting general child behavior from children in this unique situation stretches the limits of generalizability.

Rutter (1976: 147) instructs the clinician who seeks to assess separation effects to be cognizant of multiple variables in the experience. Beyond the mere fact of separation are the reasons behind the separation: the quality of caretaking during the separation, the child's age and maturity level, and the relationship in the family prior to the separation. Each of these variables influence the prediction of the impact of separation on child and family.

Perhaps more than any other person, Rutter has infused rationality into the irrational concept that the "natural family is always better." This is an inappropriate judgment in those circumstances in which the family is so physically or emotionally destructive as to endanger the child's life. Interestingly for the clinician assessing such families, *the child removed from the destructive setting may have more difficulty than that child removed from a more stable family.*

In order to understand the difficulty the maltreated child has in leaving the violent setting, the clinician must be aware of the child's internal defenses. Bowlby (1973) has offered that understanding through a process he has entitled "defensive exclusion." Through the use of this defensive process, the child has the clear capacity to rationalize the irrational, even violent, behaviors of his parents. This defensive system provides the capacity for attachment, at least within the child, even in the most difficult circumstances. The child simply denies the parent's behavior or blames himself.

The attachment that results from defensive exclusion is an "anxious attachment," in which the child is constantly fearful that there will be separation or desertion. The child lives his life under the onus of impending loss. This child has made a distorted adaptation to the attachment need, is constantly anxious regarding the predictability of his environment, but is a believer in the adage, "The devil you know is better than the devil you don't know." Separation for this child is the fulfillment of a threat he has lived with for much, if not all, of his life. Consequently, separation for this child is filled with terror.

Given this description, it is not difficult for the clinician to understand that the previously maltreated child will sometimes have a
dramatic response to what is, for him, a concluding loss. If the child
who has experienced a warm, loving attachment relationship can be
observed to respond quickly to the attachment figure's absence, that
child who has been anticipating this loss can be totally incapacitated
by it. If the clinician can see that the child is defensively excluding the
parent's negative actions toward him, this reaction can be anticipated.

The clinician who assesses separation effects within the frame of
the circumstances of the separation, the child's developmental stage
and history, and the status of current attachments (Ainsworth, 1979:
935) will find more clarity in anticipation of events to follow.

All things being equal, *the younger the child, the more difficult the
separation* (Rutter, 1972: 23). As the child progresses toward the end
of his first year of life, he develops the ability to perceive the loss but
does not yet have the coping mechanisms necessary to deal with that
perception (Bowlby, 1973: 122). This coping capacity grows pro-
gressively through the second and third years of life but may still
be overpowered by the circumstances surrounding the separation
(Bowlby, 1973: 49).

Assessing the impact of separation should focus not on the child but
on the circumstances surrounding the separation. These circumstances include what the preexisting relationship was and what the
conditions during the separation are going to be for the child. By the
age of three, the child's ability to communicate can offset some of
these frightening elements, but prior to that the effect on the child is
related directly to situational factors.

The summary information required by the clinician is that the child
has the capacity to predict unpleasant effects following separation by
the end of his first year of life. Prior to the age of three, when his own
communication powers can help him cope, the effect of separation
will depend on the circumstances constructed by the adults around
him.

The clinician assessing separation must understand that while the
separation experience is a mixture of variables that can lead to dysfunction, it is not automatic. When the separation is voluntary, there
are elements that allow the child greater exploration (Ainsworth,
1979: 935) or teach the child about independence through a graded
separation from the attachment partner (Rutter, 1972: 23). To

identify risk, the clinician should seeks out the role of each of the following: the child's age, the child's sex, the child's temperament, the attachment partnership's history, previous separation experiences, the duration of the separation, the nature of the separation environment, and the presence of consistent caretakers during the separation experience. Each of these variables holds the capacity to influence the child positively or negatively during the separation experience (Rutter, 1972). None can be ignored in assessing its impact.

The Starting Line: Understanding Acceptance and Rejection

The chapters presented to this point hold a common theme. That theme is that unimpaired attachment is possible unless mediated by one of the situations described. The clinician seeking to be alert to attachment impediments has been presented with myriad warning signals to look for at each stage of development. The general point is that the instinctive capacity to develop this partnership between parent and child is present in either partner. The child's instinctive actions stimulate the parent's instinctive caregiving and protection. Through this process a partnership in safety and growth develops. Most persons consider this a "natural" process, one that will occur unless greatly impaired functioning is present. That assumption presents only half the story.

Rejection of a child by a parent is uniformly seen as "unnatural" when it occurs after the birth of a child. The tendency is to see this "unnaturalness" as residing in the parent and to search deeply into that parent's life to find the source. It would seem that we believe that if only we can eliminate the destructive influences in the relationship, facilitative influences will spring out of that parent and a positive partnership with the child will develop. Experience suggests that this is untrue. Rejection of children by parents is a factor in our world even as acceptance of children by parents is an equal and opposite factor. Rejection is "natural," and , given the right circumstances, it will occur.

Not all persons can accept the partnership of children. As a result of their background, available physical, emotional, and environmental resources, or physiological or psychological inadequacies, some persons cannot parent successfully. We must stop assuming that everyone can. It is only because we assume that every person can parent and attach to a child that we see high rewards in the process. These rewards are most attractive to those least able to parent: the persons with fewest personal resources and those seeking a child to fulfill some of those needs. They believe that the child can compensate for what they are missing in their world; to them (before they become parents), parenting is "wonderful," "all children love their parents," and parenthood is "fulfilling." These promises are unmet for the inadequate rejecting parent. The failure in meeting these mandates, for the child of this inadequate parent, is the promise of pain.

The failure of the natural capacity for attachment predicts the occurrence of its equally natural opposite: rejection. Some elements of the impaired parent-child relationship are amenable to change and support. Others will not change. When it is attachment failure that does not change, rejection may be total.

The elements that facilitate attachment are real and present in most persons. The elements that destroy attachment capacity are also real and possible in some persons and all environments. Like lower animals in nature, some parents living in resource-scarce situations may select the path of rejection, knowing that continuation of parenting promises only continued failure. The observer of this phenomenon must understand that neither all parenting inadequacies nor all perceived scarcities can be corrected. The most difficult task of this assessment model is gaining the understanding that parental rejection of a child does have a place in our world and that this rejection is manifested first through an inability to respond to the child's instinctive attachment needs.

The following section will discuss parent and child types which are highly predictive of this potential for rejection, naturally and through no active choice on the part of either.

PART III

**THREE FALSE STARTS:
THE PREMATURE CHILD,
THE FAILURE-TO-THRIVE CHILD,
AND THE PREMATURE PARENT**

Chapter 8

EARLY STRUGGLES
Premature and Failure-to-Thrive Children

The (Too) Early Arrival:
The Premature Child

Unlike the full-term infant who presents himself fully prepared to interact with the parent, the premature infant is not equipped to conduct the task of attachment. This holds true in the most enthusiastic of families and supportive environments (Gorski et al., 1980: 270). Prior to approaching attachment, the premature child must organize for pure physical survival.

Various symptoms of growth retardation and neurologic difficulties have been isolated among premature children (Osofsky, 1972: 45), causing problems for the child seeking to develop predictable internal rhythms as well as for the child's parent in establishing predictable caretaking routines. These infants will be observed to be hypersensitive and may reject even the most loving efforts at handling them (Friedrich & Boriskin, 1976: 582). This is described by Korner (1974: 100) as a "hyperexcitability syndrome," in which all of the child's responses are exaggerated and levels of sensitivity heightened. This excitability alternates with its opposite, a difficulty in stimulating a response from the child. This confusion in behavior may provide communications that are the opposite of what they seem to indicate in the full-term infant. This, in turn, can be seen to confuse the parent.

Rather than being stimulated by environmental and parental manipulation, the premature child may become quickly overstimulated and

Problem of prematurity

forced to withdraw from attention (Gorski et al., 1980: 286-287). Typically, the parent would continue the stimulation in an attempt to receive a response. This is the opposite of what the premature child desires at that moment. *Premature children can communicate; however, their communications may differ from those of full-term children.*

Premature infants do contribute directly to the reciprocal interactions that they share (Minde, 1980: 303). The problem rests with the fact that they may stimulate inappropriate behaviors through their mixed cues and general unpredictability. This distortion in social responsiveness may be the most important difference between premature children and others in predicting later problems (Brown & Bakeman, 1977: 2).

Prematures are less alert, less responsive, and less capable of modulating their responses to stimuli than are full-term children (Goldberg et al., 1980). This confusion is destructive to parenting efforts and provides general confusion to all who provide care for the child. Should the parent already perceive the child to be "different" as a result of its prematurity, this confusing responsiveness is a dangerous confirmation (Elmer & Gregg, 1967).

The premature child's distorted responsiveness does have implications for the development of reciprocity. Not only does the impaired social responsiveness of the premature provide extreme caregiving demands, there are additional adaptions required in the development of parent-child partnerships (Goldberg et al., 1980: 4). These differences tend to persist over time, even after the child has compensated physically for its delays (Brown & Bakeman, 1979).

Kennell and his colleagues (1970: 191) describe the premature birth as a process in which the parents view a small, fragile infant that they fear will not live. This infant is largely kept away from them and housed amidst a confusing array of medical equipment, a situation that prevents most of the parents' own caretaking and creates a strange atmosphere for the initiation of reciprocal behavior. Even in that parent strong enough to initiate care, the child's response may be different from what the parent anticipated. *The parental reaction to this difference in response is a vital observational point.*

There is little doubt that some parental behaviors toward the child, such as holding, feeding, and touching, may be influenced by the condition of the infant. Some behaviors are not influenced, however, and

the parent's performance of those behaviors is a critical observational detail. The infant appears to be in a fragile state, yet the
parent still holds the option of smiling at the child, stroking the child,
talking to the child, and looking directly into his eyes. (Minde et al.,
1978: 375). *Too often, the parent's difficulty in overcoming fears
and accomplishing this basic set of interactions precludes the parent's
attempting more sophisticated interactions later.* At a later point,
these early differences translate into real differences in contact behaviors when compared to parents with full-term infants (deChateau,
1980: 151). This may be a minor expression of early separation
effects, but it is more likely that it will be observed to be a lack of
parental self-confidence, particularly with the first-birth parent
(1980: 152). This measure of self-confidence might not be missing
had the parent and child taken the opportunity to learn about each
other in the beginning. Prematurity does not preclude this opportunity. If it is observed to preclude it, the problem may be with the
parent.

   Parental involvement with a premature child is extreme. The
parent is either underinvolved or overinvolved with the child. These
extremes are easily observed. Brown and Bakeman (1977: 4) report
that parents frequently overstimulate premature infants, hoping for a
response. Goldberg and colleagues (1980: 23) support this observation, suggesting that parents of many prematures do expect *some*
delay but are not prepared to cope with delays when they compare
their children with other parents' infants. These anxious parents will
pressure their children toward levels of involvement well beyond the
child's capacity. The child's response to this overstimulation is irritability and withdrawal (Brown & Bakeman, 1979: 4). This is a pattern
of asynchronous behavior between parent and child which promises
an avoidant relationship in which neither responds to the other. This
pattern of asynchronous relating has been offered as the basis for the
notion that parents of prematures are less emotionally involved with
their children during later infancy than parents of full-term infants
(Brown & Bakeman, 1977).

   It is too simplistic to suggest that parental patience and persistence
are all that remain necessary to allow for development between parent
and child. Even as premature children are different, so are their
parents in many ways. Additionally, a premature infant, just like a
normal infant, cannot be directed continuously by a parent that is too

Loss of a dream child must be grieved

persistent or the child will fail to develop a sense of himself. There is no easy solution; both premature infants and their parents have difficult personal tasks to undertake prior to attachment development.

Two major tasks confront the parent of the premature child at his birth. First, the parents must detach from the fantasy of the normal, healthy child that was dreamed about during pregnancy. They must then attempt to attach to a child who does not relate to them in many of the ways they anticipated. These tasks imply the use of the shock and adaption mechanism characteristic of adjusting to crisis, and the grief and mourning behaviors necessary in facing the death of a child—in this case, the death of a fantasy (Drotar et al., 1975: 714). As difficult as the loss of the dream child may be, the attachment to this new and different child may be even more difficult.

The premature child develops at a different rate from that of the full-term child. He becomes alert to parental presence more slowly and gradually. The premature child demands a different level of care—more patient, less demanding, and more persistent. The premature child will be less rewarding for the parent, moving more slowly toward the adultlike behaviors that demonstrate to the parent that their ministrations are working. Finally, the *parent* of the premature child demands greater internal strength, external support, and solid information to cope with the differentness of this child (Brown & Bakeman, 1977: 4).

The clinician is likely to find that the complexity of care and slowness of response in the premature child will frighten the parent. The parents may be afraid that the child is not "making it." They are also afraid that they are not "doing the right thing" (Drotar et al., 1975: 714). Any repeat hospitalization may reactivate all of these original fears. The parent is trapped in a position of not knowing how to react. This is a trap built on a fear of interaction and a sense that this infant is somehow too fragile.

In spite of the prevalence of these fears, the clinician will find some premature child-parent relationships that develop appropriately. There are mechanisms for relating to the premature child; they simply ask more of the parent. For the most part, interactions with premature children are not that different in content. There *are* some extra demands placed on the parent. The parent of the premature child must have an extra measure of understanding toward the child's developmental capacities and limitations. The parent must have an extraordinary degree of patience regarding communications and labor put into the child-care tasks. Finally, the parents must have a strong external support system to help them when these responsibilities become more than they can bear. *It is certain that, at some time, the parent of the premature child will have this overwhelmed feeling. Just how often, to what degree, and what their response will be are pivotal assessment points.*

Moving to specific differences in the premature, it should be noted that the child has not had the benefit of some forms of physical stimulation (occurring *in utero*) that normally prepare the infant for partnership. The most glaring deficiency is that having to do with movement.

The vestibular system's maturity at term suggests its importance to early relationships in the external world. It seems clear that this system facilitates the receipt of early stimulation (Korner et al., 1975: 361). The parent of the premature must, then, provide a degree of compensation for the movement stimulation that was lost through the child's early arrival. This requirement is a fear producer for parents frightened by the fragile appearance of the infant or those parents insecure in their own abilities.

The benefits of touching, cuddling, rocking, and general movement of the premature child are legion. Various studies have demonstrated diverse effects, including weight gain, fewer apenic periods, improved central nervous system functioning, and greater responsivity (Hersh & Levin, 1979a: Klaus & Kennell, 1976). This stimulation of the vestibular sense seems to stimulate developmental progress as well as have the serendipitous benefit of improving attachment relations between parent and child through increased interactions (Korner et al., 1975: 362; Hersh & Levin, 1979a: 33). Both of these effects are also enduring. It is logical to assume that the observer who notes an absence of such stimulation can predict relatively enduring deficits in development and attachment.

Ultimately, whether they are compensating for movement loss through interaction or relating with the child while in the incubator, parents retain their critical role with their children. They may struggle with this role when the child is premature. The clinician must be sensitive to this struggle.

Reclaiming the Fantasy: Parental Behaviors with Premature Children

All parents anticipate some type of relationship with the children they will bear. The parents of the premature child not only face the loss of this anticipated relationship, but also do not know if any relationship will be reached. In order for these parents to reach even a starting point for a relationship, they must progress through a very different set of steps from those taken by parents of normal children. Klaus and Kennell (1976: 42) have described this stepwise process as: anticipating negative outcomes for the child; rearranging all life aspects to meet this unanticipated circumstance; undergoing a period of trial-and-error testing to determine how to act with this child; and struggling to know the child. These are the same steps taken by individuals confronted with an "environmental disaster" (Resnik et al., 1975: 157).

This may appears to be a cruel perspective on the birth of a child, yet ignoring the potentially destructive nature of the premature birth is inappropriate. Disturbances related to negative perceptions of the child early on are persistent even when the child's specific problems were corrected prior to going home with his parents (Klaus & Kennell, 1976: 31).

The structure and content of the interactions between a premature child and its parents becomes solidified quite early and tends to sustain itself even when specific demands within the relationship change (Brown & Bakeman, 1977: 3). *The effects of separation at birth must be considered as possible contributors to this inappropriate early structuring.*

Early contact has been described as a facilitator of early parent-child interaction. The pressures surrounding a premature birth are sufficient to transform what would ordinarily be a simple loss of facilitative time into a truly negative experience. Klaus and Kennell (1976: 160-164) set the stage for the negative sense experienced by the parent through the loss of this time through their description of the self-perceptions of the parent.

This is a parent who has not only endured the trauma of unanticipated labor and delivery, but now must cope with an "unfinished pregnancy," in which dreams, nesting behaviors and portions of the rhythmic training that occurs between parent and child have not had the opportunity to be completed. This is not only a rude experience; it is a direct loss. The process also presents the parent with a child that is somehow foreign to the parents' perception of themselves, their pregnancy, and their sense of parenthood. The longer the waiting period between the child's birth and direct interaction with the child, the more exaggerated these thoughts, fears, and sense of crisis will be for this parent.

The clinician will find that during this period the mother especially, and the father to a lesser extent, will be found to traverse the stages of reacting to crisis (Klaus & Kennell, 1976). The clinician will find the parent experiencing shock, denial, a combination of sadness, anxiety, and anger, a regaining of balanced thinking, and an eventual stabilization. These experiences tend to be sequential but are fluid enough to recur periodically throughout the early relationship with the premature child. If they are mishandled by the parents or those around them, they increase the possibility that the parents will reject the child. The frightening nature of these experiences, at the least, may cause the parents to withdraw from the caregiving and attachment requirements presented by the child.

Ultimately, parents need not experience this sense of loss and resultant crisis. Early contact seems to help reduce this risk. The evidence that early contact in the nursery does reduce parental concern and improve parental self-confidence appears solid (Seashore et al., 1973). The evidence that increased early contact will eliminate other relationship problems faced by parents and premature children is less secure.

There is a conclusion to be drawn from the work with premature children, their parents, and early contact that can guide the clinician. This conclusion is not a particularly happy one. There are three major points to be understood. The first is that the parent of the premature who misses early contact may be less responsive, and subsequently inadequately stimulating, to the infant (Barnett et al., 1970: 200); the second, that the period of separation exacerbates the parent's feelings of grief and guilt over the child's condition (Hurd, 1975); the third and most worrisome conclusion is that even those parents who are able to compensate for this early separation may demonstrate precarious relationships with the premature child.

Through a review of studies in the area, Goldberg and her colleagues (1980) have been able to identify characteristics of parents of premature children that will be commonly observed in the assessment of these parent-child pairs. These parents are described as less actively involved with their infants, having less bodily contact, spending less time face-to-face, smiling less, and talking less to their infants than parents of full-term children. The difference between these parents and those of full-term parents decreases over time but tends to stay below that demonstrated by full-term parents (1980: 21). Remember, even if these effects do slow with time, their disruptive effect on attachment building can sustain itself.

Research: link prematurity → Abuse

It is not difficult to understand why attachment may be influenced by a premature birth. The parents of the premature child must deal with multiple problems related to their child and their feelings about the child. An astute clinician should find a mix of anxiety about their parental role or their role in the child's prematurity (Drotar et al., 1975: 714); guilt, anxiety, and exhaustion (Klaus & Kennell, 1976: 118); fear during the deprivational period in which the infant will appear unresponsive to their caregiving (Goldberg et al., 1980: 25); and the possibility of long-term reduction in involvement with the child (Brown & Bakeman, 1977: 3). The juxtaposition of these factors may lead to parental inertia and a certain slowness/insecurity in reciprocating the child's behaviors. This, in turn, influences attachment development.

Obviously, this failure is not an absolute in the premature child-parent relationship. Many parents do quite well with their premature children and little difference will be found between this partnership and that with a full-term child. However, when the clinician is presented with a troubled family and there is prematurity in the past or present, these avenues to trouble must not go unexplored.

Falling Dominoes:
The Family and the Premature Child

There are degrees of casualties within the family and the prematurity crisis. Some parents are totally incapable of mastering the extra tasks; others find smooth sailing. Most that will be observed will fall between those two extremes. What is clear is that the presence of a few specific abilities can aid the parent seeking to find a positive attachment experience with the premature child.

Klaus and Kennell (1976) offer the following mandates for parents who are successfully adjusting to the premature birth experience. It goes without saying that the clinician should seek to find these strengths somewhere in the family being assessed and capitalize on them. The first capacity sought is the ability to understand problems in a realistic fashion. This requires an additional ability to be aware of their own feelings, an ability to disclose these feelings to others, and a willingness to seek help when it is needed. Obviously, meeting these requirements demands a high level of personal adjustment on the part of the parent—a level of adjustment not often found in maltreating families. Fortunately, these are not requirements that must exist in all family members—only one of them.

Earlier chapters have reflected on the need for both parents to interact with the child. The best of all attachment situations finds the parents developing their care routines jointly, in a synchronous manner. This occurs much in the same manner as the desirable synchrony between parent and child. This is a difficult task in the family with a normal child. *The family with a premature child often finds it impossible.*

The intensive care required by the premature child often contributes directly to an asynchrony between the parents or other family members. Those most at risk are those who become individually adjusted to caring for the child at different rates. Simply speaking, if Mom is spending all of her time taking care of Baby, she is not spending any time taking care of Dad. The reverse is also true. This occurs even in families with other children and practiced child-care routines. The introduction of this high-intensity caregiving into the relationship that was previously child-free cannot fail to make *that* relationship dangerously tense.

All too often, clinicians focus too much attention and sympathy on the child. The result is that the forgotten parents are left to muddle through without support. This absence of support is life-threatening for the attachment relationship between parent and child.

Those who view childbirth as "the most natural thing in the world" might well see the birth of the premature child as an opportunity for the parents to become closer. This *can* occur and is based on the presence of mutually supportive parental partners. Drotar and colleagues (1975) found the opposite effect to be a very real possibility.

The "different" (premature or congenital problem) birth can easily separate the parents and isolate them from one another. This is particularly true in the family with rigidly stereotypical behaviors toward the child or in the family where only one parent cares for the child (1975: 175). *Many potentially maltreating families will be found to approach child-care tasks in this unitary fashion, where only one parent is "responsible" for the children.*

The asynchrony and stress that result from a differential adaptation to the presence of this difficult child contributes significantly to the incidence of family stress and breakdown noted among parents of prematures. Signals of family stress, such as divorce, are many times higher in families with premature children than in families with full-term children during the child's early life (Parke et al., 1980: 129). Given the rates of family dysfunction among those families that stay together, at least physically, perhaps the divorce and relinquishment rate is not high enough.

The points regarding parental synchrony are clear. *Adequate care requires a partnership not only between parent and child but between the parents themselves.* Barnett and colleagues (1970: 203) remind the clinician that the premature birth experience is the only birth experience that equalizes the role of mother and father. In the premature experience, when the child is carried off to the nursery, both parents are relegated to the role of doing little more than observing the child. The shared frustration and helplessness of this experience has an equal opportunity to serve as a time of mutual support or mutal isolation. The clinician must study the manner this event is, or was, accepted by these two people. This is vital, for in either event the initial sense of the parent seems to carry forward into all aspects of child rearing. The father of the premature child, then, is a more equal partner in the emotional tasks of attachment than in the parenting situation involving the full-term child. It is clear that this equality must be present and responded to if the practical sharing of parenting tasks that will be required are to be accomplished. It is only with the successful conduct of these tasks that the more elaborate tasks of attachment partnership with the child can be initiated.

Most parents of premature children successfully adapt to the physical and emotional requirements placed on them. There is a small group of parents who find this burden to be unbearable, however, and whose interactive decline is readily observable (Goldberg et al., 1980: 5). Study of this group of parents belies the pronatalist notion that differences between full-term and premature parent-child relationships will automatically disappear over time. The clinician will find a vulnerability in this group of failing parents caused by a lack of social supports, the impairments of the child, and limitations placed on the facilitative aspects of early parent-child contact. All of these are familiar warning signals, for in this situation, like all other parent-child pairings, they contribute to an increased likelihood of an inadequate parent-child attachment. While these elements of potential failure focus on what the premature child brings to the relationship, there is an equally negative contribution made by the child who unexplainably struggles with growth: the failure-to-thrive child.

Recognizing Risk:
Low-Birth-Weight and
Failure-to-Thrive Children

There are several classes of weight problems among infants and young children. Although these problems present themselves somewhat differently, the implications for the family and child can be surprisingly similar. The characteristics of the family and social environment in which they occur are also surprisingly consistent.

The child who is born underweight is distinguished from the child born at normal weight and confronted by subsequent failure in weight gain. The first is termed a "low-birth-weight infant" and the second a "failure-to-thrive" child (Kretchmer, 1973: 24). The failure-to-thrive (FTT) child may suffer from a problem that is either organic and consequently explainable or nonorganic and mysterious. The focus of assessment here is on the nonorganic FTT child.

It should be noted that the low-birth-weight infant has been linked to organic complications in pregnancy related to maternal conduct of the pregnancy. Related factors may include toxemia, smoking, advanced age, malnutrition, and multiple pregnancies (Kretchmer, 1973: 25). In this assessment, the lack of maternal attachment during pregnancy that leads to this problem may be evidence of an incapacity to attach. That is certainly not always true, but the presence of a low-birth-weight history in a child requires examination by the clinician.

Even in the situation in which the low-birth-weight is not predictive of attachment problems, it does predict possible neurological, behavioral, and learning problems in the child's future (Minde et al., 1978: 373). These are secondary elements that can impinge on the attachment process.

Barbero and Shaheen (1967: 639) have provided some of the most comprehensive work regarding FTT children. For these researchers, this child can be described as follows. Nonorganic FTT differs from other weight disorders by its lack of obvious organic cause: The infant has a weight level below the third percentile and gains weight in the presence of appropriate nurturance; the infant has a developmental delay that can be accelerated with appropriate stimulation and feeding; signs of deprivation improve with a more nurturing environment; and there is a great psychological disruption in the environment of this child and his family. This is a child with growth and developmental progress behind that of other children his age. Importantly, his delayed development is not related to disease but to nutritional deficiency or emotional deprivation secondary to an inappropriate parent-child relationship (Hansen, 1974: 2). *The clinician will find no sense of sharing between this child and his parents*.

Nonorganic FTT is a syndrome built on psychological problems, family stress, and a generalized inadequacy in parenting (Elmer, 1960; Whitten, 1969: 1675; Mitchell, 1980: 971). These are psychological issues made worse by problems such as dysfunction in intestinal absorption, endocrine system malfunction, ineffective use of calories, and poor socioeconomic conditions (Whitten et al., 1969: 1675; Mitchell et al., 1980: 976). *The clinician must never assume this problem to be intrafamilial until these physical and social mediators have been ruled out.* At its core, however, FTT is a physical problem directly responsive to emotional elements in the family. While a logical connection, the sorting out of these family variables remains a difficult task.

University of Colorado physician Harold Martin (Chase & Martin, 1970: 938), is one of those maltreatment authorities who has recognized the contribution of emotional factors in FTT. He has recommended that this form of undernutrition be renamed "psycho-nutritional deprivation" as a result. This renaming would clarify the complimentary role of biological and psychological variables in the development of this problem. A short review of the literature will suggest, however, that just how much psychology and how much biology goes into this problem is, as yet, unclear.

Whitten and colleagues (1969: 1675-1680) have provided an historical overview of the early work linking psychological factors and growth retardation. Beginning with the legendary 1946 study of "hospitalism" conducted by Rene Spitz, in which Spitz identified growth retardation in institutionalized infants, these researchers point to the value of recognition of a psychological element. Whitten and colleagues point out that the children's failure in this study was not due to lack of food but a result of living in an environment with no social stimulation. A 1947 study conducted by Talbot was also reviewed and the same pattern of growth failure identified. In the Talbot work, appetite and growth improved as the psychological condition of the child improved. The Whitten review was completed with a third review of a Fried and Meyer work in which improvement of early growth failure was found when "a feeling of security and emotional tranquility" had been established. From this review, as well as their own original research, Whitten and colleagues (1969: 1675) concluded that psychological factors can depress growth despite adequate food consumption. They also concluded that the undesirable effects of the FTT syndrome were secondary to what they termed "inadequate mothering." *In this work, that would be retermed an "impaired capacity to attach."* Just how the psychological factors operate in this syndrome is uncertain.

In a later study with Fishoff and Pettit (Fishoff et al., 1971: 209), Whitten concluded that growth failure is secondary to undereating.

This undereating was a result of not being offered adequate food or not accepting food due to psychological difficulties in the relationship with the caregiver. This begins to sound again like attachment disruption.

Glaser and colleagues (1980) found still another mechanism for psychological difficulties to come into play. They reviewed research in the area and concluded that emotional disturbance in the child's environment does not lead to undereating but to problems in intestinal absorption (Patton & Gardner, 1963). Other bodily functions linked to these psychological disruptions were those of the hypothalmus, pituitary, and automatic nervous system. The conclusion must be that even in the research where the role of emotional factors is openly accepted, its direction of effects remains undefined. What is defined are the problems of the child who faces malnourishment.

Despite some disagreement (Hansen et al., 1971), there is general acceptance of the slowing of brain development as a result of inadequate calories. It is also accepted that the longer the nutritional deprivation, the more permanent the damage to the brain (Restak, 1979: 133). These are elementary points of assessment when the clinician is confronted by the child who has experienced FTT. The clinician must ask, "How long?" and "What effect on development?" Less often considered is the effect this has on the development of the parent-child partnership.

Neurologist Richard Restak (1979: 137) cites the supportive work of Pirkko Graves to reinforce his conclusion that malnutrition is really a cycle that begins with malnutrition and moves into impaired behavioral responses, reduced stimulation generally, and subsequent problems in the parent-child relationship. The clinician will find this pattern to hold true in FTT's impact on attachment.

Abnormal feeding patterns are a common element in the parent-child relationships of children subjected to FTT (Glaser et al., 1980). This feeding problem holds true in either bottle or breast-feeding partnerships (Davies & Evans, 1976). The clinician will note this in the breast-feeding situation in which there is a quiet infant and a parent who rigidly interprets the "demand" in demand feeding (Davies & Evans, 1976: 1195). The clinician will find a parent who does not feed unless stimulated to feed. The quiet child does not assert himself and goes underfed. Whitten and colleagues (1969: 1682) pinpointed the juxtaposition of the child's approach to hunger and relationship variables generally between child and parent as they "come together" to produce FTT. *The clinician must be quick to point out this mismatching of feeding behaviors to the parents and note their willingness and ability to adjust to the child's behaviors.*

Restak (1979) also reviews the work of Adolfo Chavez further to confirm the involvement of parent-child relationships in malnutrition circumstances. The mother of the malnourished infant is often malnourished herself. She is likely to be somewhat lethargic as a result. This lethargy plays itself out in many areas of her life, beginning with a lack of interest in her environment and extending to a lack of interest in child care (1979: 138). The infant, being underfed, is also lethargic and limited in energy and curiosity. Such a child demands neither attention nor stimulation (1979: 123).

This pattern encourages passive behavior from both mother and child, and the development of necessary reciprocity will be severely impaired (1979: 132). The pattern leads to a parent-child relationship in which no learning, stimulation, or attachment takes place. All of the child's proximity-inducing and attention-getting devices are subdued. Those attachment inducers that do exist are met by a parent who must be highly stimulated before a response occurs. This is a parent who does not provide reciprocal behaviors or create a stimulating environment.

This situation signals the beginning of a downward and self-perpetuating cycle of less and less reciprocal interaction, continuing malnutrition and subsequent brain damage, and the slow infusion of permanent and irreversible physiological impairment. The clinician will note that it is almost as if the child and parent had agreed to let each other drift away. This predicts major physical and psychological impairment for the child, as well as the development of a difficult child who can contribute to ongoing disruption in the already inadequate family. A follow-up study of FTT children conducted by Hansen and colleagues (1971) provides a typical picture of outcome effects in these distorted parent-child pairings.

In the Hansen et al. study, most of the children had regained near normal height and weight after a few years, but personality and intellectual problems persisted. The families of the troubled children continued to exhibit marital and economic survival problems. This would give warning that the FTT situation is one of many "family" problems in a given family. *It is the impact of the "family" problems in the life of this child, not issues of height and weight, that predict the major influence of having been an FTT victim.*

Environmental (family) effects have a strong influence over the continuation of problems in the life of the child who experiences FTT as an infant. It appears as if the FTT was really secondary to the other problems in the family. Only those children who originate in solid family situations seemed to be able to recover spontaneously (Hutton & Oates, 1977: 75; Kanawati et al., 1974: 851-852). This child, when being reared in a family with relationship problems, stands the risk not only of impairment in personality development but of being seen by his family as having "something" wrong with him even when there is not (Hutton & Oates, 1977: 75). This "special" nature of this child should be picked up quickly by the clinician, for it indicates twofold risk. Not only was this child singled out for relationship problems early in his tenure with the family; this same "specialness" may target him for a maltreating act later in childhood.

Correction of the FTT condition within the first year of life is indicative of the greatest promise of ameliorating growth retardation. Beyond that fact there are several mediating elements the clinician must relate to the problems. The age at which the FTT is or was experienced is vital. The earlier it was corrected, the better. The duration of the deprivational effects is important. The longer the duration, the worse the result. The family variables alluded to earlier are critical. A disrupted relationship between child and caregiver exacerbates the condition. Finally, the socioeconomic environment within which the child must develop, after cessation of the deprivation, plays a role. A curative environment is one full of stimuli, attachment, and good nutrition.

Any or all of the factors just mentioned may influence the direction or severity of FTT in a given child's life (Eid, 1971: 47). What is curious is that a large number of siblings of children experiencing FTT are also found to be suffering from that syndrome upon follow-up (Glaser et al., 1980: 692-694). This is evidence of clustering of problems within the same family. This is continued evidence of the interactional failures consistent with those discussed throughout this work.

Social and personal pathology is no stranger to the family with an FTT child (Mitchell et al., 1980: 973-974). Factors such as environmental deprivation, lowered socioeconomic status, and marital instability were identified by Mitchell and colleagues in more than one-third of their FTT families. Chase and Martin (1970: 938) examined FTT families and found problems such as alcohol dependency, inadequate finances, large families with many young children, and parental separation or absence to prevail within this special group. This is not to suggest that FTT does not occur in stable, intact families or that poverty generates FTT. This is simply to warn the clinician that FTT may well be a failure not only in capacity to thrive, but also in the partnership that should promote this thriving.

Pioneering FTT researchers Barbero and Shaheen (1967: 640-641) predate all the previously mentioned research in the suggestion that the FTT family holds multiple problems. These scientists found the FTT family pressured by alcohol or substance abuse, sexual incompatibility or promiscuity, financial deprivation, high-risk pregnancy and delivery, illness in other family members, frequent pregnancies that were unwanted and unplanned, unemployment, and, most important, physical abuse between the adults and toward the children. When these intrafamilial indicators of partnership break-down are combined with overcrowding, lack of recreation, poor medical attention, and a paucity of stimulation (Hansen et al., 1971: 309), the resulting environment can be easily seen to promise failure.

The observer of this family will be struck with the family's low "social functioning" (Chase & Martin, 1970), indicated by such things as poor use of resources, housekeeping standards, family health, child-rearing practices, and general family relations. The cumulative sense is that of a weakened family struggling with a weakened environment. This is an environment of "every man for himself." The child within this environment is destined to lose. Moreover, this pattern of functioning is almost impossible to alter.

When the family atmosphere of the FTT child is observed realistically as one with few resources, parental absence, undermotivated parents—a generally deprived environment—there will be little wonder in the clinician's mind that rejection and understimulation are experienced by the FTT child (Kerr et al., 1978: 778). Rejection and understimulation only worsen the child's already declining condition. The clinician is forced to ask, "What kind of parent would allow that to happen?" There is no answer.

A Partner in Failure:
The Failure-to-Thrive Parent

The descriptions of parents with FTT children range from those who are suffering from a psychiatric illness to those whose behavior is somewhat predictable given their experiences and way of life. Not only does such a parent do poorly in everyday tasks (such as getting to work); this is made worse through regular physical illness. Finally, this parent has repetitive pregnancy experiences, despite the fact that they are not wanted. The clinician will find little difficulty in assessing why such parents have problems in achieving attachment partnerships with their children.

Kerr and colleagues (1978) report that two distinct personality patterns emanate from this past and present environment. For those familiar with the child maltreatment literature, the most common type is akin to Polansky's "apathetic-futile" mother (Polansky et al., 1972a). These passive parents who are dependent and isolated. They are unkempt themselves, and their environment reflect that through its bareness and lack of stimulation. A critical observation is that most are waiting for someone to come and remove them from this circumstance. The clinician hearing this will wonder if they have plans to include the child when they fantasize themselves moving. Child care may be passed on to someone else in the environment if they are fortunate enough to have such a person available, and that may be best for the child.

Family relationships for these parents have been pathologically dependent. Often, their sole effort at independence was to move away from their own parents at an early age. This leaving frequently resulted in an adolescent pregnancy, which forced them back home again. "Home" will be a poor name for the environment in which they developed, for attachments have never been well regulated. The distorted partnerships these persons have experienced with their own parents have been marked by being alternately overwhelmed and rejected. In the worst case, they have experienced a truly hostile relationship with their parent(s). Certainly, it is little wonder that such parents find difficulty in caring for a child.

As a critical note, the clinician will find that many of these parents perceive their children as abnormal when, in fact, they are not (Hutton & Oates, 1977: 76). The child's behavior will be observed to be a disturbance in this parent. Child-care tasks are unpleasant rather than holding any promise of enjoyment. It is almost as if the parent were actively antagonistic toward any sharing with the child. This antagonism should be noted and respected for the destructive force it may become.

An opposite personality may be seen in the FTT parent, although less frequently (Kerr et al., 1978: 782). This is the parent who gives the appearance of self-confidence and high energy levels. With extended assessment, the clinician will find such parents to be shallow, less than truthful, and holding excessive control needs. There seems to be a predominating fear of rejection within these parents, and they will simply terminate a relationship or remain at a distance rather than risk failure at attachment. This makes for a difficult clinical relationship. It is worse for the child attempting to secure a relationship.

In this parent, the fear of rejection and the accompanying need for control create a disruptive pattern of relating that presents the child with a parent sometimes intense and sometimes ignoring. This constant over- and understimulation at parental whim is predictive of confusion in the child. This confusion will confound attachment opportunities, if not eliminate them completely. Leveling this out is a key role for the observer. Once FTT decline begins in a relationship of this sort, it appears that the parent will simply remove himself from the situation physically or emotionally rather than intensify efforts to help (Reinhart, 1972: 1219). Clearly, if the parent is not leveling out in this situation, an alternative attachment figure may be warranted.

It does not require a great deal of sophistication to understand that the parent-child environment generated by parents of this type is a chaotic one. Kerr and colleagues (1978) conclude that these parents are not prepared to accept responsibility and are unable to profit from obvious mistakes. The family dependencies of these parents trap them in isolated and one-track behavior styles that prohibit learning. Trust for anyone is minimal, and problems tend to be externalized. In fact, a great sense of having been victimized will be observed when emotional or child-rearing expectations are not met. There will always be an escape from responsibility or immediate disappointment. The true victim here, of course, is the child.

The mystery of nonorganic failure to thrive does not begin with the absence of known contributors to the problem. This parent will present a poor parent-child relationship in his own past. The child will be found to be living in a family with extraordinary internal and external stressors. Finally, being parented by an individual too inflexible to adjust to another's needs sets the stage completely. What does remain as a mystery to most is precisely how these family, environmental, and personality variables interact to allow this aberration to occur. It is the suggestion of this author that the precise point of failure is the failure of the necessary attachment relations between parent and child which would otherwise militate against these problems—a failure more likely in the unprepared parent.

Chapter 9

THE PREMATURE PARENT
Assessing Adolescent Parenthood

The late 1970s brought forth a great deal of information suggesting that adolescent pregnancy was reaching "epidemic" proportions. Since that burst of information, more intensive study has discovered that it is not so much an epidemic as a problem that occurs in young adults particularly unprepared to cope with its responsibilities: those under sixteen and unmarried (Furstenberg, 1981: 2). This is a predictor of problems in the parent-child partnership that are well beyond those ordinarily feared.

Early attention given to destructive influences in the adolescent parent-child pair was focused on physical problems. After controlled examination of these physical risks, however, it was determined that these risks would not exceed their prevalence in any parent-child population if adolescent parents were to avail themselves of adequate and timely prenatal care (Baldwin & Cain, 1981: 265). It remains very likely that the adolescent will not seek that prenatal care, but the inherent risk of physical problems once associated with adolescent birth can no longer be assumed. Even in the absence of physical contributors to problems associated with pregnancy or birth, adolescent childbearing represents a massive disruption of social and emotional patterns. This disruption can be destructive to the potential attachment.

Replacement or Rebellion?
The Adolescent's Search for Permanence

Change is the hallmark of the adolescent period. Change in the adolescent is predominantly internal and is marked by a vague searching and testing. This search is based on the adolescent's hope that there is one "answer" available that will settle the myriad questions he confronts (Levine, 1979: 45). This search for all-encompassing answers often extends into the fragile area of "belonging," this "belonging being an indicator of self worth and identity" (1979: 44). *One strong and relatively immediate method of achieving belonging is to have a child.* This is particularly true if (a) the adolescent's own family's sense of "belonging" has been distorted and (b) the adolescent has been led to believe that not only is childbirth "the most natural thing in the world," but also all children automatically love their parents.

Navigating adolescence demands a family with a regular, consistent, and responsive history of child care. The absence of this solid foundation leads to confusion. When parental disagreements, constant criticism, and a lack of definition of family roles are observed in the adolescent's family, the clinician is justified in exploring whether or not this adolescent feels his early attachments were inadequate. *The family with the greatest conflict with their adolescent is often a family that provided only anxious attachments.* This historical instability creates continuing anxiety in the adolescent (Perry & Millemit, 1977).

Anxiety and confusion about family relations contribute to psychological functioning in adolescents that may well predispose them to pregnancy (Abernathy, 1974: 663-664). After all, if you have been seeking love unsuccessfully throughout your life, a quick means of finding that love is to have a child of your own. At least, that is the misconception held by these needy teenagers. This type of need confusion is more familiar to the clinician as a confusion in dependencies.

It is not surprising to find pregnant adolescents who have major conflicts with their mothers (Cheetham, 1977: 64). In a large percentage of these situations, these young people are themselves products of adolescent births (Baldwin & Cain, 1981). The confused dependency needs observed are a replication of those same confused needs felt by these adolescents' own mothers at the time of their pregnancies. This pattern of aberrant need fulfillment follows a predictable course.

Often, the overwhelming dependency of the mother led her to smother her child during the child's early years. This smothering denied the individuality of the child, prohibited exploration and discovery, and imparted the message that attachment had to be "earned" by staying quietly close to the mother and doing her bidding. Discussion of this pattern will reveal it to be particularly common during those times when the mother was unable to find another adult (male) to whom she could relate in a dependent way. When a male was present this was a very different household.

During those times when the adolescent mother was able to secure an adult upon whom to thrust her dependency needs, the overly close demonstration of needs reversed itself. The clinician will find that, when an adequate relationship with another adult was available, the mother tended to reject the child (now adolescent) and her anxious attachment seeking. This alternating closeness and rejection has been titled the Deprivation-Dependency Syndrome (Daniels, 1969) and is seen frequently enough in the pregnant adolescent to be considered a major motivator in the adolescent's decision to risk pregnancy. Obviously, this attachment history does not *prepare the adolescent for adequate attachment with the child who is the product of this pregnancy.* This is a person seeking to replace or "make up for" something that was not provided in her own childhood and who does not have the smallest sense of how to do it.

Realistically, the adolescent is a powerless individual. It is a marginal position to play in our society and one that is frustrating in the best of circumstances. The adolescent who has not experienced attachment is in a more precarious position. Tolerance of her childlike behaviors has never been available, and respect for her adultlike behaviors is equally unknown. The adolescent who has been without an attachment may be an overreactor to this marginal position just because she is so tired of being "nobody." One avenue toward solving this problem is to find someone to take care of you. The other is to find someone who you can take care of—an infant, for example (Pohlman, 1969).

The child, then, is not only a symbol of independence and self-control, but someone who is dependent and "someone of my own to belong to" (Daniels, 1969: 333). When the clinician hears any reference to "belonging" from the pregnant adolescent or adolescent parent, he should begin to examine just how many ways this "belonging" has been missed in the life of this young woman.

Certain of the points of departure in the assessment of the adolescent parent are reliable. Daniels (1969) has described the family situation of this young person as one characterized by (a) the absence of a father figure, (b) being a product of an out-of-wedlock pregnancy, (c) having sibling relationships fraught with competition for attention, (d) living with frequent exposure to physical punishment, and (d) having a mother who consistently ignored emotional needs during childhood. The consequences of growing up in this family are also predictable and easily anticipated by the experienced clinician.

Reactions to this family environment would include an adolescent who (a) is seeking independence but frightened and unprepared for it, (b) is overly dependent on her peers, (c) has poor impulse control, and (d) is rebellious against and lacks respect for adults. In some small way, electing to become pregnant makes sense to this young woman.

With this family history behind her, pregnancy can be seen as a rebellion against the lack of nurturance in her own family. This act is one of the few available to express the rage she feels for them. Pregnancy also holds the additional benefit of providing a direct path to a new (and better) attachment, now that she has finally mustered the courage to risk losing the anxious attachment to her family provided by her distorted childhood.

The growing physical urgency in the adolescent to explore sexual relationships, rebellion against an unattached family, and increasing impatience to find a true attachment (someone to belong to) migrate toward each other with dangerous results in the adolescent. The willingness to risk pregnancy may be in response to a perception of lost caring and attachment that is assumed to have been deserved; an aggressive act toward a nonnurturing family; and adaptive act to provide a mechanism to leave a physically or sexually abusive home; or an accident in which the adolescent simply "drifts" into a pregnancy (Matza, 1964). Irrespective of its causes, the observer of the situation is safe in assuming that an adolescent pregnancy signals an attachment relationship that is in jeopardy from the start.

The Unbalanced Scale:
The Adolescent Parent and Child

The stress of adolescent pregnancy begins at discovery and extends throughout the parent and child's life together unless some constructive intervention occurs. This observable stress may be related to specific child-care issues that would damage any parent-child partnership. It is common that the child will serve as a focus for long-standing dysfunction that grows out of the adolescent's relationship with her own family. Pregnancy, in this sense, does not facilitate the working through of those problems; it serves as a reminder of them. Not incidentally, the presence of a child for this parent provides a mechanism for reenacting the parental failures she experienced as a child.

Adolescent parenthood is fertile ground for attachment failure. A quick look at the conduct of the pregnancy, as described by Barglow

(1967), provides a sense of why attachment failure is so common within this group.

The initial reactions of the adolescent who discovers herself to be pregnant are denial and disbelief. Her body has betrayed her, her special relationship to the world is denied, and the impossible has occurred. Early on, the denial is accompanied by rationalization of the symptoms of pregnancy ("The food in school is making me sick"); when a distortion of the somatic sensations and bodily changes are undeniable, other elements of distortion enter.

Rather than experiencing the third trimester of the pregnancy as a semipleasurable time of basic communication with the fetus, the adolescent exists in a diffused state of anxiety related to the impending delivery. Rather than nesting and building emotional space in her world through appropriate fantasy, the adolescent presents a mixed pattern of overcompensating unrealistic plans for the baby or a poverty of fantasy regarding the child's future. These extreme perceptions of the child and the pregnancy are indicative of potential attachment failure (Brazelton et al., 1974). This negative attitude is not one that will automatically shift in the presence of a child, as is so commonly assumed. If this negative sense of the experience is not mediated at some point prior to birth by a positive feeling, the prediction of attachment failure is strengthened.

It should not be assumed that the adolescent parent's feelings about the pregnancy or child will become more positive as time goes on. In studying parents' attitude shifts about pregnancy, Pohlman (1969) concluded that what we often view as a move toward acceptance of the child is mere acquiescence. When this is an unresolved acceptance, such as that of the adolescent parent, there may be some rejection sustained at the unconscious level, or it can come out in the later relationship with the child. *There is natural ambivalence in every pregnancy/parenting situation.* The adolescent holds more risk of having this ambivalence tipped in the most negative direction. The risk may be even greater in the adolescent who sought pregnancy as an "answer" to losses she perceives in her life.

The adolescent who allows pregnancy as a mechanism to escape problems is positioning herself for a downhill slide. This parent is almost certainly going to find that the pregnancy will fail in its hoped-for purposes. Regardless of the pronatalist and liberal views that prevail in many social sectors today, adolescent pregnancy remains a violation of the social order.

Parenthood does not lead to social acceptance by adults or friends surrounding the adolescent as she had hoped. It is also a very ineffective solution to other problems she has felt in her life. These two unanticipated failures in what the pregnancy was expected to bring to the adolescent's world lead to increasing disappointment across the parenting experience (Vincent, 1961: 31-35; Cheetham, 1977: 42).

Pregnancy is suddenly recognized as little more than a tactic to delay facing the true problems. The result of this realization is a quest for emotional attachment that begins with an unhealthy dose of disappointment and anger. One means of reacting to this anger is to avoid the type of prenatal care that would help guarantee a good physical beginning for the child.

Great powers of logic are not required to understand that reluctance to accept the pregnancy can lead to the subsequent reluctance to seek prenatal care. This reluctance can lead to tragic consequences for the parent and child. In the absence of prenatal care, the adolescent mother faces a greater likelihood that her child will be stillborn, born prematurely, born at low birth weight, or born with a serious congenital handicap in physical or intellectual functioning (Menken, 1981). The greatest tragedy is that the majority of these problems are completely correctable through early and adequate prenatal medical care. Not developing these good prenatal care habits during pregnancy may predict a negative outcome for future pregnancies as well.

Handicapping conditions and death occur in high numbers not only in the adolescent parent, but in the older mother as well (Anastasiow et al., 1978). An adolescent mother often becomes an older mother. Curiously, the younger a woman's age is at first birth and the greater her fertility, the more children she will bear over a fifteen-year period and the larger will be the number of out-of-wedlock and unwanted children among them. Poor initial pregnancy habits, then, may carry through to these subsequent pregnancies (Coombs & Freedman, 1970; Trussell & Menken, 1981). These interlocking phenomena create a double-jeopardy situation for the premature parent. She may have bad experiences with pregnancy and achieving relationships both now and in the future.

The case being built around adolescent pregnancy is a gloomy one. The mother is seeking something that cannot be replaced through the means she has chosen: the pregnancy. The depression and anger that flow from her disappointment in the pregnancy lead to rejection of mandatory care during the pregnancy. The pregnant woman faces multiple health risks (including toxemia, hypertension, and maternal death) as a result of the absence of medical care, and these risks are magnified if she is unmarried. The child faces greater risks of subnormality in weight, physical capacity, and intellectual ability, along with neurological problems that lead these children to be underaroused or overaroused. *The fact is that very little is right with this situation,* at least in the sense that the instinctive attachment stimuli in the child will have the opportunity to be exercised (Pakter et al., 1961; Osofsky, 1968; Lester, 1978; Ryan & Schneider, 1978).

The adolescent who is disappointed in her child and herself, who is disappointed in her environment's response to her child, and who must deal with a child who may be impaired in his responses to her faces an attachment task not often matched in its complexity. This complexity derives from the fact that the instinctive mechanisms of attachment have been removed or distorted by circumstances surrounding the birth. One major study of the attachment phenomenon in adolescent parents suggested that while infants were prepared to initiate healthy attachment if healthy themselves, the young mothers were less well prepared and often ambivalent (Williams, 1974: 74). This is just the beginning of the contribution this young parent's psychological state will make to failure between parent and child.

Nowhere to Turn:
The Environment of the Adolescent Parent

There are adolescent parents who are able to cope with and attach to a single child. The signals of a strong adolescent parent are: (a) ego strength, (b) success in the school setting, (c) independence, (d) happiness, and (e) originating in a stable home and family (Barglow, 1967). Unfortunately, many adolescent parents do not limit themselves to one child.

It is clear that the earlier a first birth, the more rapid will be the birth pace and the succession of births (Westoff & Ryder, 1977). A large family with children born in close succession is a warning signal for many forms of family crisis and dysfunction. These elements play a similarly dangerous role in the life of the adolescent parent. A short literature review reveals the staggering propensity the adolescent parent holds for repeat birth.

The landmark study of adolescent birth pace was conducted by Sarrel and Davis in 1966. A five-year follow-up of 100 adolescent parents revealed that only 5 percent had not experienced an additional pregnancy by age twenty. The mean number of children was 3.4 within this five-year period, almost all born out-of-wedlock. Similarly shocking numbers are presented by Dempsy (1970: 264), who determined that the adolescent parent is 8.4 times as likely to have another child as her peer who has not yet given birth. A study of unmarried adolescent mothers conducted by Crumidy and Jacobziner (1966: 1250) reported that 19 percent had experienced an additional pregnancy within eighteen months of the first. Finally, through a comprehensive review of doctoral dissertations, Ricketts (1973) concluded that 50 percent of adolescent mothers experience a second pregnancy within thirty-six months of their first delivery. Most frightening, perhaps, is the knowledge that *these numbers represent only pregnancies that terminate in a birth; the true rate for all pregnancies for adolescents is not really represented.* In addition, the environment into which the child is born is often a generally high-risk setting itself.

Of all children born to adolescents out-of-wedlock, 60 percent are dependent on some form of welfare for survival (Moore & Caldwell, 1981: 78-79). These children were not born to swell welfare entitlements, as is often thoughtlessly stated (Chilman, 1979). The bad news comes from the fact that these children will probably be forced to struggle with developmental tasks in understimulating, unmotivating, helpless, and hopeless surroundings. Their environment is scarce in resources in which the health, opportunities, and even survival of both child and parent are threatened. In such an environment, attachment is jeopardized.

It is certain that families in poverty and faced with particular types of resource scarcity can attach. These families are, however, more likely to face the general deprivation and competition for survival that translates into stability, stress, and crisis. *The adolescent being asked to develop an attachment with a child within this environment may be that individual provided the fewest mechanisms for escaping its scarcities.*

The life of the adolescent parent is characterized by generalized stress. As mentioned earlier, she is probably the product of an adolescent parent herself (Baldwin & Cain, 1981). She may well have developed within a family environment convoluted with unmet dependencies and deprivation. She often struggles with a reduced intellectual capacity due to this deprivation. Her future is described by financial insecurity and frequent welfare dependency. This parent finds herself isolated and introduces greater isolation by bearing of increasing numbers of children in close succession. Her stress is accompanied by an overwhelming sense of frustration, inertia, and despair, for she has terminated her educational or occupational hopes to embark on this lonely life (Bolton, 1980). As sad as this appears to be, it is even sadder that the child faces matching stresses.

It is predictable that the pregnancy experience for the child was not a good one. Undernutrition (Wallace, 1970) and the absence of pre-natal care frequently accompany such pregnancies. The delivery may well have been by Cesarean section, conducted under an anesthetic, or faced with trepidation by the child's mother (Kramer, 1978). All these factors have been reported earlier as having the potential to interfere with the partnership between parent and child in the delivery and birth experience.

The isolation at delivery is extended beyond the mother, for there is a reduced chance that this young parent will have a supportive rela-tive with her throughout labor and delivery. This is exacerbated by the increased opportunity for the child to be premature, to have a low birth weight, or to display some anomaly that will separate the mother from the child immediately and reduce the facilitative experience of early contact. This is a poor initiation into the attachment partnership.

The immediate postpartum experience is a shaky one. This young mother often elects not to breast-feed and has difficulty with the mechanical tasks of feeding. In worst case, she elects to breast-feed, and neither she nor the child is comfortable with it. She begins by basking in the attention of outsiders but becomes quickly isolated as the overwhelming and unfamiliar tasks of child care begin to take all her time. This child care is frequently conducted in isolation or under the critical eye of a mother (now a grandmother) who introduces con-flict into the perilous relationship between adolescent parent and child through her intrusions. This is not a mother, family, or child through which attachment partnerships are facilitated. Fortunately, the clinician has the means to help if it is kept to a very basic level.

The hidden destructors of the attachment between adolescent parent and child are not as hidden as most issues dealt with by the family clinician. *The first rule for dealing with the adolescent parent is: Don't look too deeply or you'll miss the problem.*

Adolescent parents are frightened, unappreciated, in need of some-one to care about them personally, and justifiably worried about what the world is going to bring them now. They have a need to be treated as children and an equal need to be treated as adults. Any approach taken with them should allow for their membership in both age groups.

Most of the immediate problems faced by the adolescent parent are those of resource scarcity. This scarcity will make the child a competitor and result in negative interactions. In many cases, if the child eats, the mother does not, and vice versa. *The first helping required is that which provides for the concrete needs in the adolescent's life: food, clothing, and shelter.*

This parent will have problems. That is inevitable. What the parent may not have is someone to call on when the problems occur. Of these young parents, 80 percent will move in with their parents. This effectively removes the parent as a source of comfort, even in those few relationships in which this was true prior to the birth. The father of the child is probably long gone. Should he be present, he is equally stressed by the birth and should not be considered a resource in most cases. The young woman probably has friends who are sometimes available, but these friends have a wealth of misinformation. The key is to have an "official" friend who is available twenty-four hours a day. The best situation is a network of "official" friends in a variety of settings, but that is not always available. *The second rule of dealing with the adolescent parent, then, is: Don't take the case unless you are nearly always accessible.*

Child care is a mystery to be solved, and some education is nearly always required. However, the greater mystery is how the child feels about the parent. The adolescent parent has a great fear that the child does not "love" her. *Point out to the parent every action the child makes that indicates a reciprocal relationship is building.* This need is short-term, for the child will quickly take over the clinician's job, as soon as the parent receives some basic skill in reading his messages.

The key to facilitating the adolescent parent's attachment is to reduce the environmental stresses that prohibit it; be available, and do some of the interpretations of the child's communication until the parent learns to do that herself. This is not a psychotherapeutic problem in the beginning. Getting too "fancy" will only make the clinician like all other adults and cause the parent to withdraw. With these early supports, the adolescent will stay with the clinician long enough to get into the issues of greater depth. Without this early "hook," there is no hope of ever reaching that level of relationship. This is a time when the clinician brings the obvious pain of resource scarcity and the hidden pain of yearning for an attachment partnership together in a constructive manner. The following chapters focus on how these two deep sources of pain interact to generate a parent who finds rejection of the child more natural than acceptance.

PART IV

RESOURCE SCARCITY

Chapter 10

STAGE ONE
Emotional Resources in
Parent and Child

A Silent Partner in Failure:
Emotional Inadequacy in the Parent

This work has so far presented a relatively commonsense message: *The quality of parent-child interactions is predictive of the success or failure of their relationship.* The first chapters suggested that failures in basic parent-child interactions are indicative of possible inadequacy in attachment capacities. When this attachment fails, the instinctive protective mechanisms in the relationship are weakened. *Should this weakened relationship be placed in an environment in which there are substantial emotional, environmental, or educational scarcities, it can be assumed to be a high-risk relationship.* Should these attachment incapacities and resource scarcities come together in an atmosphere isolated from sources of support, the child is in danger. *This juxtapositioning of these variables is the difference between the family that will maltreat a child and one that will not.*

That the abusive parent grew up in an abuse environment has become axiomatic. Psychiatrist and child abuse authority Brandt Steele (1975) noted in his research that "almost without exception" the maltreating parent has experienced childhood abuse and neglect. The clinician will find this to be a reasonably accurate statement. However, not all who grew up with abuse will become abusive. Additionally, some who grew up without abuse will follow the abusive path. Rather than listen for evidence of maltreatment in the parent's history, then, *the clinician should listen for a family history lacking*

161

in emotional capacity, the emotional capacity that builds in safe-guards against violence. The most dangerous family history is one that is lacking in *any* sensitive interaction between parent and child.

A child can attach in a maltreating environment. It is difficult, but it can be done. Some children are not given the opportunity to attach because of the degree of parental impairment in attachment capacity. Either of these situations suggests risk. If the anxiously attached or unattached child was also taught inappropriate mechanisms of dis-cipline and observed violent acts (Straus et al., 1980), the child is likely to replicate these acts. Based on that thinking, *parents who were both maltreated and unable to form an attachment during their own childhood present the greatest risk to their own children.* The degree of sensitive responsiveness experienced by parents will gen-erally translate into the degree of sensitive care and sacrifice they will be able to provide their children.

Growing up in a family that engaged in the hidden maltreatment of a failed attachment has specific impacts on these parents. Throughout their lives, these were children who were asked to avoid their own needs and thoughts in preference to the needs and thoughts of those inadequate adults around them. The constant surveillance and demand of the adults around them resulted in a slowing or retardation of nor-mal personality and emotional development. This slowing was un-avoidable. The opposite of this slowing, exploration and discovery of one's own needs, would be a testing of the anxious and insecure attachments in the family. This test was far too risky.

As a consequence of this emotional retardation, the clinician will find the absence of basic trust, self-esteem, and social confidence—all hallmarks of the potential for high-risk parenthood (Ainsworth, 1979; Bowlby, 1980). Also predictive of danger for the children of these parents is the propensity of these parents to depend on external controls rather than develop internal strength.

In exploring such a parent's life with him, the clinician will find that *external measures of success or failure are the only measures the parent can trust.* The parent's weakened sense of competence leads him to doubt his own judgment. External measures of success are fre-quently misinterpreted by this parent, and the child pays a severe price.

If the condition, appearance, and behavior of your child becomes "you" to the outside world, the demand on your child is too great ever to be fully met. *Childrearing for this emotionally inadequate parent becomes an idealized image rather than an activity.* The child is not prepared for this unidirectional taking from him. The parent responds to the images of "perfect" parenthood promoted by advertising and pronatalist descriptions and seeks unrealistic goals. In this way, the child becomes a competitor for the scant emotional rewards understood by the parent.

The perception of this inadequate parent is that childrearing is a duty. The child holds a similar "duty" toward his parent. When the child fails in his "duty" and engages in normal childhood behaviors, the parent often sees the child as having done something "to" him in a purposeful way.

The pleasures of childrearing come to this parent predominantly through outsiders' perceptions of him as a "good parent," not through shared experiences with the child. Consequently, most interactions in private are shallow and unrewarding. Interactions that take place in public, on the other hand, are elaborately choreographed to create the image that this parent is being "what a parent should be." The child cooperates with this ruse to the best of his ability out of fear or a need for some contact, however distorted.

The child is, of course, not prepared for all the tasks required of him. Deviation from his parent's distorted and narrow perception of how a child should "be" is severely punished. This image of the child builds two problems into the future relations between this child and his own children: (a) It provides him the sense that a child will do something for you as a parent. (b) It distorts his sense of how a parent relates to his child.

Misperceptions of children and their roles abound in this parent-child relationship. *The propensity for reversal of parent and child roles is great.* This reversal of roles is built on the emotional inadequacy of the parent and the misperceptions of the child's functioning in the relationship. For this parent, his own distorted attachment experience not only prevents the understanding of the child's needs but may even make him think that the child and his needs might be something to guard against. A clinical symptom of this confusion is that *fear of spoiling the child is often of great concern.* The fear of the parents is that the child will become too dependent. It does not take much for this parent to perceive the child as too dependent and too demanding.

Such a parent finds the responsibility of partnership too great to carry. If any sharing is going to take place, it will be generated by the child's instinctive attachment inducers and the parent's *limited* ability to respond to them. Should the child have some abnormality that forces the parent to generate sharing but suffer with a child who cannot reward him for his efforts, failure is predictable. This failure grows out of the parent's belief that ordinary childhood demands and testing are evidence of the child's "using" him. This parent, clearly, cannot tolerate any but the most responsive of children.

A comprehensive clinical view of the parent who did not experience adequate attachment in his own childhood is that of an immature and emotionally dependent individual who sees the child as a means to an end. There is no understanding of the child as an individual. There is no freedom of expression and self-discovery for either partner, only a mechanistic approach to child rearing. This is a rearing pattern that is conducted in the shadow of some misinterpreted model of what child rearing should be.

Cultural demands of child rearing are misinterpreted, and normal childhood deviations from this interpretation are seen as efforts on the part of the child to make the parent appear stupid and inadequate. To this parent, the child is not a child, at least not in the generally understood sense; he is more likely to be an adversary to be overcome, a competitor for limited resources.

The competition for scarce physical and emotional resources is a deadly one for the child, in that the parent's need for the child is relative and the child's need for the parent absolute. This is a balance of power bent so favorably toward the adult that the child will do almost anything to satisfy the adult's aberrant needs. This situation leads to the antithesis of everything that has been described as an adequate childhood in the previous chapters.

In-depth psychodynamic theories are not necessary to explain the intergenerational nature of violence in the family. What flows from the child of one generation to the child of the next is a failure in attachment. A failed attachment, with its attendant dependency problems, absence of empathic interaction, and emotional deprivation, is sufficient to promise continuing failure between parent and child. Competition for the limited resources available to parent and child, given this history, will trace a clear path to a vulnerability to violence.

There are warning signs for the clinician. The clinician will see an adult who *needs* rather than *wants* a child, one who perceives child rearing as a function that is structured and judged by persons other than himself. This is an adult who fears the power of the child over his own weakened self. This is an adult with low frustration tolerance and a pervasive sense of personal deprivation. Most important, this adult is a person who has failed in his attachment relationship with his own parent. Unless helped, he will fail in his attachment partnerships with his children. *Should the clinician find all these manifestations of attachment failure, it must be assumed that this individual is vulnerable to initiating violence toward the major competitor in his environment—his child.*

According to child maltreatment authority Leontine Young (1964), the maltreating parent spends the majority of his relationship with the child in one of two positions: aggressor or victim. The presence of the child evokes two major feelings in this emotionally deprived adult: weakness and possession. The child can be reacted against as an enemy who might spy the parent's weakness. The child can also generate the parent's need for possession and become the "someone of my own to belong to" mentioned earlier. These feelings occur to varying degrees within individual parents, but the environment generated as a result is remarkably similar.

When the parent is a product of a failed attachment partnership with his own parent, evidence of that failure will be available in his attitude toward their child. This will be a child-rearing environment in which *the parent holds specific requirements for the child based exclusively on his own needs.* When viewing the child, this parent fears the same absence of love and potential for manipulation that confronted him in all earlier relationships promising attachment. Being more powerful than the child, there is some hope in this parent that he can capture all of the child for himself through overcontrolling behaviors, rigid rule construction, and seeing to it that exploration and discovery of outside relationships are virtually impossible. This is the antithesis of the type of parenting behavior that generates the desired effect. This also creates a parenting environment that holds the promise of violence.

Violence against children grows out of a perception of the child as someone in need of being controlled as well as a perception of a parent as someone who needs to maintain a position of power relative to the child. In essence, the parent with this belief system is threatened by a child who would seek to exercise his own needs. If the parent has not experienced an attachment partnership in his own childhood, many ordinary child behaviors will hold this threat. Even if ordinary childhood behavior is not perceived as a threat to parental power, it may be interpreted as a threat to the attachment relationship. This is often an attachment that exists nowhere but in the mind of the parent. He cannot face its absence, but he does not have the tools to make it real.

Conflict is an essential element of all parent-child relationships. There must be a period of omnipotence and intentionality during which the child tests his control over his adult partner and maneuvers the willing adult through a series of interactions. These interactions allow the child to understand that he has the security of a strong, stable partnerhsip in which he shares resources and reciprocates giving. Should a parent be suspicious of the child's need to demonstrate this control, or should the parent be too accepting and allow the child to control every interaction, difficulty in the relationship is nearly guaranteed. Both the passive and aggressive stances described here grow out of a fear of losing the "last chance" at attachment, the potential attachment with this child This is the same fear, and the same process, by which attachment was lost to the parent when he was a child (Bell, 1979: 825).

It seems clear that *the parent who has not been able to experience an adequate attachment relationship places far too much importance on his relationship with the child.* It is not that these parents do not wish to be good parents; rather, they wish to be the *best parents* ever known. Through this drive, the actual child and his needs become almost tangential to the relationship (Laury, 1970). The relationship itself and what the emotionally inadequate parent assumes it can mean to him become more critical than the child.

A parent who holds the shape and form of a relationship more dear than the autonomy of the child within that relationship is building a partnership that will never stand the test of child rearing. This distorted relationship, in which the child is expected to perform a role dictated by parental needs, is missing the primary ingredients: love and affection (Rutter, 1972:16). The interactions in this relationship will not be those predictably based on the parent's love and respect for the child, but random and inconsistent.

Inconsistent responses to the needs of a child can distort the parent-child relationship. They may also lead to developmental anomalies in the child's behaviors (Ainsworth, 1980: 37). There is a need to experience the parent as strong, independent, and reliable. Any erratic and unpredictable or inconsistent behavior from that parent will be immediately registered by the child as a warning. Should it reach a point where the child can rarely predict the parent's behavior, the child will respond with distrust, anxiety, and even loosened emotional ties, culminating in lost attachment (Goldstein et al., 1980: 25). This is a standardized clinical picture of a child who has been subjected to maltreatment.

The child who faces an unpredictable parent will exclude some of his parent's behavior from his perceptions, watch carefully for the "right" responses to emit depending on the parent's mood, and live a cautious life of no exploration. This child will not learn to reach beyond the level of control allowed by the parent. Initially, this child did resist this control through the exercise of his instinctive attachment-generating behaviors. Gradually, because the parent really is stronger and the child must succumb to parental wishes in order to survive, the child's resistance does wane.

This relationship will eventually reach the point where the child becomes as familiar with the needs of the parent as the parent, under normal attachment circumstances, would have become familiar with the needs of the child. Any departure from responding to these needs will result in punishment in the name of "discipline" and be considered justified by the parental member of the pair. As time passes, this discipline may even be considered "justified" to the child as he learns to accept the negative messages about himself that the parent provides. This is a set of negative messages he will live with and seek to overcome only through the vehicle of *his own child's* caring.

The first link in the chain of violence in the family is the parent who is weakened through never having experienced a true attachment. This is the cornerstone of a parent-child pair in which destructive competition for emotional resources occurs. The parent is fearful, needy, inadequate, and demanding. Almost any behavior toward the child can be rationalized (as violence always is) as teaching or discipline. The behaviors toward the child are directed toward the establishment of an "ideal" relationship that changes as parental needs and perceptions change.

Changes in the child fail to influence this relationship. The child learns to accept this parental competition as inevitable and attachment falls away in favor of survival. In this way, attachment is reversed; the immature "babyness" aspects of parental behavior become the predictors of the shape of the relationship.

The child must learn to anticipate the parent's fears and needs and to prevent the parent from seeing the child's behavior as the source of these problems. This is not merely a role reversal, but a reversal of the entire natural order of animal relationships at any level. It is little wonder that this reversal contributes to a vulnerable parent-child relationship. In those situations in which the child cannot meet the needs of the parent or protect the parent from his fears, this vulnerability to failure is heightened.

The Unsuspecting Victim: Detachment and Parental Protection

It is not difficult to understand that the child and family development sought ideally is built on reciprocal interactions between parent and child. It is equally easy to understand that failure will result when the parental partner cannot or will not perform his part in this partnership. The clinician must remember, in doing the assessment, that both parent and child exist as mutually supportive members of a reward system in the positive attachment relationship. When either of the partners fails in his responsibilities toward the other, problems between the two expand geometrically. This failure is often motivated by the child. Typically, it occurs in two ways: (a) through defects that lead to a lack of responsiveness, and (b) through irritating reactions that cause frustration in the parent (Milowe & Lourie, 1964).

After study of this interactional problem, Terr (1970) has suggested that the child has a three-tiered influence on the possible generation of negative interactions. The first negative situation is one in which a physical abnormality serves as a disruption. The second is the emotional withdrawal, indifference, and psychomotor retardation that describe a child who has not been able to establish a reciprocal relationship with the parent (as in failure to thrive). The third is the older child who demonstrates an inability to discriminate between attachment figures. This is often the product of the first two negative starts with the parent. It flows out of those first two failures through the fact that the child presents a pleasing effect around all adults to ensure his own safety. This third level of the problem is troublesome to the parent because he expects the child to treat him differently from other adults in his world. This says to the parent, "you're nothing special." If the parent is not "special" to the child, he will not tolerate his demands.

The distance between parent and child can be physical or emotional. The parent vulnerable to maltreatment perpetration, as described in Part III, is particularly sensitive to this distancing. This is also a parent who is likely to ignore or be totally unaware of his own contributions to the child's distance from him. The net effect is a confused parent who is not getting what he expected to be automatic and naturally occurring. Such a parent often reports that he has never understood the child, and the child has probably never understood his parent's reactions either (Brazelton, 1980: 72).

The child victim of maltreatment has long been recognized as somehow "special" within his family. Initially, it was assumed that the "special" nature of the child was a function of something negatively different about the child that would be immediately observable to all, such as a physical deformity or developmental delay. Since that early thought, it has been determined that *the uniqueness of this child within his family is essentially unobservable to the outsider.* The emotional and behavioral pecularities that make this child "special" are most easily observed by members of his family (Martin, 1976). The child may be "different from the rest of the children," "just like Uncle Harry," "always have his nose in a book," or "must have won him in a crap game!" In any case, that "special" nature may be good or bad, but the child is always *different from others in the family.* This differentness is a creation of the emotional needs of the parent.

No child viewed from the perspective of the emotionally needy parent (described in Part III) will be void of defects. *No child can match the unreasonable expectations of that parent.* No child will gain maximal health in the presence of a parent who does not provide care, stimulation, and the security of emotional responsiveness and sensitive relating. *The emotionally disabled parent is waiting for the child to provide those things for him.* Both partners in this distorted situation are set up for failure, because both slowly turn away from each other in the absence of anticipated rewards.

When this collision of expectations occurs between parent and child, a pathological cycle of nonattachment can be seen to develop. The child can meet only minimal parental expectations, even in the presence of a supportive and forgiving parent. The inadequate parent does not "give" in the absence of initiating behaviors from the child, and perhaps not even then. As the behaviors go unreinforced, they decline in number and the relationship grows increasingly distant. Both parent and child question the other, for they are facing the failure of expectations they each held for the other. The adult once again faces a familiar sense of being unwanted, unloved, and unneeded—a sense he has carried with him since childhood. For the child, this is the beginning of the same pattern.

The pathological relationship described is not universal in families containing either inadequate parents or children with problems. Some families containing parents who did not experience particularly positive attachments are able to cope with child rearing. Some parents who originated in stable families find the responsibility of children to be overwhelming for other reasons. When the problem occurs in both parent and child, however, trouble is predictable.

When the inadequacy rests solely with the parent, positive aspects of the child or environment may compensate for this flaw. When it is the child who is difficult, a stable parent or environment may show a similar compensating mechanism. When a parent has had no attachment experience and the child is difficult to care for, the outlook is grim. The parent fears not only his own capacity for parenting, but the child himself. This sets the stage for a parent who feels that *he has been maltreated by the child.*

The elements that lead to maltreatment between parent and child are bidirectional (Bell & Harper, 1977: 56). The inadequate parent, however, sees only the unidirectional effects, or losses, imposed by the child. Many of these parents feel that they are maltreated by the child in the sense that the child is the *cause* of all the relationship problems (Bell & Harper, 1977). The chld has repeatedly demonstrated behavior in contradiction to parental need or expectation.

The child's "inappropriate" behavior is sustained in the face of what the parent feels is reasonable pressure to change. It sustains itself through the fact that it is normal child behavior. Ultimately, this "reasonable pressure" or "all my efforts" will collapse into anger. Unrestrained by the parent's attachment sense, this anger progresses into violence. Again, the parent feels the child has brought this anger on himself.

Parent-child behavior exchanges such as those described become a self-fulfilling prophecy. Having been treated in this angry and hostile manner, the child becomes even more distant and this behavior is regenerated. The more fixed the parent's needs are regarding the child, the more likely the child will fail to meet these needs, causing the downward cycle to continue.

Many find it curious that a single child may be targeted for maltreatment in a given family (Martin, 1976). It is not a mystery that *this child is more difficult to care for, one who is less rewarding, or both.* This "difficulty" may grow out of the physiological problems discussed earlier or may be as simple as a mismatching of parent and child tolerance levels.

When the parent and child are mismatched, the parent will have little ability to adjust to the child's individual differences. This will be followed by a failure in the regulation of child and parent behavior in a way that facilitates reciprocal behavior. Given the maltreating parent's propensity to perceive the child as troublesome from the beginning, these failures are often learned dysfunctions that build on themselves. *This is the common high-risk partnership in which the parent is inadequate and the child disarmed.* In the presence of parental inconsistency, insensitivity, and unavailability, the child's instinctive attachment inducers are virtually useless.

In the absence of physical limitations, the child should enter the partnership with adaptive capabilities. If the parent is unable to provide an atmosphere in which these adaptive capabilities can be exercised, due to either his own inadequacy or environmental events, the partnership will express itself inconsistently. This is a situation into which the child enters with false expectations of building a partnership with an adult who responds to his need for protection and care. Should the child be entering a relationship with a parent who has not experienced a prior attachment relationship, these expectations will be reversed. *The parent will be looking for care and protection from the child.*

The parent still seeking his first attachment will expect behaviors from the child well beyond the child's emotional capacity. Anything less than this level of behavior indicates a "difficult" child. Unfortunately for this parent, all children begin life acting on their own needs. The child enters the attachment relationship only to gain the strength and self-confidence to leave it. This is the contradiction of parenting: You are to give your all in order to allow your child to leave you one day. In sociobiological terms, this is the parental mechanism for maximizing fitness.

Maltreating parents, especially those who have not experienced attachment, have little capacity to understand the natural investment in tomorrow; they are riveted in their past. The inadequate parent has sought parenthood not to maximize fitness and draw pleasure from the child's increasing independence, but to have the child stay close and serve him as long as he (the parent) wishes. As a result, the early years of the child's life, with its budding independence behaviors, are at particularly high risk for a child in this type of relationship.

The early years of a child's life present two paths to danger: (1) This is the time most demanding for the parent. (2) It is a time when the child is least likely to understand parental needs. It is probable that the parent at risk for attachment failure and subsequent maltreatment has fantasized life with a child much older, in behavioral terms, than the infant. It is only the older child who can perform the emotional tasks that these parents have been waiting for virtually their entire lives. Anticipation of this role from an infant is a guarantee of failure. This child is not prepared to compensate for inadequacies in the parental environment either emotionally or physically. But, this is precisely the role immediately assigned the child by his needy parent. Failure to carry out his role successfully, in the eyes of the parent, makes the child one more person in that parent's life to promise love and affection and then fail to keep that promise.

The clinician will find that *the parent feels this child to be a disappointment.* The adults surrounding this child will respond to him in inconsistent and inappropriate ways. The mood of the parent at any given moment will dictate the tone of his approach to the child. Finally, this child will pay a price or be punished for what would, in the eyes of a stronger parent, be considered normal behavior (Martin, 1976). Should these emotional problems be joined by physiological problems in the child, the risk for maltreatment is magnified.

Battling Baby's Biology: Physical Precursors to Attachment Failure

At best, the environment provided for the development of reciprocal relationships is a precarious one. Many things can and do go wrong. Under ordinary circumstances, adjustments are made by each partner to allow for less than optimal performance of the other. However, *when one partner has no capacity for compensation as a result of physical impairments and the other partner has a weak ability to adjust due to his own emotional inadequacies, the system may fail.* Higher rates of violence are found within families pressured by such circumstances.

Multiple studies of the relationship between maltreatment and early health problems in the child conclude that a "disproportionately large number" of maltreated children were premature or had other neonatal health problems (Elmer & Gregg, 1967; Klein & Stern, 1971, Lynch, 1975; Campbell & Taylor, 1980: 6). This is an additional risk faced by children born at low birth weight (Hurd, 1975: 37; Bell & Harper, 1977). With the numbers of these children who survive increasing, there is likely to be a complementary increase in maltreatment.

The landmark works in the study of the introduction of impaired children into families were those of Klein and Stern (1971) and Stern (1974). Based on the then inviolate acceptance of critical periods and the importance of early separation, these researchers feared indifference from parents at best and total rejection in the worst cases. Although the total acceptance of critical periods and early contact has been moderated since these works, the concern over disruptions in attachment remains realistic. This is particularly true of the inadequate parent who demands an even closer relationship with and higher response level from his child than would the normal parent. Should stress levels be raised for both parent and child, as they are in this circumstance, the potential for maltreatment increases (Minde et al., 1978).

Despite the minimizing of the effects of early separation in recent years, it remains true that the course of early life for the infant who is premature or ill is quite different from that of the child who is simply not allowed early contact. This is especially true for the child who is admitted to an extended care nursery for more than forty days (Hunter et al., 1978: 633). It is not uncommon for the parent of this child to feel that the child belongs more to those caring for him in the nursery than to his family. Even as this time passes, earlier sections of this work have predicted that this is to be a child who is difficult to care for, difficult to stabilize behaviorally, and difficult to read in a sensitively responsive manner. These are realities that are immediately disruptive to the attachment relationship (Ainsworth, 1980: 43). Should this child be born into a partnership with an adult who needs an extra measure of the child's guidance to establish a solid relationship, there is an even greater potential for failure.

The largest problem for the child saddled with impairments at birth is that he does not have the capacity to play his intended role in the reciprocal system. Similarly, this child has no opportunity to help the parent compensate for the extra caring that his condition demands. This extra layer of "unshared" stress will frequently increase the risk of violence. In the absence of the child's instinctive aid, support, and reinforcement for his parent's actions, the parent's (even the most prepared parent's) resources are overtaxed.

The child who is ill or who has abnormal birth experiences has been described as having "deviant" characteristics according to the per-tion of his parent (Bell, 1979: 824). This deviance magnifies the strength of the child's effect on the parent. For example, the tendency for the parent of the premature to become "overinvolved" has been previously noted. When the concept of caring for a child generally overwhelms the parent, the idea of caring for this utterly helpless creature is certain to overwhelm him (Terr, 1970: 667).

For a closing statement regarding the risks faced by the child who enters a family prematurely, the reader is referred to Garbarino (1980: 59), who summarizes the work of Lynch (1975) to bring the risks of maltreatment and prematurity into causal order.

Garbarino notes that for the parent faced with a premature or congenitally handicapped child, the prospect of abnormal pregnancy, difficult labor and delivery, neonatal separation, separation in the first six months of life, and illness in the first year of life sets the stage for violence. This work would suggest that, should the parent be faced with inadequacies of his own through emotional failure, the risk is magnified. However, risk does not begin and end with factors in parent and child. *If the inadequate parent and child are asked to develop this beleaguered attachment relationship in an environment that denies growth and development due to scarce resources, violence is virtually assured.* Mechanisms for assessing this environmental risk will be discussed in the chapter to follow.

[handwritten margin note: Women wounded → difficult or premature labor → sets stage for violence]

Chapter 11

STAGE TWO
Environmental and Educational
Resources

No Place to Raise a Child:
Environmental Victimization

While the "whys" and "hows" of internal family operations influence the development of maltreatment, the "where" of the environment in which this family exists also plays a role. Weakened attachment relationships, personal inadequacies, *and stressful environments* come together in the lives of maltreating families in such a way as to provide an open path to violence.

The assessment of the stress level of the family environment begins with the discovery of two major warning signals: (1) *an environment that presents a high potential for crisis* and (2) *a stressful environment from which there is little hope for escape.* Assessment of this environment's potential to generate violence demands examination not of single pressure points, but of the interactive nature of all its negative elements.

The influence of single aspects of environmental stress cannot be assessed as though they functioned independently. Stress-producing factors in the world of the violent family are interactive to the point that it is difficult to determine which occurred first among them. A level of stress sufficient to generate violence is an individual matter, but within the poor and socially isolated families being discussed here, the rapidly accumulating interactive stresses in their environment can easily be seen as holding the potential for crisis.

After years of seeking alternative explanations (that the poor are more likely to be reported, for example), it is now reasonable to suggest that poverty increases the likelihood of violence in the family (Pelton, 1978; Holmes, 1978). This does not suggest that family violence is exclusive to the poor. Neither does it suggest that the persons within these families are inherently more likely to maltreat others. What this does recognize is that families who originate in lower SES environments are more often reported for child maltreatment.

The poverty-ridden environment is seen as raising the potential for crisis (Helfer, 1975) as well as generating anger and frustration through situations in which the family's resources for dealing with problems are restricted (Goode, 1971). While resources are scarce in this environment, problems requiring greater resources are abundant. *When these two elements (resource scarcity and high resource need) come together, crisis is the result.*

The pivotal environmental element moving a weakened attachment into a violent confrontation is the repetitive exposure to crisis (Helfer, 1973). When repeated experiences of crisis proportion are introduced into a family that does not have the capacity to respond to crisis or to adapt in such a way as to avoid the recurrence of crisis, the accumulated frustration may result in a violent act.

It has already been noted that the family that has failed in its attachment relationship has a limited range of emotional alternatives for dealing with problems. Should these problems extend to a limitation of physical resources in their environment, the child becomes a competitor for these limited resources. When the parent feels the need for a given resource (physical or emotional) and the environment is restricted in its ability to provide this necessary element, the resultant frustration may lead to a violent act toward the competitor—the child. These sources of resource limitation and consequent frustration and crisis are well known.

An arbitrary point at which to begin the search for sources of crisis in the maltreating family's environment might be their relative youthfulness. These families tend to be younger than nonmaltreating families when taking on the roles of childbearing and/or marriage (Lincoln et al., 1976; Maden & Wrench, 1977; Bolton, 1980). This youthful parenting is the foundation on which multiple stresses are built.

As noted earlier, the mother's early age at first birth is related to an increased level of fertility and subsequent childbearing. The stress of childbearing for this parent is intensified in that large numbers of children are born in rapid succession. This rapidity leads to inappropriate child spacing and the presence of many small children in a single family at one time. According to sociobiological theory, this generates a family environment that exceeds its "carrying capacity" (Barash, 1979: 93).

Family size among animals is determined in two ways. Some species have massive numbers of offspring so that a few will survive to carry on parental fitness. Others, human beings among them, have a very small number of offspring. The number of offspring produced accords with the capacity of the environment to provide resources as well as the time the parent has to concentrate on the parent-child relationship. Animals with large numbers of offspring are termed "R-selected," while those with smaller families are termed "K-selected." When the K, or carrying capacity, of the family environment is exceeded, competition for resources among all members becomes a problem (Barash, 1979: 93).

Among humans, the financial stress on such an overloaded young family is obvious, but too many people see this financial stress as the sole pressure point. For the parent who has difficulty in attachment, the presence of many small children, who demand emotional investment over a long period, may be a greater problem than immediate financial stress. Together, financial and emotional stress may become deadly.

The children in this overloaded family are asking for affective development and reciprocal partnering. The parent fears that he cannot even feed all the mouths, much less answer emotional needs. A child who has special needs because of impaired physical or intellectual capacity—a child often present in these poor young families—makes for additional pressure. This pressure may become unbearable for the parent.

While there are good compensating mechanisms by which the children relate to each other in partnership fashion, the parent is left alone to fend for himself. This isolation, when combined with the hopelessly overextended resources of the family, may induce the parent to reverse natural feelings of attachment. When this occurs, one or more of the children face the potential for parental rejection. This is sometimes directed toward saving others in the family and sometimes directed toward the survival of the parent himself.

All too often, this young parent feels the imposition of child-centered needs, competition for limited physical resources, and competition for limited emotional supports and retreats from the child or children. The shallow and inadequate relationships of earlier life have provided this parent with no security or individuals to turn to in this time of crisis. The parent is socially and emotionally isolated. There is no relief to be found in work, for the undereducation common among parents in these families leads to a low level of employability. If either parent *is* working, he is likely to be struggling with a low-paying and frustratingly menial job. *This family is trapped in an ever-widening cycle of isolation and marginal participation in the world outside the family.* The frustration and anger generated by this developmental path is given vent in the family through violence toward those being rejected.

A large number of children is not the sole predictor of violence toward children. The responsibility of caring for even one child may be too much to ask of parents trapped in an environment in which they feel themselves to be constantly "circling the drain and about to go under." This is a particular risk when these pressures are being faced by the single parent.

The responsibility for responding to child-rearing demands and addressing the attachment needs of the child to the exclusion of the parent's own needs may be a blow to this young parent's expectation of what parenthood promised. Parenthood was the mechanism by which escape from this oppressive environment was to be possible, but it only drags him further into it. Given the pressures of both the dynamic and environmental elements that accompany this high-risk situation, it is little wonder that a sense of hopelessness may enter this relationship from the beginning.

This work has been concerned with the dynamics of the violent family. These are dynamics that cannot be separated from the environment in which the family exists. The environment of the violent family has been characterized as one of poverty (Gil, 1970; Pelton, 1978) and social isolation (Solomon, 1973); such families are exposed to crisis at a very early point in their development (Holmes, 1978; Bolton, 1980), face underemployment and undereducation (Prescott & Letko, 1977), include many single-parent households (Hertz, 1977), and are saddled with high rates of marital disruption (Ensminger-Vanfossen, 1978). Most important, the presence of many children born in close succession (Light, 1973; Klerman, 1975; Trussell & Menken, 1981) causes the environment to exceed its carrying capacity (Barash, 1979). This excess leads to the possibility of competition between parent and child for scarce resources and of subsequent parent rejection. *This is the worst possible set of cir-*

cumstances in which to place any individual, parent or child, already suffering the emotional trauma of inadequate attachment. This trauma is not compensated for by educational efforts.

Panacea or False Sense of Security? Parental Awareness of Child Rearing

A logical fallacy exists in the thinking of many persons as they consider violence between parents and their children. Many persons assume that violent parents are either inadequately aware of child development and child-rearing tasks or do not understand either. That thinking is based on the superficially logical assumption that if these parents were trained in child-rearing skills, they would conduct themselves appropriately, and if they understood child development, they would better understand their children. When parents *drift* into violent acts against their children, this is an accurate conceptualization. When parents are *repeating a lifelong set of behaviors,* founded on their search for attachment, this is not true.

The assessment of parental knowledge regarding child rearing and child development is essential. Often the general public is aghast at the low level of parenting information held by some maltreating parents and conclude that it is this ignorance that has led to their violent acts. This is true in a certain percentage of cases and will be found to be more common in events involving neglect, overdiscipline, and physical injury due to lack of understanding (of diaper rash, for example). This is also common among parents and children who exhibit some feeding disorders and those who present with a grossly overprotective sense.

When these events can be traced to lack of education or understanding, a great sense of relief is justified, as the path to correcting the problem is clear: provide the education or understanding. That is not to suggest this is an easy task or one that automatically provides enduring changes, but it is a place to begin clinical work. *The larger problem is that a greater number of parents do hold adequate parenting and child development knowledge but do not exercise it.* It is for these parents that the level of understanding must be assessed.

Parental understanding of children and the ability of "put themself in their child's place" have long been of great concern to those working with abusive parents. The parent who views the child only in terms of his own needs, without any consideration of the individuality of the child, is a known culprit in child maltreatment clinical studies. It has been commonly assumed that this parent was focused in this direction by ignorance or through socioeconomic factors. While this is accurate for some parents, it is rare that socioeconomic pressure is a "necessary and sufficient" causal factor in child maltreatment (Newburger & Newburger, 1978) even when combined with parental ignorance. The more dangerous and difficult parent is that one with a solid understanding of the child who elects not to deal with the child as an individual because his own needs are too great for the child: *the parent seeking a resolution to an unanswered attachment.*

Most parents can be taught something new about parenting, something new about their child, or a new disciplinary skill. Myriad research works relating to parenting education illustrate its success with some groups of parents. There remains a dearth of information relating to its success with maltreating parents and a pervasive lack of information proving its enduring effects. Irrespective of long-term research evidence, early suggestions are that parenting education retains some value. This value is demonstrated through its ability to facilitate some reciprocal behavior on a short-term basis.

Family sociologists Robert Burgess and Rand Conger have attempted to teach behavioral skills to abusive parents to increase the frequency of positive interactions in the home (Burgess et al., 1981). The results were moderately successful in the short term but tended to decline as time went on. However, there was an important lasting effect in some families.

When the behavioral skills were utilized in the short term, this opened the door for reciprocal behaviors from the child. If the parent was taught to be more positive, the child returned this positive affect. This is not surprising to those who view the parent-child relationship as a reciprocal partnership. With the Burgess parents, the negative interactions with their children did not decrease significantly, but the incidence of positive interactions did increase. Even when the child continues to be stressed by the parent, the moderate sense of attachment provided by the limited number of positive interactions would predict a better chance at being an adequate parent himself. This experience holds a message for the clinician.

It is clear that inadequate parental skills and knowledge of child development can influence the development of a maltreating situation. Some maltreatment is little more than the accidental commission or omission of an act as a result of such ignorance. This can also interact with socioeconomic and environmental variables. For example, if you are poor you may well cut corners in child care or believe medical care is too expensive. *It is when these inadequacies interact with emotional failings that they become most dangerous.*

Merely teaching a skill does not guarantee its use. It is the effect of using that skill for the person using it for the first time that maintains its use. For the parent who is suffering from never experiencing an attachment relationship, the teaching and supervised use of very minor relationships can provide the beginning of an answer. Even for the parent aware of the "shoulds" of parenting who elects not to use them, behaviorally based supervised practice can open some doors. It is unlikely that this practice effect will benefit this parent-child relationship in any substantial way, but it may well benefit the relationship that child builds with children of his own.

Parenting and child development education is not a panacea. Many maltreating parents will not relate to the affective elements presented in the more humanistically oriented parent training programs. The affective vocabulary of these programs is at such a distance from these parents' operational sense that it borders on a foreign tongue. Behavioral skills, in the other hand, do offer some hope.

The parent who is simply ignorant can find some protection for his child in new disciplinary skills less physically severe than those used by his own parent. The parent who has a confused idea of what children are all about can be taught behaviorally to find order in the chaotic world of child care. Most important, for that parent with the minimal attachment impairment, behavioral skills may open the door to minor reciprocal behaviors that allow the child to utilize his instinctive attachment inducers. If this parent has been afraid to allow this to happen before, supervised encouragement may reduce this fear.

There is a false sense of security in providing parenting knowledge. It is not a complete answer, only a beginning. It should never be assumed that "all this family needs" is a "little parenting education." Even when disciplinary patterns change, the elements in that parent's life motivating the need to discipline do not. Additionally, it cannot be assumed that the parent who does not exercise appropriate parental skill is not aware of what those skills may be. This is the most dangerous parent of all—the parent whose history, environment, and emotional makeup have built a person who is able to parent but whose inability to attach makes it difficult for the child to release sufficient caring to allow the parent to exercise those known skills.

Parental awareness, parental conceptions of the child, and parental knowledge of child rearing are important assessment point. Most important is the assessment of why that knowledge is not being applied. Knowledge can be a compensating factor in the development of risks within a family; but knowledge translates into action only if attachment needs are met. Placing all of these variables into a "family map" from which assessment can be drawn is the topic of the next chapter.

Chapter 12

SOME THINGS BEGGED AND
SOME THINGS BORROWED
From Theory to Practice

An Early Warning System:
Using Graduated Resource
Assessment to Examine Problem Potential

The struggle against maltreatment of children often feels like a losing battle, particularly to the clinicians who wage that war. The high rate of burnout among clinicians in this area is testimony to the level of stress involved. One reason for this stress is that child maltreatment is an intense problem that stands in contradiction to "what ought to be." Another is that a small number of families return time and again, regardless of the time and effort invested in them. Perhaps the major source of frustration, however, is that services are often not provided to that failed parent-child relationship until something negative has already occurred. Treatment for maltreatment is focused on the rehabilitation phase. The recidivism rate among maltreating families is evidence that this "after the fact" approach is inadequate.

Family Resource Theory suggests *resource scarcity* as a contributor to stress between parent and child. This is also true of clinicians in the maltreatment area; they are a scarce resource. The traditional response to increasing numbers of cases and fewer clinicians has been to tighten standards for admission to treatment. The consequences of maltreatment must be more severe now than five years ago before the case "merits" attention. This could be a contributor to even fewer clinicians due to frustration.

Case severity screening is a source of frustration, for the clinician knows (a) a child is being injured despite the fact that he is not injured "enough" to secure help; (b) maltreatment does escalate, so the child will eventually have a more severe problem; and (c) perhaps something could have been done if the family had been identified earlier. For the clinician, living with this knowledge and fear is a wearisome experience. Other problems exist among families who *do* secure treatment.

The maltreating family may be drawn from a wide distribution of social/emotional/parenting pathology. These families range from those who repeatedly inflict grievous injury on their children and seem impervious to treatment to those who make minor child-care errors out of ignorance. The major problem with this distribution of families is that *the extremes require a disproportionate share of clinical attention,* a disproportionate share based on its effectiveness with these extreme families. This concentration of attention leaves the troubled family in the middle range of this distribution, with less clinical time than necessary. This is a misapplication of resources, for it is the mid-level family that most needs and can benefit from treatment.

It is a risk to suggest that any person should be provided a lower level of treatment than another person with the same problem. However, *it is time to apply a certain degree of triage to allocating treatment resources to maltreating families.* Triage does not suggest that the person with the worst problem is seen first exclusively. Rather, this concept offers that the person with the worst *correctable* problem is seen first.

Until clinicians working in this frustrating area are provided a mechanism to identify those families who will respond to care and those families in which maltreatment may be prevented through non-clinical services, the care system for maltreating families will continue in its overloaded state. Through the use of Graduated Resource Assessment, the initial mechanism exists for the identification of necessary levels of treatment through early screening of the family. This is a process, however, that must conform to certain standards.

Perhaps the most often-cited authorities for standards in early screening are Frankenberg and Camp (1975). These authorities have put forth the following minimal standards for the initiation of a screening program: (1) There is little utility in screening for a problem that is not severe. (2) There is no utility in screening unless this early detection improves prognosis and can occur prior to the best time for treatment. (3) The problem should be one that is not only widespread, but for which adequate diagnostic tools, valid tests, and productive treatment are available. (4) The costs of the problem should outweigh the costs of screening.

When examining parent-child relationship failure that culminates in violence through these criteria, it is obvious that most of the criteria are easily met. That criterion in question is the availability of adequate diagnostic tools and treatment. The purpose of developing a Family Resource Theory has been to provide the elements necessary to design such a tool, one that will enable the clinician to predict the probability of failed partnerships culminating in violence. *Clinical knowledge of parent-child behavior is at a point where assignment of risk potential can occur prior to the onset of a maltreating behavior.* This knowledge *must* be applied prior to the violent act if maltreatment of children within their families is to be substantially reduced.

Tool Building: Threads of Theory in the Fabric of Practice

This effort at building an early screening/assessment model through Family Resource Theory used three separate but related points of parent-child study. The first body of knowledge is that described by sociobiology. Sociobiological thinking has been present in many forms throughout recent decades but has gained increasing interest in the past ten years through its application of evolutionary principles to the behavior not only of animals but of humans as well.

A second body of knowledge brought to bear on the development of Family Resource Theory was that of attachment theory. Although older, this literature is often traced back to John Bowlby's work on relationship development between parents and children. This theory base has experienced a surge of interest in the past fifteen years through complementary research in the area of mother-infant bonding. Taken together, they form a body of knowledge that is not limited to early childhood but prevails on events of an entire childhood to predict personality and social development.

The third interactive fund of knowledge used in the development of Family Resource Theory is the research on child maltreatment. This literature has been subjected to criticism for methodological inadequacy and a propensity to examine the same elements of the problem repeatedly. It is precisely this overattention to demographic risk factors that makes it desirable for use in a theoretical formulation such as that proposed by this work.

While sociobiology provides some of the "nature" sense of Family Resource Theory and attachment theory supplies a significant portion of the "nurture" elements, child maltreatment research provides a solid sense of the environmental mediators and focuses the assessment at the appropriate point—at the level of the practical survival problems faced by the family at risk. It was from these three separate bodies of study that the basic postulates of Family Resource Theory were drawn.

The sociobiological study of human and animal behavior provides the most fundamental statement within Family Resource Theory. That postulate may be understood as follows: *While most parents will with little question accept and guard their offspring from danger, there are those situations and events that allow the rejection of a child to be as natural as the more frequently occurring acceptance.*

Attachment theory provides Family Resource Theory with a postulate that is not as sweeping as that from sociobiology, but one vital to the prediction of parental behavior. Attachment theory would suggest that *a positive attachment relationship must have been experienced with one or more persons during the course of an individual's development if he is to be able to attach with others in his adult years.*

Finally, in a more mundane but equally critical vein, child maltreatment knowledge postulates that *the physical environment and demographic reality of the family may generate sufficient stress to push a marginal parent-child relationship into violent confrontation.*

These global statements have identified the cornerstones of Family Resource Theory. It is a more specific set of constructs from these three areas of study that identifies the building blocks of Family Resource Theory's Graduated Resource Assessment.

Narrowing the Gap:
From Thought to Action

Sociobiology was introduced in the first chapter of this work as a "big" concept. It covers all aspects of behavior. As such, it presents arguments for some behaviors that are stronger than others. One of the strongest is a set of concepts that have been applied here to describe the mechanisms that fail in the maltreating parent-child relationship. Child maltreatment is not "natural," but when one or all of the natural mechanisms shown in Table 12.1 fail, the controls against child maltreatment may be weakened to a dangerous point.

TABLE 12.1   Sociobiological Constructs Applied to Graduated Resource Assessment

1. The parent holds the capacity to nurture, protect, and educate his child in a manner that will maximize the child's opportunity for survival *(fitness)*.
2. The child holds an instinctive ability to generate care giving behaviors on the part of the parent, unless child or parent are impaired *(attachment)*.
3. In order to facilitate survival, the parent and child must engage in altruistic behaviors toward each other for which reward is anticipated but not immediately received *(altruism)*.
4. In order to facilitate survival, the parent and child must have the capacity to develop a reciprocal reward system between them in which the behavior of the other is perceived as rewarding *(reciprocity)*.
5. Both parent and child are limited in the level of altruism they are willing to submit to for the other. Neither will offer total sacrifice under ordinary conditions *(pure altruism)*.
6. Competition for physical and emotional resources can arise between parent and child *(competition)*.
7. The parent is most committed to a child carrying his own genes *(kin selection)*.
8. The environment in which the parent and child exist has a limited carrying capcity *(habitat capacity)*.
9. Any environment is limited in the availability of natural (survival) resources it has available *(resource scarcity)*.
10. The major motivator in the relationship is survival of self over maximization of fitness.

The natural capacity of the parent to rear a child is a strong but imperfect system. The human animal is first and foremost an animal. His own survival will transcend all other matters of importance. Built into the parent-child system is the parent's capacity to provide care, make sacrifices, and develop a reciprocal reward system with the child. A complementary system is built into the child to facilitate those operations in the parent, but both members of this pair have limits on the amount they will sacrifice. The parent does want to move toward fitness and maximize the child's survival. The child wants to maximize its own fitness through its own survival. Unfortunately, the environment in which they exist has limited resources, and the striving for those resources can lead them into a competitive relationship. When this occurs, the elements working against violence in the stronger member (the parent) are reduced, and violence can result. This is a perspective echoed by the attachment literature. (See Table 12.2.)

Attachment is a process that ordinarily flows in an unimpeded manner from the time the parent understands that she is carrying a

TABLE 12.2   Assessment Theory Concepts Applied to Graduated
              Resource Assessment

1. Parents and children will begin attachment process during pregnancy and move steadily toward a lifelong permanent relationship *(bonding)*.
2. Early contact with the child immediately following birth is not required to facilitate attachment, but may help, especially if the parent believes it necessary *(early contact)*.
3. The child's appearance factors can facilitate or impair the progress of the attachment relationship, especially as it pertains to the parent's willingness to protect *(babyness)*.
4. The child and parent must develop a system of mutual rewards for each other *(reciprocity)*.
5. Both the child's ability to communicate and the parent's ability to understand the child's communications are critical for the sucessful progress of the relationship *(sensitive responsiveness)*.
6. Attachment can occur in a home where parental behavior is less than adequate.
7. The child can ignore, defend against, and rationalize the parent's negative behavior *(defensive exclusion)*.
8. The child will form multiple attachments that respond to different needs in his development as an individual.
9. Should the child attach in a maltreating home, that attachment will be an insecure one promising constant anxiety and fear of loss of the attachment figure *(anxious attachment)*.
10. The child who has missed an attachment opportunity or lived with an anxious attachment will demonstrate behavioral effects. A common sequel to this experience is the premature seeking of an attachment with a child of his own.

child. It is influenced by factors in the history and personality of the parent as well as the environment in which the attachment must develop. Early contact is not mandatory for such attachment but may facilitate the rapid bonding of parent and child in those cases where the parent has been led to believe in its necessity.

The child has been given natural tools to facilitate attachment through the helpless appearance he presents initially and the rapidly increasing ability to communicate that characterizes the growth of a normal child. If that appearance or ability to communicate is impaired, or if the parent is unable to interpret these communications, the attachment will suffer. It may be that this attachment will then be fixed to another parent or sibling. In other cases, the child will simply defend against the irrationality of the parental behavior (often accepting it as his fault) and move into an anxious attachment.

When anxious attachment occurs, the child is never certain the attachment is firm and will dedicate much of his energy to answering

TABLE 12.3   Child Maltreatment Concepts Applied to Graduated
             Resource Assessment

1. The hallmark of the violent parent-child relationship is the environment that repeatedly exposes this parent and child to crisis situations of all types.
2. Life in a poverty-ridden environment increases the potential for crisis and the potential for violent reactions.
3. The violent parent-child relationship is one isolated from sources of aid in time of crisis. Social support systems on a personal level are weak, and official support systems are inappropriately and inadequately utilized.
4. Childbirth and marriage occur at an unusually young age for most parents at risk for violence.
5. The youthful childbearing of high-risk parents leads to the presence of large numbers of children born in close succession.
6. A high incidence of marital disruption and single parenthood results in enduring stress and crisis.
7. The combination of undereducation and underemployment often found provides little hope that this crisis prone environment will be escaped.
8. Through ignorance of parenting skills, child development, or personal need, the high-risk parent holds unreasonable expectations for the child.
9. This environment of crisis and resource scarcity may make the child a competitor, unwanted, or perceived as "different."
10. The parental history will have been one of deprivation, indifference, rejection, and hostility in early childhood, which leads to low self-esteem, inability to delay gratification, and fear of rejection.

to the parent's wishes in an attempt to secure the attachment. As the child reaches the age of conception, the answer to compensating for this missed or anxious attachment becomes having a child of his own, and the failed attachments of his childhood are replicated in the next generation. When this occurs, particularly in a stressful environment, the potential for violence between parent and child is enhanced. (See Table 12.3.)

The environment of the parent at risk for violence toward his child is characterized by resource limitations and stress. The parent's youth has terminated his educational career, led to underemployment, and guaranteed difficulty in escaping the pressures of this environment.

The parent's youth also leads to having large numbers of children in very close succession. This is particularly unfair, for this is a parent whose lack of knowledge about children, personal needs, and inadequate resources come together in competition against the children who are overloading the stressful environment. The children contribute stress, lack of resources contributes stress, and the adults around this parent contribute stress. This must be tolerated, since the parent has no caring personal support system surrounding him and is not competent at using the "official" support programs designed for families under stress.

This is a frightened, inadequate, and insecure individual. Low frustration tolerance, poor impulse control, and fear of rejection collide with the child's needs when the child is unable to compensate for other pressures in the parent's environment.

Just how these sociobiological, attachment, and child maltreatment concepts interact to generate a violent act will be described in the section to follow.

Three to Tango:
Interactive Pressures on the
Violent Parent-Child Relationship

It is the thesis of Family Resource Theory that it is not an event or series of events that culminates in a violent act between parent and child. Rather, a combination of obstacles to the natural partnership mechanisms in parent and child, historical factors and subsequent needs in the parent, and pressures from the environment intertwine to increase risk. The three theoretical bases previously described capture the mechanisms through which this danger develops.

It is assumed here that parent and child do hold the capacity and the desire to contribute to each other's ongoing survival and satisfaction. The child has the instinctive ability to draw caregiving behaviors from the parent, and the parent has the capacity to provide that caregiving unless impaired by the child's inability to seek those behaviors, his own inability to understand the child's actions, or environmental pressures that inhibit communication between them. Tables 12.1, 12.2, and 12.3 describe necessary elements for the success or failure of this "natural" partnership.

Altruism is implied in the relationship between parent and child. Each must be able to give to the other at no cost. The parent who has never been "given to," however, sees the child more as a tool to receive the giving he has missed in the past. In some cases, the environment is so saturated with needy beings and so short on resources that any giving is prohibited, even when desired.

Reciprocity is implied in the successful relationship between parent and child. These two individuals are capable of developing a communication system that provides understanding more intense than any other human pairing. This is a system built on the rewards each can offer the other. However, this reward system is relative and the interpretation of mutual communication something to be learned by trial and error over time.

Should the parent not find the rewards the child has to offer (growth, development, and increasingly independent functioning) reinforcing, the motivation to engage in shared communication declines. If the environment of the parent and child is at a level where physical survival comes into question regularly because of inadequate resources, communiting with the child will become secondary. In the worst case, the pressures for survival will find the parent more concerned about his own survival than that of his child. This is an environment in which the child is not a "gift" but a competitor.

It has long been assumed that the human parent will sacrifice himself for his offspring. Those who work in the family violence area know this assumption to be invalid in some families. Some parents simply do not want their children. Still others want them for aberrant reasons and reject them when expectations are not met. Others cannot support another child within their world, for the emotional and physical resources are simply too limited. The fact remains that *the parent has the capacity totally to reject a child.* Until this is admitted to by those who would seek to help families, resources will continue to be misplaced and ill used. Attachment is not infallible.

In the absence of gross deprivation in emotional capacity or environmental scarcity, most parents hold the ability to attach and protect a child if they have experienced a similar attachment at some point in their own life. Work in the maltreatment area has offered repeated mention of a parental "history of deprivation" or "inadequate and harmful mothering" (Court & Kerr, 1971), "disturbed family background" and "absence of good enough mothering" (Steele, 1975), or "personal rearing deprivation and subsequently mistaken notions of child rearing" (Spinetta & Rigler, 1972) as impairments to relationship development between parent and child. It seems that the absence of this attachment in one's childhood contributes mightily to an inadequacy in the ability to develop this attachment with one's own child. This is an inadequacy with multiple manifestations.

When a parent is driven to assume the child will fulfill unmet attachment needs for him, the *thoughts of the child begin and end with this need.* The child is seen as a giving, not a taking, new element of their life. Pregnancy is not recognized as a shared time with another individual; it is a period of waiting until lifelong needs will be met. Early contact is not engrossing but troubling when the helplessness of the child is seen. The helpless appearance of the child in the beginning does not induce altruistic care but a grudging acceptance of child care and a sense of being taken advantage of by the child. Not too much care can be given or the child will be spoiled; you cannot "let them take advantage of you," the way everyone else has. The child is not rewarding because he does not provide that narrow range of rewards the parent anticipated. The time to develop a communication system is not developed. When the child recognizes this distortion, a reversal takes place.

Seeking his own survival, the child will reverse roles with the parent. Assuming he survives the early months of life, the child will begin to anticipate the parent's needs. The child will excuse the irrational behavior of the parent. It will be the child who faces anxiety over loss of the parent rather than the parent who worrries when he is unaware of what the child is doing. This child will also grow to replicate this failed relationship with his own child. However, impairment of the attachment relationship is not always built on parental inadequacy.

The child who is physically, intellectually, or emotionally impaired from birth may prove to be an obstacle to the development of the attachment relationship that would protect him. Should this congenital impairment be matched with an inadequate parent and/or in an extraordinarily stressful environment, failure is nearly guaranteed. Even with the most adequate of parents, the mismatching and emotional turmoil associated with this impaired child can lead to the rejection of the child at worst and unstable attachment at best.

The child who is "different" faces the greatest risk in the parent-child relationship. It does not matter whether this differentness comes from an original impairment or the child's behavior is different from that which the parent expected. Should any element of this child serve to reduce the parent's investment in him, attachment will be weakened and violence will be more likely. If the environment is one that exaggerates the child's "different" nature or causes the child to compete with the parent, the violent die is cast.

If the environment in which the parent and child live is overloaded, danger is increased. Should this be an environment in which physical and emotional resources are unavailable, the child becomes a competitor for those few resources that become sporadically available. When the child competes with the parent, unless willing to submit to extreme sacrifice or extraordinarily clever, the child will ultimately suffer. The child forced to watch the adults around him as a guide to his behavior becomes the adult who fails to trust, fears love and affection, and is confident only with those things he controls totally. This is not an individual who will find comfort in the uncontrollable elements of parenthood.

In summary, the risk of parental rejection can be seen through the impaired development of the attachment relationship. Survival issues are evidenced through the mechanisms by which the parent and child deal with resource scarcity and competition. Physical and emotional inadequacy in parent or child is a contributor to potential failure in any case. The warning signs of this interactive decline are many, but the major warning signals for the clinician can be illuminated (see the following tables).

An exhaustive listing of all possible warnings signs of relationship failure is neither possible nor desirable for a work such as this. This information is to serve to stimulate the clinician's thinking, not to capture it in some rigid framework. There are, however, some suggestions for its use:

(1) These warning signs are not stage-specific. They are problems that can and do occur at all points in the parent-child relationship independently. Once they have begun, they tend to persist. However, this is not a limited assessment of parent and infant. For example, reciprocity is as strong a requirement in adolescence as it is in infancy.

(2) This is information that can be observed in the present or gleaned from questioning about the past. It is certain that all stages of the parent-child relationship must be explored irrespective of the stage at which the relationship is when it first presents itself. For example, the clinician assessing an adolescent and parent requires thorough information about how that parent dealt with the carrying of the child, important issues in delivery, and early child care. It is unimportant whether the information comes from observation or recall.

(3) No single variable within this listing (other than overt rejection of the child) holds the power to imply a relationship at risk for violence. The key to the use of these factors is an assessment of their interdependence on the development of risk.

Similar warning signals are present in the clinician's observations of or retrospective report about the child.

As was the case with the warning signs in the adult being assessed, these factors are not stage-specific, can be used to assess in the present or retrospectively, and become most significant when interacting with one another.

TABLE 12.4   Assessment of the High-Risk Parent: Warning Signals

I. *Historical Factors*

1. Missed or distorted attachment relationships in the parent's childhood.
2. Impaired intellectual or emotional functioning on the part of the parent.
3. Repeated exposure to parental rejection, hostility, and deprivation in parent's childhood.
4. Alternate exposure to deprivation and dependency during the parent's childhood.
5. Impaired ability to form relationships of any depth on the part of the parent (poor peer relationships and history of failed romantic relationships).
6. Historical pattern of self-imposed isolation and withdrawal from persons and events outside the nuclear family.
7. Demonstrated impairment in ability to trust; propensity to externalize blame *(distortion in trustability)*.
8. Low self-esteem and self-confidence; pervasive anxiety and insecurity *(sense of personal inadequacy)*.
9. Poor frustration tolerance, inability to delay gratification, poor impulse control *(Weakened self-control)*.
10. Absence of available social support and poor utilization of support when available *(inability to ask for help)*.

II. *Environmental Factors*

1. Poverty or extreme financial insecurity. May be absence of financial resources or misuse of adequate resources.
2. Early marriage, marital distress, repetitive marital or marriage-like cohabitation during which the parent felt he was "taken advantage of" by his partner.
3. Early childbirth.
4. Frequent child birth; birth in rapid succession; presence of large number of children, which "overloads" physical and parenting environment.
5. Remarriage after childbirth with childbearing in new marriage. Places original child in jeopardy through Cinderella Effect.
6. Prematurely terminated education, sooner than desired.
7. Underemployment; participating in menial and frustrating job.
8. Ignorance of child development.
9. Ignorance of child-care necessities.
10. Adequate awareness of child development and parenting skills but refusal to employ this knowledge with the child.

III. *Behavioral Factors*

1. Overt rejection of child at any stage.

TABLE 12.4 (Continued)

---

2. Denial of pregnancy; failure to receive prenatal care, failure to prepare environment, failure to acquire necessary knowledge.

3. Distortions of pregnancy; absence of fantasy, rigid expectations of child in fantasy, seeking child to compensate for perceived emotional loss during childhood.

4. Negative reaction to childbirth; failure to respond to child, negative statements about child or father. absence of desire for contract, fear.

5. Postnatal disappointment or depression; ignoring child, child does not meet expectations, child is "taking advantage" of parent or fails to respond to parental needs and commands.

6. Rigid expectations of child that do not alter during first days of child care; inability to perceive child's helplessness.

7. Rejection of major child-care tasks: feeding, soothing, touching.

8. Perception of child as extension of the parent rather than as individual.

9. Inability to perceive child's behavior as rewarding.

10. Absence of reciprocal interaction between parent and child.

11. Inability to interpret child's cues and respond to the cues in a sensitive manner.

12. Perception of child as competitor for physical and emotional resources in the environment.

13. Requiring child to play parental (giving) roles.

14. Disallowing opportunity for relationships between the child and other persons.

15. Concentration on the external appearances of parenting: dressing the child, but not changing diapers, for example.

16. Absence of reaction to separation from the child; hands to strangers, does not keep child in sight, welcomes opportunity to focus attention on himself.

Using these parent and child warning signals in an interactive manner enables the clinician to identify a *degree of risk*. This is not a procedure for risk assignment that lends itself to a scoring technique. These problems cannot be scored, in that the impact of each will vary across the range of parent-child relationships seen. What is possible is the application of the clinician's diagnostic experience in consort with the tenets of Family Resource Theory to develop a typology of risk that describes broadly based relationship failure encountered on the road to violence between parent and child. Before study of that typology, consider the following warning.

Two critical elements in the application of Graduated Resource Assessment are the clinician's perception of the problem and the parent's perception of the problem. The parent's definition of the problem as well as the clinician's experienced eye are necessary to gain understanding of *how to apply* the concepts from sociobiology,

TABLE 12.5   Assessment of the High-Risk Child: Warning Signals

I. *Historical*

1. Product of difficult pregnancy.
2. Product of difficult delivery.
3. Infant with congenital anomalie, prematurity, or low birth weight.
4. Birth situation contributing to prolonged separation.
5. Factors contributing to difficulty in early care: prematurity neurological impairments, mismatching of parental and child stimulation levels.
6. Distortions in growth and development; failure to thrive.
7. Feeding difficulties.
8. Difficulty in soothability.
9. Perceived by parent as "difficult" child to care for or as "different" from siblings or other children.
10. Perceived by parent as having "something wrong" or not being "understandable" from the point of birth.

II. *Behavioral Factors*

1. Failure to reciprocate parental actions.
2. Failure to seek parental attention; withdrawn, lethargic.
3. Frightened, anxious, and insecure; over-or under reactions to separation from parent.
4. Emotionally too "adult" for chronological age.
5. Distortions in affection; fear of love and affection despite obvious craving or indiscriminate affection.
6. Continuous seeking of parental approval.
7. Justification of parental actions; frequently accepting blame.
8. Lack of ability to trust.
9. Impaired self-esteem and self-confidence.
10. Waiting for his own parenthood to "make things all rights."

attachment, and maltreatment that constitute Family Resource Theory.

In many ways, the behavior descriptions offered by the sociobiological and attachment elements of Family Resource Theory are so "big" and universalistic as to escape specific application. At the same time, they do apply to human behavior and have been essentially ignored for too long. Defining these concepts as "big"does not define them out of usefulness. *The key to making them useful is the clinician's ability to bring them to bear on the situational variables he sees in the case as well as those the parent and child define for him through their perceptions of the situation.*

The "big" concepts used to structure Family Resource Theory and Graduated Resource Assessment are not closed systems. There is no cause and effect implied. Neither sociobiology nor attachment "causes" child maltreatment. Parents who misperceive these large roles when strapped by situational factors may "cause" maltreatment through inappropriate responses to these pressures. It is the interaction of misplayed universal roles with difficult situational variables that will be presented to the clinician for evaluation.

It is the clinician's role to (1) grasp the meaning of that parent's definition of the problem, (2) evaluate it against the stresses of the situation and the family's resources for dealing with the situational variables, (3) estimate any compensation that will come from an adequate understanding of the "universals" required in parenting, and (4) place this family on a risk continuum. Some guidelines for the clinician are offered in Table 12.6

Examination of this typology reveals that differing situational factors or misperceived roles demand differential assignment of risk. The history of parental attachment and possible impairments in the child are considered to be the highest risk-producing elements. That is understandable, for it is confusion growing out of these areas that impairs the "universals" of parenthood and parental investment. A second level of risk is represented by environmental or situational factors that may force a functioning relationship into a resource-scarce competition for survival. Finally, the parental knowledge factors are included as elements that may allow for a "drift" into a violent controntation. The parent at extraordinarily high risk and the parent at very low risk make the clearest statement regarding resource allocation.

The highest-risk parent in this typology holds the capacity, if not the propensity, to reject his child. At the other extreme, the lowest-risk parent may simply err into a violent act through lack of understanding. *Both of these extremes are consuming professional resources far beyond what is justified.* Failing to admit that parents can reject a child focuses professional energies on that family through a succession of maltreating events. This constant contact terminates only when the child receives a major injury or leaves that particular system. Focusing clinical attention on the unknowledgeable parent is similarly unnecessary. This parent may show a better response to a more familiar and less imposing helper. What has been ignored for too long is the need for help in families living between these extremes. From what has gone before in this work, it can be concluded that it is the 80 percent of the families between those who reject and those who are underprepared that should receive the greatest amount of clinical attention. Those who are rejecting may be beyond our help; those who are unprepared can be prepared through prevention, not rehabilitation, programs.

No paper-and-pencil test will soon provide the same power of assessment as a caring professional in face-to-face discussion, at least as that assessment pertains to violent parents. Like any other assessment, however, interdependent "systems" within that family require individual assessment and subsequent integration. These systems are, obviously, the parent, child, and their environment. Importantly, it is not only current behavioral observation that is telling; the history of each element requires exploration as well.

The broadly based "universals" of developmental history can no longer be lumped into a diffuse "social history." The developmental points that generate the risk of violence in a given parent extent backward well beyond the situational variables being presented to the clinician. The influence of these historical "universals" and situational factors may be understood through a combination of the elements of Graduated Resource Assessment, intuitive directions taken by the clinician, and the perceptions of a parent who does not understand but can describe himself. The key to the exploration of all things, broad and specific, touching that parents behavior with his child. It is only through this level of detail that accurate prediction of risk will eventually be ours.

Matching Treatment to Source of Risk

What has been described in this work as Graduated Resource Assessment is a screening program. A screening program is of little utility unless supported by a solid treatment program. Most treatment for maltreating families has met with less success than would be hoped. Based on the perspectives offered by Family Resource Theory, that is because the treatment begins at the wrong point, may be directed toward the wrong problems, and may even offer the wrong service.

Far too little effort is directed toward preventive services for the maltreating family. This is not only true, it is understandable. Child protection laws, as they should be, are written with family privacy and protection in mind. Additionally, the expense associated with a prevention program is often beyond that of a rehabilitation program. It would be ideal to provide prevention services (such as home health visitors) to all families, or even just families under stress, but that is not realistic. What is realistic is a shift in focus in current clincal work to prevention efforts within the population known to be troubled.

TABLE 12.6 A Typology of Failed Relationship Types

Risk Level Assignment	Description	Parent	Child	Environment
Level I (highest)	Total parental rejection	Never experienced an attachment	Physically or intellectually impaired	Low resource availability. High competition between parent and child
Level II	Unidimensional (self-directed) parenting	Distorted attachment experience	Functional	Adequate
Level III	Progressive decline	Adequate	Severely impaired (e.g., premature)	Adequate
Level IV	Fixated	Adequate	Adequate	High stress and crisis. Low resource availability. High parent-child competition
Level V (lowest)	Adrift	Inadequate knowledge	Adequate	Adequate

Awaiting a severely abusive act prior to the initiation of treatment focuses on events rather than processes in the family. This promotes the use of "Band-aid" solutions to complex and long-standing family problems. Not unexpectedly, the same troubled families repeatedly show up in caseloads across the "system." As a result, the treatment programs apply their best services to the least responsive families. This provides time for mildly troubled families to decine and "catch up" to the level of maltreatment sufficient to "merit" treatment. This builds a self-perpetuating overload of the system. Until we begin to recognize that some families are going to be helped and others are not, we will continue to overload our treatment programs with all-consuming impossible cases.

If we have shown ourselves to be only mildly successful at helping parents compensate for needs that were not met in their childhood, it seems that the beginning of "prevention" is to focus more of our efforts on the children of these inadequate parents. It is these children who will fail to meet the attachment needs of the next generation of families. This requires a difficult recognition, the recognition that some parents will always find the task of parenting too much to ask, irrespective of our treatment efforts. If our prevention efforts toward the total family are necessarily limited, we should focus them within the family where it seems they will be most effective. This should be a prevention effort that begins with solving practical problems first.

Treatment often begins at the wrong point in the spectrum of family problems. It often begins by seeking behavior change without consideration of the environment in which these new behaviors are intended to occur. Behavior change in the maltreating family will come about only if stress in the physical environment is reduced. This is the only mechanism for providing a sense of control or options to this family. Clinicians tend to charge headlong into diffuse problems such as self-identify, self-esteem, and self-confidence. Admittedly, these are important problems, but they become much more easily managed if issues such as shelter, hunger, and control over one's economic destiny are attacked first. These problems are less glamorous than typical "psychotherapeutic" problems, but solving them is mandatory before the positive elements of therapy and insight can be experienced by these family members.

It must be remembered that this problem evolves out of interactive elements of the parent, the child, and the world in which they live. Each piece of that therapeutic puzzle holds elements that contribute to the family failure. There is an order in which they should be approached. Some elements are not responsive to our current treatment techniques. Choices must be made regarding whom to help, for how long, and at what cost to the other family members. What follows are some suggestions for approaching those questions.

Now What?
The Postassessment Approach
to the Failed Family

Noted child and family therapist Sally Provence (1973: 106-107) offers some rules for dealing with the high-risk family. These rules as offered here are a guide to the clinician seeking to treat the family who has fallen into maltreating behavior as a result of confused attachment experiences or needs.

The first demand in working with this family is flexibility in attitude and practice. It is unlikely that one therapeutic modality will serve to capture all problems facing this family. In essence, we are dealing with a person who has not had the opportunity to become a person (that is, one whose basic needs have not been respected, recognized, and met). Nevertheless, we expect this person to react as if he were able to trust, see himself in a positive light, and seek to make changes in his life. This individual's needs are much more basic. Forget rules and inflexibility; they are too familiar to this individual and the family structure that he constructs for himself.

The second demand is to identify the concrete resources this person and his family need before doing anything else. This requires an assessment of strengths and weaknesses, absolute deficits that are unlikely to change, areas of conflict in all parts of the individual's world, and how much you as the clinician are going to have to do for the family because they will not initially do it for themselves.

Once the tasks of resource development are assigned to family members and a plan for achieving resource expansion is in place, the next task is to organize the ability to mobilize these extrafamilial resources quickly in the event of an emergency. Remember, this is a family who does not hold an accurate perception of either "family" or "community" and may have learned not to reach out to either in a crisis event. The clinician must "direct traffic" during crisis, for it is only through consistent reliance on the clinician for a period of time that these family members learn to rely on each other and, ultimately, themselves. This type of crisis management should be available in all problem areas in the family, not just parenting.

The child in this family must be understood from a developmental perspective. Where has he been? Where is he going? What has he missed? These questions must be asked again and again each time the child faces a new situation, for his unique developmental path plays independently on each activity he undertakes. As is his parent, this is a child who does not trust, feels helpless, and will view the clinical with the same jaundiced eye as he does all persons who make the promise of caring. Consistency and predictability are the keys to clinical success.

These thoughts are not new to the clinician. They are presented here simply as a reminder. It is not easy to care for a family that is "unlikeable." Maltreating parents have spent years proving their "unlikeability"—their parents convinced them of it early on. Maltreating families will not suddenly take charge of their lives and grow. These individuals learned that they were helpless in their infancy. Some will pretend to take hold so as to steer the clinician away from them. Some will engage in a passive-aggressive game of "almost" taking hold, then failing, also to frustrate the clinician and drive him away. This cannot be allowed. Fortunately, there are techniques that show promise in breaking down this resistance and litany of dangerous familial behaviors.

The potential for maltreatment casts its shadow over a given parent and child from multiple directions. As has been repeatedly noted, factors in the child, the parent, and their environment all play into the development of that maltreating event. Too much clinical effort has been expended on the psychodynamic condition of the parent. That is less than adequate clinical work.

A major motivator in the development of risk for maltreatment is the competition between parent and child that occurs in the low-resource environment. There may be an accompanying competition for distorted emotional resources, but the clinical work must begin with the alleviation of the more basic physical resource competition. Far too much violence occurs in families who are reacting to *understandable stress and crisis* in their physical environments—crisis brought about through not enough to eat, no shelter, no clothes, and other physical stress. Should physical resource scarcity be identified as a major contributor to violence potential, it is resource scarcity that must be attacked—not the psyche.

In Family Resource Theory, parents are seen as having the ability to drift into violence through ignorance and lack of understanding. Child psychiatrist Selma Fraiberg (1980: 55) of the University of

Michigan's Child Development Project, responds to this need through a technique termed "developmental guidance," in which the clinician introduces bits and pieces of parenting or child development information at each meeting. This is not parenting education that comes from a book, but suggestions from a friend—one who cares about the parent and the child, one who points things out about the child as the parent holds him, not through pictures in a book, movies, or slides.

In some cases, neither the parent nor the environment is inadequate and the child is. It is no longer unthinkable to suggest that the child contributes to his own victimization in some cases. Digging into those cases, it is often the parent's lack of understanding of the child's condition, fear of his own inadequacy in the face of that condition ("I know I'm going to do something wrong!"), and the absence of support in caring for the child that allows for the decline into maltreatment. Someone to turn to in these times of stress will remove that risk, not during a fifty-minute hour, but more frequently. There is certainly a place for the clinical hour in work with maltreating families, but the place and time may not be in the beginning of the clinician's relationship with them.

Recognition of the multiple influences on the development of maltreatment demands a recognition of the need for multiple treatment modalities. Too often in the history of treatment programming for high-risk parents the courts, clinics, and child protective services programs have been afraid *not* to offer the most extensive treatment (traditional psychotherapy) available, regardless of the type of developmental problems or resource scarcity they present.

This standardized approach has caused a drain on the system, the overloading of clinicians, and a generally poor record for psychotherapy as a service for maltreating and potentially maltreating parents. Given that maltreatment is built on many causal factors beyond a damaged psyche, there is little wonder that psychotherapy has not proven itself to be a panacea.

Matching the causal factors in the development of violence in a given parent-child pair to any service that will reduce the presence of that factor in their life is the key. Early identification of those causal factors and their treatment holds the promise of prevention or reduction in severity of later acts. Some suggested principles behind this systematic preventive treatment follow. (See Table 12.7.)

Obviously, these principles can be nothing more than a general set of suggestions for the clinician or program designer. Two major suggestions are critical, however. The first is that the work with mal-

TABLE 12.7   A Sequential Approach to Treatment Provision

1. The clinician managing the parent-child relationship at risk for mal-treatment is just that: more manager than therapist. Management of these cases cannot and should not be attempted alone.

2. The first step in managing the early-identified, high-risk parent-child relationship is the maximization of environmental resources. This may include the securing of housing, food, or employment. All efforts should be directed toward providing small and achievable successes in practical living skills for the maltreating parent.

3. Having achieved maximum environmental (concrete) resources for this parent and child, an assessment of their use of these resources must be conducted.

4. Should the parent reveal a dangerous lack of understanding in the use of available resources, a nondidactic program of guided and supportive ex-perience should be instituted. Appropriate behaviors for resource use should be modeled and rewarded.

5. When environmental resource availability and use are secure, attention will turn toward assessment of parental understanding of normal child development and child-care requirements.

6. Errors in parental understanding will be discussed with the same non-threatening individual who provided support during the resource utili-zation training. This discussion will include the child and be conducted in the parent's home. Appropriate behaviors with the child will be mod-eled, practiced, and rewarded. Generous attention shall be paid to any at-tachment-inducing behavior exhibited by the child toward the parent, and liberal repetition of the meanings behind the child's cues shall be offered. *Note:* If the child is over the age of three, he should be included in the discussion selectively (Fraiberg, 1980).

7. If the child is suffering from a physical or intellectual impairment, the full implications of this impairment will be pressented by the appropriate professional. This presentation should include the clinician; however, the presenting professional should be available on a continual basis to answer parental questions.

8. The role of the clinician with the parent who has an impaired child is education, continuous availability, encouragement where appropriate, and the pointing out of the normal aspects of the child. Clinical dis-cussion should be directed toward removing parental quilt.

9. As each disruptive factor is dealt with, the potential for maltreatment is again assessed.

10. Should assessment reveal that no change has come about through func-tional alterations, education, and resource improvement, intensive psy-chotherapy must begin. The focus of this therapy rests on the parent's inability to parent in an otherwise unimpaired environment.

treating parents need not be the exclusive purview of the high-priced and busy clinician. The second is that much of the best work with maltreating parents takes place in their home, over a long period of time, during which there is no particular focus for any one session.

The individual able to function in the parent's home not only reaches more powerful assessment measures, but also is better able to understand day-to-day crisis in this parent's environment. It is the early elimination of day-to-day crisis potential in the environment of the high-risk parent and child that will ultimately serve to reduce the potential for a violent confrontation.

We are concentrating our child protection resources at the wrong points in the spectrum of maltreating behaviors. Until we seek prevention, rather than rehabilitation, we will continue to be confronted by high levels of maltreatment. Until we give our child maltreatment professionals permission to fail and permission to admit that some families cannot be helped, we will continue to focus resources on those families, taking them away from families that can be helped. Successful treatment to follow Graduated Resource Assessment demands the use of the right type of person, in the right place, at the right time. It demands defining and dealing with the "real" problem in the family.

It should be obvious that talking to a parent who is frustrated and angry about being unemployed will not find him employment. It should be obvious that some parents had a childhood so distorted as to prohibit the successful parenthood they so desire. It is time we gave another permission—permission to be angry about not having a job, then helping the person to find one, and permission not to be a parent, and helping to find another way to have those needs of caring met. Child maltreatment professionals have been asking too much of themselves and too much of parents for too long. The time has come to examine both our natural resources and our limitations, and live within them.

A Word to Researchers

Like a young adult, at some age between eighteen and twenty-one years, child maltreatment research is beginning to be perceived by those looking at it as "grown up." The first symptom of this maturity is the criticism of the research now appearing regularly in the literature. The second manifestation of this growth is that individual schools of thought (such as psychological versus sociological) are sufficiently entrenched to motivate comparisons. Unfortunately, after twenty years of research and writing, much that is being written is repetitive and not leading to real progress.

After twenty years of study of the maltreating family, child maltreatment rates continue to rise. After twenty years of discussing the risks in youthful parenthood and children with special problems, unwed adolescent parenthood is larger than ever, and there are more high-risk parents who do not understand the child's limitations. After twenty years of studying risk factors, there is still no study of success factors that allow families burdened by intense personal, social, and environmental pressure to avoid violent acts. After twenty years of study, it is time to synthesize what we know and move forward in a somewhat different direction.

The study of the violent family is one of the more compartment-alized areas of study in the behavioral and social sciences. At one level, there is a real protectiveness among persons and agencies hold-ing the data regarding violent events in families. As these record systems have developed, the child maltreatment records "belong" to social services, the interspousal abuse records "belong" to law enforcement agencies, and the adolescent pregnancy records rest securely in the bowels of various medical settings. *This isolation of records and other sources of information leads to an isolation of knowledge.*

For some unknown reason, individual types of violence within violent families have evolved with independent bodies of knowledge about them. The child maltreatment researcher does not often seek out the adolescent pregnancy researcher. Those who study the abuses directed toward the elderly do not tend to examine the abuses those now-elderly persons faced as children. Very few researchers are studying the commonalities between those families who abuse, become pregnant adolescents, move into adult victimization as a battered spouse, and perhaps even abuse elderly persons in their homes. There is a haunting sense that, much in the same manner that the public isolates violent families in order to view them as "different," *family violence researchers isolate their areas of study to legitimize them as focusing on "real" problems.* The time has come to study the violent family across the full spectrum of its violent behavior. This research task must concentrate on the commonalities among these families as well as the differences between them and those who are not violent despite similiar pressures.

A final danger is found in the tendency for much of the child maltreatment research to be internally isolated. It is often designed around problems consisting of (a) an isolated *perpetrator* (that is, a parent), (b) an isolated victim (a child), (c) causal factors isolated by person (problems in the parent's personality), and (d) isolation in out-come variables (consequences for the child). There is too great a focus on *events* and far too little focus on the *reciprocal roles* played by all of these elements in the *process* of child maltreatment. As the research in this work has pointed out, none of these roles is isolated in the development of a situation that holds the risk of maltreatment.

Rather than concentrate solely on problems within the research, there is the opportunity here to offer a suggested solution. That solution is to present a hypothetical process for family violence that can be examined. The *process* through which a child maltreatment situation is generated has been described at length through Family Resource Theory. The mechanisms for identifying that process have been described in detail through Graduated Resource Assessment. What is yet to be offered is some suggestion as to how that plays into other forms of family violence.

A suggested research hypothesis, built on Family Resource Theory, is that all forms of family violence have their beginning in a failed attachment and the accompanying parental rejection associated with that failure. The failed attachment leads to a higher risk of child maltreatment. Failed attachment, when added to child maltreatment victimization, increases the risk of adolescent pregnancy. Failed attachment, child maltreatment victimization, and adolescent pregnancy increase the likelihood of seeking a relationship with a similarly inadequate individual, which increases the risk of interspousal abuse. Ultimately, this process leads to increased risk of child maltreatment perpetration in the next generation. If the research regarding the abuse of the elderly were not as scant, perhaps a continuing relationship would be seen even in this form of maltreatment. The point of study is simply this: Family violence must begin *somewhere* in a family's history. *The failed attachment with subsequent parental rejection is that somewhere.* There are some simple questions to ask this family to identify the *growth of violence within it.*

Any question asked of a violent family must be asked not only of individuals in this generation, but also of past generations of this family. It must be determined whether this family has *ever* been a unit or attachment has always been elusive, a group of individuals living in the same household without hope or desire of sharing the reciprocity of a family. Is each individual in the family truly recognized for the role he plays in this process, or is the researcher presuming a role for him? Are childbearing and child rearing essential functions in this family, or have they really always been out of place? If child rearing has been out of place, where did that family fail in seeking permission not to raise children? Where were the benefits of child rearing for that family, and where were they expected to be? Finally, why was child-bearing a crisis for this family, and why did the family (and those of us who observe families) fail to recognize the signs of crisis? Finally, there is the massive question we must ask ourselves: How has our overly positive public perspective on the family and childbearing contributed to the process and development of violence in this and all other families?

The tasks of the researcher in this third decade of child maltreatment research are difficult. The research must move from one level to the next. Ordinarily, research on behavior would move to the next level of abstraction in order to capture a wider perspective. The need within the family violence knowledge is to move downward to reduce abstraction and maximize applied knowledge. It is hoped that Family Resource Theory will provide one point from which to begin that reductionistic process.

One Last Hurrah: Concluding Statement

Any effort to summarize a work of this length, and the thought of so many researchers, writers, and teachers, is virtually impossible without missing some significant point. A summary view would be different for each group reading this material, as well. Perhaps the most graceful exit is a simple concluding statement to be made to the major audiences for which this work was developed: family violence practitioners and clinicians.

Family Resource Theory brings a plea to the researcher to begin an examination of the commonalities within violent families of all types. Most important among those commonalities are those that allow the stressed family to decay into violent interaction. Family Resource Theory focuses on characteristic elements of some families (resource scarcity, failed attachment, and rejection) that seem to hold a logical pattern across all types of violent families. Together, these generate the "failed" family as compared to the warm, loving environment we would like families to provide for their members.

This failure in the family motivates the adolescent to bear a child to provide her the love she feels she missed. This failure leads the battered wife to be blind to inadequacies in her partner, as assaults continue, with promises that "it will never happen again." This failure grows out of a desperate need to belong and a fear of being alone again. This failure prohibits recognition of the needs of family members as they make normal human demands on those who share that "family" with them. Family Resource Theory does not prove the existence of this pattern of failure; researchers motivated by this thought will prove or disprove its existence.

Family Resource Theory and Graduated Resource Assessment bring the clinician a plea to begin where the most basic failings in the family are and treat the family as an interactive unit. The clinician is urged to seek the basic caring skills the members of the family have missed and assess each individual and generation to determine the depth of that absence. The clinician is encouraged to seek the individual strengths and weaknesses of family members and measure their effects as they position themselves against the strengths and weaknesses of the other members of the family. Most important, the clinician is taught to eliminate any perspective held solely about isolated victims, perpetrators, or outcomes. All of the potential failings exist in each member of that failed family.

This work brings its biggest challenge to the teacher. That challenge is to transmit the many pieces of information presented in this work to the student in such a way that they are questioned and reorganized. The failures of the family in motivating the violent act are many. Only one perspective on those failures has been described here. It is the job of the teacher to stimulate the evolution of others. It is hoped that this evolution will move us closer to a greater understanding.

It is likewise hoped that the collection of research, theory, and practical suggestions offered in this work will serve as a challenge to all who have been exposed to it. Family Resource Theory is not really a beginning point; it is a beginning thought, one that should offer a challenge to the researcher to seek a greater depth of knowledge. This is a challenge to the clinician to serve the violent family with compassion and understanding. It is a general challenge to seek to eliminate the misunderstanding and misdirection that exist in the knowledge of violent families, and to offer this new understanding to others as a teacher would a student. Family Resource Theory, as presented by this work, may well have generated more questions than answers. If that is so, then this work as been a success, for *it is the asking of these questions and the seeking of their solutions that will lead to hope for violent families.*

REFERENCES

Abernathy, V. Illigitimate conception among teenagers. *American Journal of Public Health,* 1974, *64,* 662-665.

Ainsworth, M.D.S. The effects of maternal deprivation: A review of the findings and controversy in the context of research strategy. Public Health Papers No. 14, *Deprivation of maternal care: A reassessment of its effects.* Geneva: World Health Organization, 1962.

Ainsworth, M.D.S. Patterns of attachment behavior shown by the infant in interaction with its mother. *Merrill-Palmer Quarterly,* 1964, *10,* 51-58.

Ainsworth, M.D.S. *Infancy in Uganda: Infant care and the growth of love.* Baltimore: Johns Hopkins University Press, 1967.

Ainsworth, M.D.S. Infant-mother attachment. *American Psychologist,* 1979, *34*(10), 932-937.

Ainsworth, M.D.S. Attachment and child abuse. In G. Gerbner, C. Ross, & E. Ligler (Eds.), *Child abuse: An agenda for action.* New York: Oxford University Press, 1980.

Ainsworth, M.D.S., & Bell, S. M. Some contemporary patterns of mother-infant interaction in the feeding situation. In A. Ambrose (Ed.), *Stimulation in early infancy.* New York: Academic Press, 1969.

Ainsworth, M.D.S., & Bell, S. M. Attachment, exploration, and separation: Illustrated by the behavior of one-year-olds in a strange situation. *Child Development,* 1970, *41,* 49-67.

Ainsworth, M.D.S., Bell, S. M., & Slayton, D. J. Individual differences in strange situation behavior of one year olds. In H. R. Schaffer (Ed.), *The origins of human social relation.* New York: Academic Press, 1971.

Ainsworth, M.D.S., Bell, S. M., & Slayton, D. J. In M.P.M. Richards (Ed.), *The integration of a child into a social world.* New York: Cambridge University Press, 1974.

Ainsworth, M.D.S., Blehar, M. C., Waters, E., & Wall, S. *Patterns of attachment.* Hillsdale, NJ: Erlbaum, 1978.

Ainsworth, M.D.S., & Wittig, B. A. Attachment and exploratory behavior of one year olds in a strange situation. In B. M. Foss (Ed.), *Determinants of infant-behavior* (Vol. IV). London: Methuen, 1969.

Aleksandrowicz, M. K. The effect of pain-relieving drugs administered during labor and delivery on the behavior of the newborn. *Merrill-Palmer Quarterly,* 1974, *20,* 121-141.

Alexander, Richard D. The search for a general theory of behavior. *Behavioral Science,* 1975, *20,* 77-100.

American Psychologist (Special issue, Psychology and children: Current research and practice). 1979, *34* (Whole No. 10).

Anastasiow, N. J., Everett, M., O'Shaughnessy, T. E., Eggleston, P. J., & Eklund, S. J. Improving teenage attitudes toward children, child handicaps and hospital settings: A child development curriculum for potential parents. *American Journal of Orthopsychiatry,* 1978, *48,* 663-671.

Anonymous. Obstetric analgesia and the newborn baby. *Lancet,* 1974, *1,* 1090.

Bakan, David. *Slaughter of the innocents: A study of the battered child phenomenon.* Boston: Beacon Press, 1971.

Baldwin, W., & Cain, V. S. The children of teenage parents. In F. F. Furstenberg, Jr., R. Lincoln, & J. Menken (Eds.), *Teenage sexuality, pregnancy and childbearing.* Philadelphia: University of Pennsylvania Press, 1981.

Barash, David P. Sociobiology: Evolution as a paradigm for behavior. In M. S. Gregory, A. Silvers, & D. Smith (Eds.), *Sociobiology and human nature: An interdisciplinary critique and defense.* San Francisco: Jossey-Bass, 1978.

Barash, David P. *The whisperings within.* New York: Penguin, 1979.

Barglow, P. Some psychiatric aspects of illegitimate pregnancy during early adolescence. *American Journal of Orthopsychiatry,* 1967, *37,* 266.

Barnett, C. R., Leiderman, P. H., Grobstein, R., & Klaus, M. H. Neonatal separation: The maternal side of interactional deprivation. *Pediatrics,* 1970, *45,* 197-205.

Bell, R. Q. Contributions of human infants to caregiving and social interaction. In M. Lewis & L. A. Rosenblum (Eds.), *The effect of the infant on its caregiver.* New York: John Wiley, 1974.

Bell, R. Q. History of the child's influence: Medieval to modern times. In R. Q. Bell & L. V. Harper, *Child effects on adults.* New York: John Wiley, 1977.

Bell, R. Q. Parent, child and reciprocal influences. *American Psychologist,* 1979, *34*(10), 821-826.

Bell, R. Q., & Harper, L. V. *Child effects on adults.* New York: John Wiley, 1977.

Belsky, J. Early human experience: A family perspective. *Developmental Psychology,* 1981, *17*(1), 3-23.

Bettleheim, B. *Love is not enough: The treatment of emotionally disturbed children.* New York: Avon, 1950.

Blehar, M. C., Lieberman, A. F., & Ainsworth, M.D.S. Early face-to-face interaction and its relation to later infant-mother attachment. *Child Development,* 1977, *48,* 182-194.

Bolton, F.G., Jr. *The pregnant adolescent: problems of premature parenthood.* Beverly Hills, CA: Sage, 1980.

Bolton, F.G., Jr., & Laner, R. H. Maternal maturity and maltreatment: Expanding the definition of the abusive adolescent mother. *Journal of Family Issues* (Special issue, New research in family violence), 1981, *2,* 485-508.

Bolton, F.G., Jr., Laner, R. H., & Gai, D. S. For better or worse? Foster parents and foster children in an officially reported child maltreatment population. *Children and Youth Services Review,* 1981, *3*(1, 2).

Bolton, F.G., Jr., Laner, R. H., Gai, D. S., & Kane, S. P. The "study" of child maltreatment: When is research. . .research? *Journal of Family Issues,* 1981, *3*(4), 531-539.

Bolton, F.G., Jr., Laner, R. H., & Kane, S. P. Child maltreatment risk among adolescent mothers: A study of reported cases. *American Journal of Orthopsychiatry,* 1980, *50*(3), 489-504.

Bowlby, J. The influence of early environment in the development of neurosis and neurotic character. *International Journal of Psychoanalysis,* 1940, *21,* 154-178.

Bowlby, J. Forty-four juvenile thieves: Their characters and home life. *International Journal of Psychoanalysis,* 1944, *25,* 19-52; 107-127.

Bowlby, J. *Maternal care and mental health* (2nd ed.). Monograph Series No. 2. Geneva: World Health Organization, 1951.

Bowlby, J. *Can I leave my baby?* New York: National Association for Mental Health, 1958. (a)

Bowlby, J. The nature of a child's tie to his mother. *International Journal of Psychoanalysis,* 1958, *39,* 350-373.

Bowlby, J. The Adolf Meyer lecture: Childhood mourning and its implications for psychiatry. *American Journal of Psychiatry,* 1961, *188,* 481-497.

Bowlby, J. *Maternal care and mental health.* Geneva: World Health Organization, 1962.

Bowlby, J. Effects on behavior of disruptions of an affectual bond. In J. D. Thoday & A. A. Parks (Eds.), *Genetic and environmental influences on behavior.* London: Oliver & Boyd, 1968.

Bowlby, J. *Attachment and loss. I: Attachment.* New York: Basic Books, 1969.

Bowlby, J. *Attachment and loss. II: Separation anxiety and anger.* New York: Basic Books, 1973.

Bowlby, J. *Separation anxiety: A critical review of the literature.* New York: Child Welfare League of America, 1975.

Bowlby, J. *Attachment and loss. III: Sadness and depression.* New York: Basic Books, 1980.

Bowlby, J., Ainsworth, M., Boston, M., & Rosenbluth, D. The effects of mother-child separation: A follow-up study. In N. L. Corah & E. N. Gale (Eds.), *The origins of abnormal behavior.* Reading, MA: Addison-Wesley, 1971.

Brazelton, T. B. Psychophysiological reaction in the neonate. *Journal of Pediatrics,* 1961, *58,* 513-518.

Brazelton, T. B. The early mother-infant adjustment. *Pediatrics,* 1963, *32,* 931-938.

Brazelton, T. B. *Neonatal behavioral assessment scale.* Clinics in Developmental Medicine No. 50. New York: Spastics International Medical Publications, 1973.

Brazelton, T. B. Behavioral competence of the newborn infant. In P. Taylor (Ed.), *Parent-infant relationships.* New York: Grune & Stratton, 1980.

Brazelton, T. B., Kowslowski, B., & Main, M. The origins of reciprocity: The early mother-infant interaction. In M. Lewis & L. Rosenbaum (Eds.), *The effect of the infant on its caregiver.* New York: John Wiley, 1974.

Brazelton, T. B., Tronick, E., Adamson, L., Als, H., & Wise, S. Early mother-infant reciprocity. In M. A. Hofer (Ed.), *Parent-infant interaction.* Amsterdam: Elsevier, 1975.

Bromwich, R. M. Focus on maternal behavior in infant intervention. *Orthopsychiatry,* 1976, *46*(3), 439-446.

Bronfenbrenner, U. Early deprivation in mammals: A cross-species analysis. In G. Newton & S. Levine (Eds.), *Early experience and behavior.* Springfield, IL: Charles C Thomas, 1968.

Broussard, E. R. Assessment of the adaptive potential of the mother-infant system: The Neonatal Perception Inventories. In P. Taylor (Ed.), *Parent-infant relationships.* New York: Grune & Stratton, 1980.

Brown, J. V., & Bakeman, R. *Behavioral dialogues between mothers and infants: The effect of prematurity.* Paper presented at the American Pediatric Society and the Society for Pediatric Research, San Francisco, April 1977. (Supported by Grant No. MH26131, Center for the Study of Crime and Delinquency, NIMH DHEW.

DHEW Publication No. [OHDS] 79-30225, September 1979).

Burgess, R. L., Anderson, E. A., Schellenback, C. J., & Conger, R. D. A social inter-actional approach to the study of abusive families. *In Advances in family assessment and theory* (Vol. 2). Greenwich, CT: JAI Press, 1981.

Caffey, J., Silverman, F. N., Kempe, C. H., Venters, H., & Leonard, M. Seek and save. *Medical World News,* 1973, *131,* 21; 25; 28; 32-33.

Campbell, S.B.G., & Taylor, P. M. Bonding and attachment: Theoretical issues. In P. M. Taylor (Ed.), *Parent-infant relationships.* New York: Grune & Stratton, 1980.

Caplan, G. *Emotional implications of pregnancy and influence on family relationships in the healthy child.* Cambridge, MA: Harvard University Press, 1960.

Caplan, G. Patterns of parental response to the crisis of premature birth. *Psychiatry,* 1960, *23,* 365-374.

Caplan, G., Mason, E., & Kaplan, D. Four studies of crisis in parents of prematures. *Community Mental Health Journal,* 1965, *1,* 149.

Card, J. J., & Wise, L. L. Teenage mothers and fathers: The impact of early childbearing on the parents' personal and professional lives. *Family Planning Perspectives,* 1978, *10,* 199-205.

Chase, H. P., & Martin, H. P. Undernutrition and child development. *New England Journal of Medicine,* 1970, *282*(17), 933-939.

Cheetham, J. *Unwanted pregnancy and counselling.* London: Routedge & Kegan Paul, 1977.

Chilman, C. *Adolescent sexuality in a changing American society: Social and psychological perspectives.* Bethesda, MD: DHEW Public Health Service, 1979. (NIMH No. [NIH] 79-1426)

Cohen, R. L. Maladaptation to pregnancy. In P. M. Taylor (Ed.), *Parent-infant relationships.* New York: Grune & Stratton, 1980.

Condon, W. S. A primary phase in the organization of infant responding behavior. In H. R. Schaffer (Ed.), *The origins of human social relations.* New York: Academic Press, 1977.

Coombs, L. C., & Freedman, R. Premarital pregnancy and status before and after marriage. *American Journal of Sociology,* 1970, *75,* 800-820.

Court, J., & Kerr, A. The battered child syndrome—2: A preventable disease? *Nursing Times* (London), 1971, *67*(23), 695-697.

Crumidy, P., & Jacobziner, H. A. Study of young unmarried mothers who kept their babies. *American Journal of Public Health,* 1966, *56,* 1242-1251.

Daniels, A. M. Reaching unwed mothers. *American Journal of Nursing,* 1969, *69,* 332-335.

David, M., & Appell, G. Mother-child interaction and its impact on the child. In A. Ambrose (Ed.), *Stimulation in early infancy.* New York: Academic Press, 1969.

Davies, D. P., & Evans, T. I. Failure to thrive at the breast. *Lancet,* November 27, 1976, 1195-1196.

deChateau, P. Effects of hospital practices on synchrony in the development of the infant-parent relationship. In P. M. Taylor (Ed.), *Parent-infant relationships.* New York: Grune & Stratton, 1980.

deChateau, P., & Wiberg, B. Long-term effect on mother-infant behavior of extra contact during the first post partum hour. I. First observations at 36 hours. *Acta Paediatrica Scandanavia,* 1977, *66,* 137. (a)

deChateau, P., & Wiberg, B. Long-term effect on mother-infant behavior of extra contact during the first hour post partum. II. A follow-up at three months. *Acta
Paediatrica Scandanavia,* 1977, *66,* 145-151. (b)

Dempsey, J. J. Illegitimacy in early adolescence. *American Journal of Obstetrics and
Gynecology,* 1970, *106,* 260-265.

DiVitto, B., & Goldberg, S. The development of early parent-infant interaction as a
function of newborn medical status. In T. Field, S. Sostek, S. Goldberg, & H. H.
Shuman (Eds.), *Infants born at risk.* Holliswood, NY: Spectrum, 1983.

Drotar, D., Baskiewicz, A., Irvin, N., Kennell, J., & Klaus, M. The adaption of parents
to the birth of an infant with a congenital malformation: A hypothetical model. *Case
Western Reserve Pediatrics,* 1975, *56*(5), 710-717.

Dubignon, J., Campbell, D., Curtis, M., & Partington, M. W. The relationship between laboratory measures of sucking, food intake, and perinatal factors during the
newborn period. *Child Development,* 1969, *40,* 1107-1120.

Dunn, J. B., & Richards, M.P.M. Observations on the developing relationship between mother and baby in the neonatal period. In H. R. Schaffer (Ed.), *The origins
of human social relations.* New York: Academic Press, 1977.

Eid, E. E. A follow-up study of physical growth following failure to thrive with special
reference to a critical period in the first year of life. *Acta Paediatrica Scandanavia,*
1971, *60,* 39-48.

Eisenberg, R. B. Auditory behavior in the human neonate: Functional properties
of sound and their ontogenic implication. *Ear, Nose, and Throat Audiology,* 1969,
9, 34.

Elmer, E. Failure-to-thrive role of the mother. *Pediatrics,* April 1960, 717-725.

Elmer, E. *Children in jeopardy: A study of abused minors and their families.* Pittsburgh:
University of Pittsburgh Press, 1967.

Elmer, E., & Gregg, G. S. Developmental characteristics of abused children. *Pediatrics,* 1967, *40,* 596-602.

Emde, R. N. Emotional availability: A reciprocal reward system for infants and
parents with implications for prevention of psycho-social disorders. In P.M. Taylor
(Ed.), *Parent-infant relationships.* New York: Grune & Stratton, 1980.

Ensminger-Vanfossen, B. *Battered women and cultural beliefs about them.* Paper
presented at the Eastern Sociological Society, April 1, 1981.

Eppink, H. An experiment to determine a basis for nursing decisions in regard to time
of initiation of breast feeding. *Nursing Register,* 1969, *18,* 292.

Epstein, S. The stability of behavior. I: On predicting most of the people most of the
time. *Journal of Personality and Social Psychology,* 1979, *37,* 1097-1126.

Fantz, R. L., Fagan, J. F., & Miranda, S. B. Early visual selectivity as a function of
pattern variables, previous exposure, age from birth and conception and expected
cognitive deficit. In L. B. Cohen & P. Salapatek (Eds.), *Infant perception from sensation to cognition.* New York: Academic Press, 1975.

Finkelhor, D. *Sexually victimized children.* New York: Macmillan, 1979.

Fishoff, J., Whitten, C. F., & Pettit, M. G. A psychiatric study of mothers of infants
with growth failure secondary to maternal deprivation. *Journal of Pediatrics,*
1971, *79*(2), 209-215.

Fitzhardinge, P., & Ramsey, K. The improving outlook for the small prematurely born
infant. *Developmental Medicine in Child Neurology,* 1973, *15,* 447.

Fitzhardinge, P., & Steven, E. The small-for-date infant. II. Neurological and intellectual sequalae. *Pediatrics,* 1972, *50,* 50. (a)

Fitzhardinge, P., & Steven, E. The small-for-date infant. I. Later growth patterns. *Pediatrics,* 1972, *46,* 67. (b)

Fontana, V. *Somewhere a child is crying: Maltreatment causes and prevention.* New York: Macmillan, 1973.

Fox, R. *Encounter with anthropology.* New York: Harcourt Brace Jovanovich, 1973.

Fraiberg, S. *Clinical studies in infant mental health: The first year of life.* New York: Basic Books, 1980.

Frankenberg, William K., & Camp, B. W. *Pediatric screening tests.* Springfield, IL: Charles C Thomas, 1975.

Fried, R., & Mayer, M. F. Socio-emotional factors accounting for growth failure in children living in an institution. *Journal of Pediatrics,* 1948, *33,* 444-456.

Friedrich, W. N., & Boriskin, J. A. The role of the child in abuse: A review of literature. *American Journal of Orthopsychiatry,* 1976, *46,* 580-590.

Fullard, W., & Reiling, A. M. An investigation of Lorenz' "babyness." *Child Development,* 1976, *47,* 1191.

Funke, J., & Irby, M. *A study of predictive criteria in relation to behavior.* Unpublished research, University of Colorado, 1973.

Furstenburg, F.F. Jr., *Unplanned parenthood: The social consequences of teenage childbearing.* New York: Macmillan, 1976.

Furstenberg, F.F., Jr., Lincoln, R., & Menken, J. *Teenage sexuality, pregnancy, and childbearing.* Philadelphia: University of Pennsylvania Press, 1981.

Garbarino, J. Changing hospital childbirth practices: A developmental perspective on prevention of child maltreatment. *American Journal of Orthopsychiatry,* 1980, *50*(4), 588-597.

Garbarino, J., & Gilliam, G. Understanding abusive families. Lexington, MA: D. C. Heath, 1980.

Gelles, R. J. Child abuse as psychopathology: A sociological critique and reformulation. *American Journal of Orthopsychiatry,* 1973, *43,* 611-621.

Gelles, R. J. The violent home. Beverly Hills, CA: Sage, 1974.

Gelles, R. J. Family violence. Beverly Hills, CA: Sage, 1979.

Gelles, R. J. Violence in the family: A review of research in the seventies. *Journal of Marriage and the Family,* November 1980, 873-885.

Gerbner, G., Ross, C. J., & Zigler, E. (Eds.). *Child abuse: An agenda for action.* New York: Oxford University Press, 1980.

Gerrard, J. W. Breastfeeding: Second thoughts. *Pediatrics,* 1974, *54,* 757.

Gil, D. G. *Violence against children.* Cambridge, MA: Harvard University Press, 1970.

Glaser, H. H., Heagarty, M. C., Bullard, D. M., & Pivchik, E. C. Physical and psychological development of children with early failure to thrive. *Journal of Pediatrics,* 1980, *73*(5), 690-698.

Goldberg, S., Brachfeld, S., & Divitto, B. Feeding, fussing, and play: Parent-infant interaction in the first year as a function of early medical problems. In T. Field, S. Goldberg, D. Stern, & A. Sostek (Eds.), *High risk infants and children interactions with adults and peers.* New York: Academic Press, 1980.

Goldstein, J., Freud, A., & Solnit, A. J. *Before the best interest of the child.* New York: Macmillian, 1979.

Goode, W. J. Force and violence in the family. *Journal of Marriage and the Family,* 1971, *33,* 624-636.

Gorski, P.A., Davison, M. F., & Brazelton, T. B. Stages of behavioral organization in the high-risk neonate: Theoretical and clinical considerations. In P. M. Taylor (Ed.), *Parent-infant relationships.* New York: Grune & Stratton, 1980.

Greenberg, M., & Morris, N. Engrossment: The newborn's impact on the father. *American Journal of Orthopsychiatry,* 1974, *44*(4), 520-531.

Greenberg, M., Rosenberg, I., & Lind, J. First mothers rooming in with their newborns: Its impact upon the mothers. *American Journal of Orthopsychiatry,* 1973, *43,* 783-788.

Grey, J., Cutler, C., Dean, J., & Kempe, C. H. Perinatal assessment of mother-baby interaction. In R. E. Helfer & C. H. Kempe (Eds.), *Child abuse and neglect: The family and community.* Cambridge, MA: Ballinger, 1976.

Guttmacher Institute. *Teenage pregnancy: The problem that hasn't gone away.* New York: Author, 1981.

Hansen, C. M. *Failure-to-thrive: A manual prepared for social workers.* Piscataway, NJ: Protective Services Resource Institute, Rutgers Medical School, Department of Pediatrics, 1977.

Hansen, J.D.L., Freesemann, C., Moodie, A. D., & Evans, D. E. What does nutritional growth retardation imply? *Pediatrics,* 1971, *47*(1, Part II), 299-313.

Harlow, H. F., & Harlow, M. K. Developmental aspects of emotional behavior. In P. Black (Ed.), *Physiological correlates of emotion.* New York: Academic Press, 1970.

Harlow, H. F., & Harlow, M. K. Psychopathology in monkeys. In H. D. Kimmel (Ed.), *Experimental psychopathology.* New York: Academic Press, 1971.

Harlow, H. F., Harlow, M. K., & Hansen, F. W. The maternal affectional system of rhesus monkeys. In H. L. Rheingold (Ed.), *Maternal behavior in mammals.* New York: John Wiley, 1963.

Harlow, H. F., & Zimmerman, R. R. Affectional responses in the infant monkey. *Science,* 1959, *130,* 421-432.

Haselkorn, F. (Ed.). *Mothers at risk: The role of social work in prevention of morbidity in infants of socially disadvantaged mothers.* Garden City, NY: Adelphi University School of Social Work, 1966.

Helfer, R. E. The etiology of child abuse. *Pediatrics* (Supplement), 1973, *51*(3), 777-779.

Helfer, R. E. *The diagnostic process and treatment programs.* Washington, DC: Government Printing Office, 1975. (DHEW Publication No. [OHD] 75-69)

Helfer, R. E. *Childhood comes first: A crash course in childhood for parents.* East Lansing, MI: Author, 1978.

Hersh, S. P., & Levine, K. How love begins between parent and child. In S. P. Hersh & K. Levin (Eds.), *Selected readings in mother-infant bonding.* Washington, DC: Government Printing Office, 1979. (a) (DHEW Publication No. [OHDS] 79-30225)

Hersch, S. P., & Levin, K. (Eds.). *Selected readings in mother-infant bonding.* Washington, DC: Government Printing Office, 1979. (b) (DHEW Publication No. /OHDS/ 79-30225)

Hertz, D. G. Psychological implications of adolescent pregnancy: Patterns of family interaction in adolescent mothers-to-be. *Psychodynamics,* 1977, *18,* 13.

Herzog, E. Social and economic characteristics of high risk mothers. In F. Haselkorn (Ed.), *Mothers at risk.* Garden City, NY: Adelphi University Press, 1966.

Hetherington, E. M., Cox, M., & Cox, R. Divorced fathers. *Family Coordinator,* 1976, *25,* 417-428.

Holmes, M. B. *Child abuse and neglect programs: Practice and theory.* Washington, DC: National Institute of Mental Health, 1978. (DHEW Publication No. [ADM] 78-344)

Hunter, R. S., Kilstrom, N., Kraybill, E. N., & Loda, F. Antecedents of child abuse and neglect in premature infants: A prospective study in a newborn intensive care unit. *Pediatrics,* 1978, *61*(4), 629-635.

Hurd, M. J. Assessing maternal attachment: First step toward prevention of child abuse. *Journal of Gynecological Nursing,* 1975, *4*(4), 25-30.

Hutton, J. W., & Oates, R. K. Nonorganic failure to thrive: A long-term follow-up. *Pediatrics,* 1977, *59*(1), 73-77.

Jones, S. D., & Moss, H. A. Age, state, and maternal behavior associated with infant vocalizations. *Child Development,* 1971, *42,* 1039-1051.

Joy, L. A., Davidson, S., Williams, T. M., & Painter, S. L. Parent education in the perinatal period: A critical review of the literature. In P. M. Taylor (Ed.), *Parent-infant relationships.* New York: Grune & Stratton, 1980.

Kanawati, A. A., McLaren, D. S., & Darwish, O. Failure to thrive in Lebanon. IV: Longitudinal health and growth data. *Acta Paediatrica Scandanavia,* 1974, *63,* 649-654.

Kempe, C. H., & Helfer, R. E. *The battered child* (2nd ed.). Chicago: University of Chicago Press, 1972.

Kempe, C. H., Silverman, F. J., Steele, B. F., Droegemueller, W., & Silver, H. K. The battered child syndrome. *Journal of the American Medical Association,* 1962, *181,* 17-24.

Kennell, J. H., Chesler, D., Jerauld, R., Kreger, N., Steffa, M., Wolfe, H., McAlpine, W., & Klaus, M. H. Maternal behavior one year after early and extended postpartum contact. *Developmental Medicine and Child Neurology,* 1974, *16,* 172-179.

Kennell, J. H., & Klaus, M. H. Early mother-infant contact. *Bulletin of the Meninger Clinic.* 1979, *43,* 69-78.

Kennell, J. H., & Rolnick, A. Discussing problems in newborn babies with their parents. *Pediatrics,* 1960, *26,* 832-838.

Kennell, J. H., Slyter, H., & Klaus, M. H. The mourning response of parents to the death of a newborn infant. *New England Journal of Medicine,* 1970, *283,* 344-349.

Kennell, J. H., Trause, M. A., & Klaus, M. H. Evidence for a sensitive period in the human mother. In M. A. Hofer (Ed.), *Parent-infant interaction.* Amsterdam: Elsevier, 1975.

Kennell, J. H., Voos, D., & Klaus, M. Parent-infant bonding. In R. E. Helfer & C. H. Kempe (Eds.), *Child abuse and neglect: The family and community.* Cambridge, MA: Ballinger, 1976.

Kerr, M.A.D., Bogues, J. L., & Kerr, D. S. Psychosocial functioning of mothers of malnourished children. *Pediatrics,* 1978, *62*(5), 778-784.

Kinard, E. M., & Klerman, L. V. Teenage parenting and child abuse: Are they related? *American Journal of Orthopsychiatry,* 1980, *50,* 481-488.

Klaus, M. H., Jerauld, R., Kreger, M., et al. Maternal attachment: Importance of the first postpartum days. *New England Journal of Medicine,* 1972, *286,* 460-463.

Klaus, M. H., & Kennell, J. H. Mothers separated from their newborn infants. *Pediatric Clinics of North America,* 1970, *17,* 1015-1037.

Klaus, M. H., & Kennell, J. H. *Maternal-infant bonding: The impact of early separation or loss on family development.* St. Louis: C. V. Mosby, 1976.

Klaus, M. H., Kennell, J. H., Plumb, N., & Zuehlke, S. Human maternal behavior at first contact with her young. *Pediatrics,* 1970, *46*(2), 187-191.

Klein, M., & Stern, L. Low birth weight and the battered child syndrome. *American Journal of Diseases of Childhood,* 1971, *122,* 15-18.

Klerman, L. V. Adolescent pregnancy: The need for new policies and new programs. *Journal of School Health,* 1975, *45,* 263-267.

Korner, A. F. Individual differences at birth: Implications for child-care practices. In D. Bergsma (Ed.), *The infant at risk.* New York: Intercontinental Medical Book Corporation, 1973.

Korner, A. F. The effect of the infant's state, level of arousal, sex and ontogenetic stage on the caregiver. In M. Lewis & L. A. Rosenblum (Eds.), *The effect of the infant on its caregiver.* New York: John Wiley, 1974.

Korner, A. F., Kraemer, H. C., Haffner, M. E., & Cosper, L. M. Effects of waterbed flotation on premature infants: A pilot study. *Pediatrics,* 1975, *56*(3), 361-367.

Kramer, R. *Giving birth: Childbearing in America today.* Chicago: Contemporary Books, 1978.

Kretchmer, N. Ecology of the newborn infant. In D. Bergsma (Ed.), *The infant at risk.* New York: Intercontinental Medical Book Corporation, 1973.

Lamb, M. E. *The role of the father in child development.* New York: John Wiley, 1976.

Lamb, M. E. The development of parental preferences in the first two years of life. *Sex Roles,* 1977, *3,* 495-497. (a)

Lamb, M. E. Father-infant and mother-infant interaction in the first year of life. *Child Development,* 1977, *48,* 167-181. (b)

Lamb, M. E. The father's role in the infant's social world. In J. H. Stevens & M. Mathews (Eds.), *Mother/child, father/child relationships.* Washington, DC: National Association for the Education of Young Children, 1978.

Lamb, M. E. Paternal influences and the father's role: A personal perspective. *American Psychologist,* 1979, *34*(10), 938-943.

Laury, G. V. The battered child syndrome: Parental motivation, clinical aspects. *Bulletin of the New York Academy of Medicine,* 1970, *46*(9), 676-685.

Leiderman, P. H., & Seashore, M. J. Mother-infant separation: Some delayed consequences. In M. A. Hofer (Ed.), *Parent-infant interaction.* Amsterdam: Elsevier, 1975.

Leifer, A. D., Leiderman, P. H., Barnett, C. R., & Williams, J. A. Effects of mother-infant separation on maternal attachment behavior. *Child Development,* 1972, *43,* 1203-1218.

Leonard, M. F., Rhymes, J. P., & Solnit, A. J. Failure to thrive in infants: A family problem. *American Journal of Diseases in Children,* 1966, *3,* 600.

Lester, B. M. *Relations between teenage pregnancy and neonatal behavior.* Washington, DC: National Institute for Child Health and Development, March 1978. (Progress report)

Levine, S. V. Infantile stimulation: A perspective. In A. Ambrose (Ed.), *Stimulation in early infancy.* New York: Academic Press, 1969.

Levine, S. V. Adolescents believing and belonging. In S. C. Feinstein & P. L. Giovacchini (Eds.), *Adolescent psychiatry: Developmental and clinical studies* (Vol. 8). Chicago: University of Chicago Press, 1979.

Lewis, M. State as an infant-environment interaction: An analysis of mother-infant interaction as a function of sex. *Merrill-Palmer Quarterly,* 1972, *18,* 95-121.

Lewis, M., & Rosenblum, L. A. (Eds.). *The effect of the infant on its caregiver.* New York: John Wiley, 1974.

Light, R. L. Abused and neglected children in America: A study of alternative policies. *Harvard Educational Review,* 1973, *43*(4), 556-598.

Lincoln, R., Jaffe, F. S., & Ambrose, A. *11 million teenagers.* New York: Guttmacher Institute, 1976.

Lorenz, K. *On aggression.* New York: Harcourt, Brace & World, 1966.

Lozoff, B., Birttenham, G. M., Trause, M. A., Kennell, J. H., & Klaus, M. The mother-newborn relationship: Limits of adaptability. *Journal of Pediatrics,* 1977, *91*(1).

Lynch, M. A. Ill-health and child abuse. *Lancet,* August 16, 1975.

Lynch, M. A., & Roberts, J. Predicting child abuse: Signs of bonding failure in the maternity hospital. *British Medical Journal,* 1977, *1,* 624-626.

Maccoby, E. E., & Masters, J. C. Attachment and dependency. In P. H. Mussen(Ed.), *Carmichael's manual of child psychiatry* (3rd ed.). New York: John Wiley, 1970.

Maden, M. F., & Wrench, D. F. Significant findings in child abuse research. *Victimology,* 1977, *2*(2), 196-224.

Mahler, M. S., Oine, F., & Bergman, A. *The psychological birth of the human infant: Symbiosis and individuation.* New York: Basic Books, 1975.

Martin, H. P. *The abused child: A multidisciplinary approach to developmental issues and treatment.* Cambridge, MA: Ballinger, 1976.

Matza, D. *Delinquency and drift.* New York: John Wiley, 1964.

McCall, R. B. A hard look at stimulating and predicting development: The cases of bonding and screening. *Pediatrics in Review,* 1982, *3*(7), 205-212.

Menken, J. The health and social consequences of teenage childbearing. In F. F. Furstenberg, Jr., R. Lincoln, & J. Menken (Eds.), *Teenage sexuality, pregnancy and childbearing.* Philadelphia: University of Pennsylvania Press, 1981.

Menken, T. C. Teenage childbearing: Its medical aspects and implications for the U.S. population. In C. Westcalf & R. Parks (Eds.), *Demographic and social aspects of population growth.* Washington, DC: Government Printing Office, 1972.

Milowe, D., & Lourie, R. S. The child's role in the battered child syndrome. *Journal of Pediatrics,* 1964, *65,* 1079-1081.

Minde, K. L. Bonding of parents to premature infants: Theory and practice. In P. M. Taylor (Ed.), *Parent-infant relationships.* New York: Grune & Stratton, 1980.

Minde, K. L., Trehub, S., Corter, C., Boukydis, D., Celhoffer, L., & Marton, P. Mother-child relationships in the premature nursery: An observational study. *University of Toronto Pediatrics,* 1978, *61*(3), 373-379.

Mitchell, W. G., Gorlee, R. W., & Greenberg, R. A. Failure to thrive: A study in a primary care setting, epidemiology and follow-up. *Pediatrics,* 1980, *65*(5), 971-977.

Moore, K. A., & Caldwell, S. The effect of government policies on out-of-wedlock sex and pregnancy. In F. Furstenberg, Jr., R. Lincoln, & J. Menken (Eds.), *Teenage sexuality, pregnancy and childbearing.* Philadelphia: University of Pennsylvania Press, 1981.

Murphy, L. B., & Moriarity, A. E. *Vulnerability, coping, and growth from infancy to adolescence.* New Haven, CT: Yale University Press, 1976.

Newberger, C. M., & Newberger, E. H. *The search for a theory on child abuse.* Paper presented at the Conference on Child Abuse: Cultural Roots and Policy Options, Annenberg School of Communications, University of Pennsylvania, November 1978.

Newson, J. An intersubjective approach to the systematic description of mother-infant interaction. In H. R. Schaffer (Ed.), *The origins of human social relations.* New York: Academic Press, 1977.

Newton, N., & Newton, M. Mothers' reactions to their newborn babies. *Journal of the American Medical Association,* 1962, *181,* 206-211.

Osofsky, H. J. *The pregnant teenagers.* Springfield, IL: Charles C Thomas, 1968.

Osofsky, H. J. Poverty, pregnancy outcome and child deveopment. In D. Bergsma (Ed.), *The infant at risk.* New York: Intercontinental Medical Book Corporation, 1972.

Osofsky, H. J., & Osofsky, J. D. Normal adaptation to pregnancy and new parenthood. In P. M. Taylor (Ed.), *Parent-infant relationships.* New York: Grune & Stratton, 1980.

Osofsky, J. D., & Osofsky, H. J. Teenage pregnancy: Psychosocial considerations. *Clinical Obstetrics and Gynecology,* 1978, *21,* 1161-1172.

Pakter, J., Rosner, H. J., Jacobziner, H., & Greenstein, F. Out of wedlock births in New York City: Sociological aspects. *American Journal of Public Health,* 1961, *51,* 683.

Parens, H. Indices of the child's earliest attachment to his mother, applicable in routine pediatric examination. *Pediatrics,* 1972, *49*(4), 600-603.

Parke, R. D. Parent-infant interaction: Progress, paradigms, and problems. In G. Sackett (Ed.), *Observing behavior. Volume 1: Theory and applications in mental retardation.* Baltimore: University Park Press, 1978.

Parke, R. D., Power, T. G., Tinsley, B. R., & Hymel, S. The father's role in the family system. In P. M. Taylor (Ed.), *Parent-infant relationships.* New York: Grune & Stratton, 1980.

Parkes, C. M., & Stevenson-Hinde, J. *The place of attachment in human behavior.* New York: Basic Books, 1982.

Patton, R. G., & Gardner, L. L. *Growth failure in maternal deprivation.* Springfield, IL: Charles C Thomas, 1963.

Pawlby, S. J. Imitative interaction. In H. R. Schaffer (Ed.), *The origins of human social relations.* New York: Academic Press, 1977.

Pedersen, F. A., & Robson, K. S. Father participation in infancy. *American Journal of Orthopsychiatry,* 1969, *39,* 466-472.

Pelton, L. H. Child abuse and neglect: The myth of classlessness. *American Journal of Orthopsychiatry,* 1978, *48*(4), 608-617.

Perry, N., & Millemit, C. R. Child rearing antecedents of low and high anxiety eighth grade children. In C. D. Spielberger & T. G. Sarason (Eds.), *Stress and anxiety,* Washington, DC: Hemisphere, 1977.

Pohlman, E. *The psychology of birth planning.* Cambridge, MA: Schenkman, 1969.

Polansky, N., Borgman, D., & DeSaix, C. *Child neglect: Understanding and reaching parents.* New York: Child Welfare League of America, 1972. (a)

Polansky, N., Borgman, D., & DeSaix, C. *Roots of futility.* San Francisco: Jossey-Bass, 1972. (b)

Prescott, S., & Letko, C. Battered women: A social psychological perspective. In M. Roy (Ed.), *Battered women: A psychosociological study of domestic violence.* New York: Van Nostrand Reinhold, 1977.

Provence, S. Early intervention: Experiences in a service-centered research program. In D. Bergsma (Ed.), *The infant at risk.* New York: Intercontinental Medical Book Corporation, 1973.

Reinhart, J. B. Failure to thrive: 50 year follow-up. *Journal of Pediatrics,* 1972, *81*(6), 1218-1219.

Resnik, H. L. P., Ruben, H. L., & Ruben, D. D. *Emergency psychiatric care: The management of mental health crisis.* Bowie, MD: Charles Press, 1975.

Restak, R. M. *The brain: The last frontier.* New York: Warner Books, 1979.

Ricketts, S. S. *Contraceptive use among teenage mothers: Evaluation of a family planning program.* Unpublished doctoral dissertation, University of Pennsylvania, 1973.

Robson, K. S. The role of eye-to-eye contact in maternal infant attachment. *Journal of Child Psychology and Psychiatry,* 1967, *8*, 13.

Robson, K. S., & Moss, H. A. Patterns and determinants of maternal attachment. *Journal of Pediatrics,* 1970, *77*(6), 976-985.

Rutter, M. Parent-child separation: Psychological effects on the children. *Journal of Child Psychology and Psychiatry,* 1971, *12*, 233-260.

Rutter, M. *Maternal deprivation reassessed.* Baltimore: Penguin, 1972.

Rutter, M. Separation experiences: A new look at an old topic. *Journal of Pediatrics,* 1976, *95*(1), 147-154.

Rutter, M. Protective factors in children's responses to stress and disadvantage. In M. W. Kent & J. E. Rolf (Eds.), *Primary prevention of psychopathology: Promoting social competence and coping in children* (Vol. 3). Hanover, NH: University Press of New England, 1978.

Rutter, M. Maternal deprivation, 1972-1978: New findings, new concepts, new approaches. *Child Development,* 1979, *50*, 283-305.

Ryan, G. M., & Schneider, J. M. Teenage obstetric complications. *Obstetrics and Gynecology,* 1978, *21*, 1191-1197.

Sander, L. W. Issues in early mother-child interaction. *Journal of the American Academy of Child Psychiatry,* 1962, *1*, 141-166.

Sarrel, P. M., & Davis, C. D. The young unwed primipara: A study of 100 cases with five year follow-up. *American Journal of Obstetrics and Gynecology,* 1966, *95*.

Schaffer, H. R. Cognitive structure and early social behavior. In H. R. Schaffer (Ed.), *The origins of human social relations.* New York: Academic Press, 1977. (a)

Schaffer, H. R. *Mothering.* Cambridge, MA: Harvard University Press, 1977. (b)

Schaffer, H. R. (Ed.). *The origins of human social relations.* New York: Academic Press, 1977. (c)

Schaffer, H. R. (Ed.). *Studies in mother-infant interaction.* Proceedings of the Loch Lomond Symposium, Ross Priory, University of Strathclyde. New York: Academic Press, 1977. (d)

Schwarzbeck, R., III. Identification of infants at risk for child neglect: Observations and inferences in the examination of the mother-infant dyad. In S. P. Hersch & K. Levin (Eds.), *Selected readings in mother-infant bonding.* Washington, DC: Government Printing Office, 1979. (DHEW Publication No. [OHDS] 79-30225)

Seashore, M. H., Leifer, A. D., Barnett, C. R., & Leiderman, P. H. The effects of denial of early mother-infant interactions on maternal self confidence. *Journal of Personality and Social Psychology,* 1973, *26*, 369-378.

Shaheen, A., Alexander, D., Truskowsky, M., & Barbero, G. J. Failure to thrive: A retrospective profile. *Clinical Pediatrics,* 1968, *7*, 255-261.

Shapiro, M. *The sociobiology of Homo sapiens.* Kansas City, MO: Pinecrest Fund, 1978.

Solnit, A. J., & Provence, S. Vulnerability and risk in early childhood. In J. D. Osofsky (Ed.), *Handbook of infant development.* New York: John Wiley, 1979.

Solnit, A. J., & Stark, M. H. Mourning and the birth of a defective child. *Psychoanalytic Study of the Child,* 1961, *16,* 523.

Solomon, T. History and demography of child abuse. *Pediatrics* (Supplement), 1973, *51*(4), 775-776.

Spinetta, J. J., & Rigler, D. The child-abusing parent: A psychological review. *Psychological Bulletin,* 1972, *4,* 296-304.

Spitz, R. A. Hospitalism: An inquiry into the genesis of psychiatric conditions in early childhood. *Psychoanalytic Study of the Child,* 1945, *1,* 53-74.

Spitz, R. A. Anaclitic depression. *Psychoanalytic Study of the Child,* 1946, *2,* 313-342. (a)

Spitz, R. A. Hospitalism: A follow-up report. *Psychoanalytic Study of the Child,* 1946, *2,* 113-117. (b)

Spitz, R. A. *The first year of life.* New York: International Universities Press, 1965.

Sroufe, L. A. *Knowing and enjoying your baby.* Englewood Cliffs, NJ: Prentice-Hall, 1977.

Sroufe, L. A. Attachment and the roots of competence. *Human Nature,* October 1978, 1050-1059.

Sroufe, L. A. The coherence of individual development: Early care, attachment, and subsequent developmental issues. *American Psychologist,* 1979, *34*(10), 834-841.

Steele, B. F. *Working with abusive parents from a psychiatric point of view.* Washington, DC: Government Printing Office, 1975. (DHEW Publication No. [OHD] 75-70)

Stern, D. N. Mother and infant at play: The dyadic interaction involving facila, vocal and gaze behaviors. In M. Lewis & L. A. Rosenblum (Eds.), *The effect of the infant on its caregiver.* New York: John Wiley, 1974.

Stern, D. N. *The first relationship: Infant and mother.* Cambridge, MA: Harvard University Press, 1977.

Straus, M. A., Gelles, R. J., & Steinmetz, S. K. *Behind closed doors: Violence in the American family.* Garden City, NY: Doubleday, 1980.

Sugarman, M. Paranatal influence on maternal-infant attachment. *Orthopsychiatry,* 1977, *47*(3), 407-421.

Tanner, J. M. Variability of growth and maturity in newborn infants. In M. Lewis & L. A. Rosenblum (Eds.), *The effect of the infant on its caregiver.* New York: John Wiley, 1974.

Taylor, P. M. (Ed.). *Parent-infant relationships.* New York: Grune & Stratton, 1980.

Terr, L. C. A family study of child abuse. *American Journal of Psychiatry,* 1970, *127*(5), 665-671.

Thoman, E. F., Leiderman, D. H., & Olson, J. P. Neonate-mother interaction during breast feeding. *Developmental Psychology,* 1972, *6,* 110-118.

Thomas, A., & Chess, S. *Temperament and development.* New York: Brunner/Mazel, 1977.

Trivers, R. L. Parent-offspring conflict. *American Zoologist,* 1974, *14,* 249-264.

Trussell, J., & Menken, J. Early childbearing and subsequent fertility. In F. Furstenberg, Jr., R. Lincoln, & J. Menken (Eds.), *Teenage sexuality, pregnancy, and
   childbearing.* Philadelphia: University of Pennsylvania Press, 1981.

Van Den Berghe, P. L. Bridging the paradigms: Biology and the social sciences. In
   M. S. Gregory, A. Silvers, & D. Smith (Eds.), *Sociobiology and human nature: An
   interdisciplinary critique and defense.* San Francisco: Jossey-Bass, 1978.

Verny, T. *The secret life of the unborn child.* New York: Summit Books, 1981.

Vincent, C. *Unmarried mothers.* New York: Macmillan, 1961.

Wallace, H. Factors associated with perinatal mortality and morbidity. *Clinical
   Obstetrics and Gynecology,* 1970, *13,* 13-43.

Watzlawick, P., Beavin, J. H., & Jackson, D. D. *Pragmatics of human communication: A study of international patterns, pathologies, and paradoxes.* New York:
   Norton, 1967.

Westoff, C. F., & Ryder, N. B. *The contraceptive revolution.* Princeton, NJ: Princeton
   University Press, 1977.

Whitten, C. F., Pettit, M. G., & Fishoff, J. Evidence that growth failure from maternal
   deprivation is secondary to undereating. *Journal of the American Medical Association,* 1969, *209*(11), 1675-1682.

Williams, T. M. Childbearing practices of young mothers: What we know, how it
   matters, why it's so little. *American Journal of Orthopsychiatry,* 1974, *44*(1), 70-
   75.

Wilson, E. O. *On human nature.* Cambridge, MA: Harvard University Press, 1979.

Wolfe, P. H. The natural history of crying and other vocalization in early infancy. In B.
   M. Foss (Ed.), *Determinants of infant behavior* (Vol. 4). London: Methuen,
   1969.

Wolfe, T. *The right stuff.* New York: Dell, 1979.

Young, L. *Wednesday's children.* New York: McGraw-Hill, 1964.

Zalba, S. R. The abused child: I. A survey of the problem. *Social Work,* 1966, *11*(4),
   3-16.

Zax, M., & Stricker, G. (Eds.). *The study of abnormal behavior.* London: Macmillan,
   1969.

Zenick, M., & Kantner, J. Sexual activity, contraceptive use, and pregnancy among
   metropolitan-area teenagers: 1971-1979. *Family Planning Perspectives,* 1980,
   12(5), 230-237.

ABOUT THE AUTHOR

Frank G. Bolton, Jr., is Coordinator of Psychological Services for the Arizona Department of Economic Security. In addition, he is Director of the Maricopa Medical Center's Adolescent Parenting/Mother-Infant Bonding Program. His numerous publications include *The Pregnant Adolescent* (Sage, 1980) and other books, training manuals, and articles dealing with child maltreatment, adolescence, and the family.

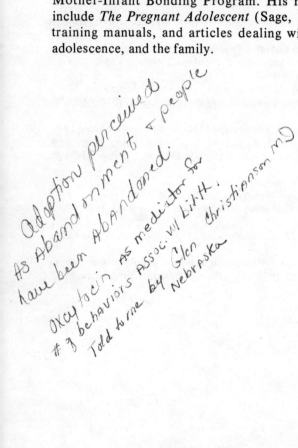

Adoption perceived as Abandonment + people have been Abandoned.

Oxytocin as mediator for
3 behaviors Assoc. w/ birth.
Told to me by Glen Christianson MD
Nebraska